2019

Berlin

Shortlist

timeout.com / berlin

WITHDRAWN

100

ONE WEEK W!

130

Contents

103

View from the Siegessaule

ABOUT THE GUIDE

The *Time Out Berlin Shortlist* is one of a series of pocket guides to cities around the globe. Drawing on the expertise of local authors, it distils their knowledge into a handy, easy-to-use format that ensures you get the most from your trip, whether you're a first-time or return visitor.

Time Out Berlin Shortlist is divided into four sections:

Welcome to Berlin introduces the city and provides inspiration for your visit.

Berlin Day by Day helps you plan your trip with an events calendar and customised itineraries.

Berlin by Area is the main visitor section of the guide. It includes detailed listings and reviews for the very best sights and museums, restaurants & cafés ⑩, bars & pubs ⑩, shops & services ⑩ and entertainment venues ⑩, all organised by area with a corresponding street map. To help navigation, each area of Berlin has been assigned its own colour.

Berlin Essentials provides practical visitor information, including accommodation options and details of public transport.

Shortlists & highlights

We have selected a Shortlist of stand-out venues in each area, which are marked with a heart ♥ in the text. The very best of these appear in the Highlights feature (*see p10*) and receive extended coverage in the guide.

Maps

There's an overview map on *p8* and individual street maps for each area of the city. Venues featured in the guide have been given a grid reference so that you can find them easily on the maps and on the ground.

Prices

All our **restaurant listings** are marked with a euro symbol category from budget to blow-out (€-€€€€), indicating the price you should expect to pay for an average main course: € = under €10; €€ = €11-€20; €€€ = €21-€30; €€€€ = over €30.

A similar system is used in our **Accommodation** chapter based on the hotel's standard prices for one night in a double room: **Budget** = under €70; **Moderate** = €70-€120; **Expensive** = €120-€190; **Luxury** = over €190.

Introduction

The German capital is home to approximately 3.6 million inhabitants and welcomes five million visitors per year; a number that is set to rise with Berlin's increasing popularity as a tourist destination. However, the city rarely feels cramped. Sprawling across nearly 900 square kilometres, Berlin is nine times larger than Paris, closer in size to New York, but, with half the population of the Big Apple and 12 times fewer annual visitors, it can sometimes feel more like a village… sometimes like a reclaimed, post-apocalyptic metropolis.

It's not just the lack of crowds that makes the city appear sparse; from the remaining symbols of Prussian greatness to the brutalist remnants of GDR town-planning, the style of Berlin's architecture and the weight of its history can seem to overshadow its citizens. Fortunately, the city's vast reach means there's plenty of room for green spaces too: Tiergarten, Tempelhofer Feld and countless neighbourhood parks offer respite from the concrete urban environment and from reminders of the city's fascinating but troubled past.

As in any other city, public transport is best avoided at rush hour, supermarket queues can be atrocious, finding a table for brunch, especially on a Saturday, is nigh-on impossible, and there's always something sticky on the steps leading down to the U-Bahn. But there's ample compensation to be found in Berlin's first-rate museums and cutting-edge galleries, its street food and flea markets, third-wave coffee and vegan doughnuts, kite-flying and roller-blading, impeccable orchestras and trail-blazing techno. Above all, it's the anything-goes attitude of this über-cool city that is sure to win you over.

Welcome
to Berlin

Flughafen Berlin Tegel

Osloer

Hohenzollernkanal

Volkspark Jungfernheide

Volkspark Rehberge

Saatwinkler Damm

Seestrasse   Müllerstrasse

WEST OF THE CENTRE

Tegeler Weg

Berlin by boat ♥

Spree

Otto-suhr-allee

Beusselstr

Alt-moabit

Stromstr

Paulstr

Heidestr

Berlin Hauptbahnhof

TIERGARTEN & AROUND

Reichstag ♥

Str des 17. Juni

Tiergarten

Philharmonie ♥

Berlinale ♥

Kaiserdamm

Kantstrasse

Kurfürstenstr

Str

CHARLOTTENBURG & SCHÖNEBERG

Berlin brunch ♥

KaDeWe ♥

Hohenstaufenstr

Grunewaldstr

Potsdamer Str

Hauptstr

♥ **Bathing lakes**

Grazer Damm

TEMPELHOF

Bergstrasse

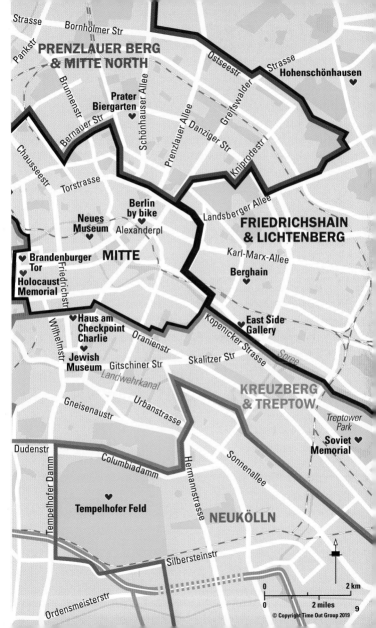

Strasse

Bornholmer Str

**PRENZLAUER BERG
& MITTE NORTH**

Pankstr

Ostseestr

Strasse

Hohenschönhausen

Greifswalder

Brunnenstr

**Prater
Biergarten** ♥

Schönhauser Allee

Prenzlauer Allee

Danziger Str

Bernauer Str

Kniprodestr

Chausseestr

Torstrasse

Landsberger Allee

**Berlin
by bike** ♥

**Neues
Museum** ♥

**FRIEDRICHSHAIN
& LICHTENBERG**

Alexanderpl

Friedrichstr

MITTE

Karl-Marx-Allee

**Brandenburger
Tor** ♥

Berghain
♥

**Holocaust
Memorial** ♥

♥**Haus am
Checkpoint
Charlie**

Wilhelmstr

Oranienstr

Kopenicker Strasse

**East Side
Gallery** ♥

♥**Jewish
Museum**

Gitschiner Str

Skalitzer Str

Spree

Landwehrkanal

Urbanstrasse

**KREUZBERG
& TREPTOW**

Gneisenaustr

Treptower
Park

Dudenstr

Columbiadamm

Hermannstrasse

Sonnenallee

Soviet ♥
Memorial

Tempelhofer Damm

♥

Tempelhofer Feld

NEUKÖLLN

Silbersteinstr

Ordensmeisterstr

| 0 | | 2 km |
| 0 | | 2 miles |

© Copyright Time Out Group 2019

Highlights

Visiting Berlin can seem an overwhelming prospect. The city is so big; its history, so daunting; its reputation, so cool that it's hard for the first-time visitor to know where to start. Fortunately, this guide is here to help, with a shortlist of Berlin's highlights, from museums and memorials to biking and bathing.

01

Reichstag *p103*

This neo-Baroque edifice housing the German Bundestag (Parliament) survived wars, Nazis, fire, bombing and the country's division, only to return as a symbol of a new era in German politics. A tour around the iconic dome, designed by Sir Norman Foster, is thoroughly recommended.

02

Brandenburger Tor *p72*

Berlin's long-suffering victory arch, the Brandenburg Gate, served as a visual flashpoint for much of the trauma to have beset Germany in the 20th century – standing alone in no-man's-land during the GDR era and providing the backdrop to the euphoria of 1989. Restored to its rightful place at the heart of the city, this monument to unity is a must-see on any Berlin itinerary.

03

Neues Museum *p84*

It's hard to pick just one of the five museums on Berlin's UNESCO-listed Museumsinsel, but the Neues Museum is an unmissable highlight. David Chipperfield's award-winning rebuild is a suitably stunning home for a treasure trove of artefacts from pre- , early and ancient history, including the Ancient Egyptian bust of Queen Nefertiti.

04

Tiergarten *p101*

This vast park in the heart of the city comes into its own during spring and summer, when you can happily lose yourself amid its woodlands, lakes and miles of greenery.

05

Soviet Memorial *p77*

One of Berlin's most impressive public monuments, this memorial to Soviet soldiers killed in World War II is located in a peaceful riverside park. It's as bombastic and intimidating as you would expect.

06

Holocaust Memorial *p75*

Architect Peter Eisenman's Memorial to the Murdered Jews of Europe (Denkmal für die ermordeten Juden Europas) is intentionally disorienting; a striking sculptural statement that invites visitors in, only to create a feeling of unease. It is rightfully at the forefront of the city's attempts to come to terms with its past.

07

Haus am Checkpoint Charlie *p84*

Once the flashpoint between East and West, today the former Checkpoint Charlie border crossing offers tacky souvenir stalls, coachloads of trippers, and actors pretending to be US and Soviet guards. But it also features this intriguing little museum.

08

Tempelhofer Feld *p158*

The vast 1920s airport west of Neukölln now stands empty, but the surrounding airfields and runways have become a huge park for cycling, kite-flying and open-air festivals.

09

East Side Gallery *p126*

One of the few remaining strips of the Berlin Wall is still festooned with the murals that became iconic across the world after reunification. The riverside views are great, too.

10

Gedenkstätte Berlin-Hohenschönhausen *p134*

Former inmates of this Stasi internment facility lead chilling tours through the depths of their former jail, describing the horrors inflicted on them by the GDR's notorious secret police.

11

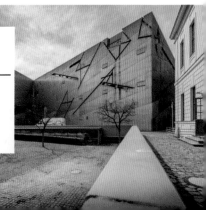

Jüdisches Museum *p82*

Daniel Libeskind's beautiful, yet deliberately oppressive building houses a masterful museum devoted to the turbulent history of Judaism in Germany.

12

Philharmonie *p110*

Designed by architect Hans Scharoun and home to one of the best orchestras in the world, an evening spent in the Philharmonie is one of Berlin's most exquisite pleasures – if you can get a ticket.

13

KaDeWe *p41*

The legendary department store is more than a century old and has stood at the heart of the city's shopping scene through thick and thin. Today it's as opulent as ever, especially the food hall on the sixth floor.

14

Berlin by boat *p168*

Winding through the centre of Berlin, the River Spree offers a different perspective on this once-divided city. There's no shortage of tour operators offering trips along the river, the Landwehrkanal or across the lakes, and some services are included on the city travelcard.

COME
HERE, YOU

Get to know the Berlin attractions with pulling power, and book them for less with Time Out.

Sightseeing

Berlin covers a vast 891 sq km, but the area inside the
Ringbahn (the 37-km/23-mile overground railway that
loops round the city centre) is where you'll find most
of the sights, museums, restaurants, shops, bars and
entertainment options.

In the days of division, **Mitte** (*see p68*) lay on
the eastern side of the city, but today it is once again
the centre in every respect – historically, culturally,
politically and commercially. The Fernsehturm on
Alexanderplatz is the unmissable landmark in the east
and can be seen from all over the city. Mitte's main
thoroughfare is Unter den Linden, a grand east–west
avenue full of mighty neoclassical paeans to the imperial
era, such as the recently renovated Staatsoper. At its
eastern end is the UNESCO World Heritage Museuminsel
(*see p81*), incorporating a cluster of major museums,

❤ **Shortlist**

Most iconic sights
Brandenburger Tor p72, East Side Gallery p126, Fernsehturm p94, Museumsinsel p81, Reichstag p103, Tiergarten p101

Best viewpoints
Fernsehturm p94, Klunkerkranich p159, Reichstag Dome p103, Siegessäule p100, Teufelsberg Berlin p180

Best German history lessons
Deutsches Historisches Museum p73, Gedenkstätte Berliner Mauer p120, Gedenkstätte Berlin-Hohenschönhausen p134, Jüdisches Museum p140, Museum in der Kulturbrauerei p114, Schloss Charlottenburg p171, Story of Berlin p165

Best family museums
Bode-Museum p83, Deutsches-Technikmuseum Berlin p139, Haus am Checkpoint Charlie p138, Museum für Naturkunde p79

Best memorials
Holocaust Memorial p75, Kaiser-Wilhelm-Gedächtnis-Kirche p165, Neue Wache p74, Soviet Memorial p150

Best art collections
Alte Nationalgalerie p82, Brücke-Museum p180, Gemäldegalerie p106, Hamburger Bahnhof p104, Museum Berggruen p171

the Berliner Dom and the rebuilt Stadtschloss. South of Unter den Linden, there are glitzy shops along Friedrichstrasse, and cathedrals and concert halls around the Gendarmenmarkt. Things get more bohemian to the north, particularly around the Scheunenviertel, Berlin's historic Jewish quarter. At the western end of Unter den Linden is the iconic Brandenburger Tor (see p72), once the ceremonial entrance to the city; the undulating concrete blocks of the Holocaust Memorial (see p75) lie just to the south.

The Brandenburg Gate marks the border between Mitte and **Tiergarten** (see p97), with the huge wooded park of the same name stretching away on the western side (see p101) as far as the Zoologischer Garten. This district also incorporates the Reichstag (see p103), complete with glass cupola, and other key buildings of the government quarter along the Spree. South of the park, the postmodern entertainment and commercial zone of Potsdamer Platz adjoins the Kulturforum, home to institutions such as the Neue Nationalgalerie, the Philharmonie (*see p110*) and a whole slew of embassies. To the north of Tiergarten is the relatively central but unassuming district of **Moabit**.

Kastanienallee leads north-east from Mitte into **Prenzlauer Berg** (*see p111*), easily Berlin's most picturesque residential neighbourhood and Mitte's fashionable adjunct in terms of nightlife and gastronomy; east Berlin's gay district is focused on the northern reaches of Schönhauser Allee. Just to the west, there's an evocative history lesson to be had at the Berlin Wall memorial on the edge of working-class **Gesundbrunnen** (*see p120*). East of Prenzlauer Berg is **Friedrichshain** (*see p123*), which has the most 'East Berlin' feel of the inner-city districts. Its spine is the broad GDR-era Karl-Marx-Allee; photographers gravitate to the East Side Gallery (*see p126*), while bohos, students and young tourists flock to the lively area around Simon-Dach-Strasse. Heading further east out of town, **Lichtenberg** (*see p133*) has a few reminders of Stasi oppression and the East Berlin Zoo.

Berliner Dom

Oberbaumbrücke

Crossing the River Spree south from Friedrichshain (via the photogenic Oberbaumbrücke) takes you into the former West Berlin neighbourhood of **Kreuzberg** (*see p135*), once the city's main alternative-lifestyle nexus and the capital of Turkish Berlin. The northern part of Kreuzberg, bordering Mitte, contains some important museums, including the Jüdisches Museum (*see p140*), as well as Friedrichstrasse's Cold War landmark, Checkpoint Charlie (*see p138*). Bergmannstrasse is lively with cafés and retro shops, while bars and clubs line Oranienstrasse and the eastern area around Schlesisches Tor. South of Kreuzberg, hip and happening **Neukölln** (*see p151*) provides access to the vast expanse of Tempelhofer Feld (*see p158*), while large and leafy Treptower Park contains the imposing Soviet Memorial (*see p150*).

West of Kreuzberg lies **Schöneberg** (*see p174*), a residential district centred around Winterfeldtplatz,

In the know
Museums and collections

Note that most museums are closed on Mondays but are open and free between 6pm and 10pm Thursdays.

Highlight

♥ Berlin by bike

Cycling through Berlin with the wind in your hair is an experience not to be missed. Flat, with lots of cycle routes, parks and canal paths, the city is best seen by bike. That said, caution is required. Cobbles, tram lines, aimless pedestrians, other cyclists and careless drivers all pose hazards. Few locals wear helmets, but you'd be wise to get your hands on one, especially if you're used to riding on the left.

Bicycles can be carried on the U-Bahn (except during rush hour, 6-9am and 2-5pm) in designated carriages, up to two per carriage. More may be taken on the S-Bahn at any time of day. In each case an extra ticket (€1.90 for zones A and B) must be bought for each bike. This means you can train it back to the city after a cycle ride to the lakes, or if you get hopelessly lost. A good guide to cycle routes is the *ADFC Fahrradstadtplan* (€6.90), available in bike shops, but most bus shelters also have city maps which will help you regain your bearings.

These days, there's a surplus of bike-sharing apps in Berlin, such as **Mobike** (mobike.com), **Donkey Republic** (www.donkey. bike), **Lidl Bike** (www.lidl-bike. de) and **Deezer Nextbike** (www. deezernextbike.de). Typically,

there's a small sign-up fee of around €10, and then rates are charged by the half hour (€1-€1.50). Maximum full-day fees are around €15. Bikes can be picked up all over the city (you'll notice all sorts of colourfully branded cycles) and at designated docking stations. However, if you're planning an excursion or want to explore Berlin's streets more fully, you'd do well to pick up a bicycle from a hire shop. Not only are the bikes better quality, but you'll also get free servicing and advice; €8-15 euros a day is the going rate. Some of the best are **Berlin on Bike** (Knaackstrasse 97, Kulturbrauerei, Prenzlauer Berg, www.berlinonbike.de); **Fahrradstation** (Dorotheenstrasse 30, Mitte, www.fahrradstation. com) and **Wicked Wheels** (Grossbeerenstrasse 53, Kreuzberg, www.wicked-wheels.de).

Once you've got your chariot, it's time to hit the road. Cycling around Tempelhofer Feld (*see p158*), along the Landwehrkanal or through Treptower Park to the site of the Soviet Memorial (*see p150*) all make for unforgettable rides. If you're feeling more ambitious and you've a couple of days to spare, it's possible to cycle the whole 160-km (99-mile)route of the Berlin Wall.

with its popular market. Berlin's historic gay district stretches along and around Motzstrasse and Fuggerstrasse, while Wittenbergplatz, at Schöneberg's north-west corner, is the location of KaDeWe (*see p41*), continental Europe's biggest department store. It marks the beginning of the well-heeled district of **Charlottenburg** (*see p161*), Berlin's West

End, whose main artery is the Kurfürstendamm, a typical high-end shopping drag. The palace that gives the district its name is to the north. **West of the Centre** (*see p177*) is the Olympiastadion, the biggest single example of Nazi-era architecture still extant. The forested Grunewald and a cluster of bathing lakes (*see p182*) entice residents out of the city in warmer weather, while the sculptured gardens and royal residences of **Potsdam** (*see p181*), the capital of Brandenburg, make it a popular day trip for tourists.

Discount cards, visitor passes and tours

Most of the major museums and galleries are administered by the **Staatliche Museen zu Berlin** (SMB; www.smb.museum/home.html), which offers a three-day card (€29; €14.50 reductions), for access to any of its museums.

There are also excellent-value tourist discount cards, which combine unlimited transport within designated zones, with a bundle of other discounts and deals. The **Berlin CityTourCard** (www.citytourcard.com) costs

Olymplastadion

€16.90 for a 48-hour pass for zones A and B, €23.90 for 72 hours and is available from tourist offices, BVG and S-Bahn ticket machines and from the airports. The **Berlin WelcomeCard** (www.berlin-welcomecard.de) costs €19.90 for 48 hours in zones A and B, €28.90 for 72 hours (€45 including access to museums at Museum Island). Another option is the **Berlin Pass** (www.berlinpass.com, €89 for three days), allows entry to over 50 attractions and free hop-on, hop-off bus tours around the city.

There are heaps of tours to help you learn about the history, architecture, street art and culture of Berlin, by bike, boat, bus or on foot. **Insider Tours** (www.insidertour.com) are led by very well-informed English-speaking guides who reveal the history of the city in a series of themed walks. **Alternative Berlin** (http://alternativeberlin.com) offers a look at the counter-culture of the city, taking you through squats, street art and skateparks. If you'd rather see the city on two wheels, try **Fat Tire Tours** (www.fattiretours.com/berlin). For a full list of available tours, see www.visitberlin.de/en/sightseeing-tours-berlin.

Key Events

All the Berlin dates that matter

12th century Foundation of the twin settlements of Berlin and Cölln, which are later united as a single trading centre.

1416-1701 The Hohenzollern dynasty rules the city as Electors of Brandenburg.

1618-1648 Thirty Years War.

1701 Elector Friedrich III is crowned King Friedrich I of Prussia.

1713-86 King Friedrich Wilhelm I and his son Friedrich II (the Great) turn Prussia into a major power.

1806-1808 Berlin is occupied by Napoleonic troops.

1814-1840 Political reform stalls but cultural life thrives in the city.

1862 King Wilhelm I appoints Otto von Bismarck as Prime Minister.

1869 The left-wing SPD is founded and starts to dominate Berlin politics.

1870 A united German army led by Prussia defeats the French.

1871 King Wilhelm I is proclaimed Kaiser of Germany at Versailles. Berlin becomes the capital of the German Empire.

1888 Kaiser Wilhelm II is crowned.

1914-1918 World War I.

9 Nov 1918 The Kaiser abdicates.

1919-1933 Weimar Republic. Despite political and financial instability, Berlin overtakes Paris as the entertainment capital of Europe.

1932 The Nazi party gains 40% of the vote, becoming the largest party in the Reichstag.

1933 Adolf Hitler becomes Chancellor. The Nazis use the Reichstag Fire as an excuse to arrest political opponents.

July 1934 Night of the Long Knives. Hitler declares himself Führer.

1935 Nuremberg Laws strip German Jews of citizenship.

1936 Olympic Games in Berlin.

9 Nov 1938 Kristallnacht. Jewish businesses are vandalised; 12,000 Jews are sent to Sachsenhausen concentration camp.

1939-1944 World War II.

1942 Nazi leaders meet at Wannsee to decide on the 'Final Solution' to the Jewish question.

1943 Battle of Berlin.

1945 The city surrenders to the Red Army and is divided into four sectors overseen by the Allied powers.

1948 The Berlin Airlift supplies West Berlin, following a blockade by the Soviets.

1949 Founding of the Federal Republic of Germany in the West, and the German Democratic Republic in the East.

1961 The GDR government builds the Berlin Wall, sealing off West Berlin from East Germany.

1967-1968 Student protests in West Berlin.

1971 Quadripartite Agreement between the Western powers formally recognises the city's divided status.

9 Nov 1989 Fall of the Berlin Wall.

3 Oct 1990 German reunification.

1999 Berlin becomes the official capital of the Federal Republic of Germany.

2006 Germany hosts the FIFA World Cup.

2017 The CDU's Angela Merkel wins her fourth term as Chancellor, but there are significant gains for the far-right AfD party.

Eating & Drinking

Dining out in Berlin, while easy on the wallet, was once an uninspiring experience. If you liked fatty pork, you were in luck: traditional restaurants served hearty, stick-to-your ribs fare and plenty of it. Turkish and Vietnamese eateries added some variety, but only in a standardised, blandified version of their national cuisines. And then there was *Currywurst*...

Now, three decades since the fall of the Wall, eating out in Berlin has undergone a sea change. Finally, the city's appetite for exciting gastronomy has caught up with its craving for every other pleasure in life. An influx of global expats, combined with the ambition of the city's chefs and entrepreneurs, is redefining the parameters of the Berliner palate, and new levels of diversity have driven up standards. Formerly drab districts, such as Mitte and Kreuzberg are emerging as foodie havens, while Neukölln's

Cocktail kings
Becketts Kopf *p117*, Buck and
Breck *p89*, Green Door *p175*,
Galander Kreuzberg *p142*, Newton
Bar *p76*, Rum Trader *p173*,
Würgeengel *p147*

Snacktime superstars
Azzam *p152*, Konnopke's
Imbiss *p115*, Imren Grill *p155*,
Markthalle Neun *p147*, Vöner *p128*

Best German food
Café Einstein *p108*, Einstein Unter
den Linden *p76*

Best dive bars
Ankerklause *p152*, Bar 3 *p89*,
Barbie Deinhoff's *p146*, Bei
Schlawinchen *p146*

Best coffee & cake
Anna Blume *p115*, Barcomi's *p86*,
Bonanza *p115*, Five Elephant *p144*,
Konditorei Buchwald *p102*,
Princess Cheesecake *p88*

Best fine dining
Borchardt *p74*, Cinco *p108*,
Eins44 *p154*, Grill Royal *p80*,
Horváth *p145*, Katz Orange *p88*

hipster population has invigorated a groundswell of
pop-ups and street food. The only aspect of eating out
that has remained wonderfully and reassuringly the
same is Berlin's legendarily brusque service (*see p36*
Service with a Smile).

At the upper reaches of the market, there are still a
few trusty warhorses serving the great and good their
allocation of upmarket meat and veg. Much-revered
venues such as **Borchardt**, **Grill Royal**, **Lutter und
Wegner** (Charlottenstrasse 56, Mitte, 2029 5415, www.l-
w-berlin.de), and **Pauly Saal** (Auguststrasse 11-13, Mitte,
3300 6070, paulysaal.com) are sprinkled with Michelin
stars and attract a plutocratic clientele. These have
been joined by more contemporary ventures, such as
Cinco, **Hugos** (*see p108*), **Nobelhart & Schmutzig**
(*see p141*) and **Eins44**, which provide welcome
culinary innovation. Chefs such as Sebastian Frank
(**Horváth**) and wunderkind Dylan Watson-Brawn (**Ernst**,
Gerichtstrasse 54, Wedding, www.ernstberlin.de) have
gained superstar status.

Meanwhile, at the other end of the scale, there has
been a mini-revolution in the quality and diversity
of the city's street food, with Berliners showing an

unquenchable appetite for new experiences and flavours. The proliferation of eclectic pop-ups and foodie events demonstrates the dynamic new DIY ethic invigorating the city's eating-out scene, with intrepid young cooks creating anything from tapioca dumplings to ceviche, Nigerian *fufu* to Korean buns. Plenty of new, promising spots close almost as soon as they've opened, but, if a stall or pop-up proves its chops, it may graduate to more permanent premises.

German cuisine

If you want a taste of old Berlin, there are a few places, such as Mitte's **Kellerrestaurant im Brecht-Haus** (Chausseestrasse 125, 282 3843, www.brechtkeller.de) and Prenzlauer Berg's **Prater** (*see p118*), that still bear some resemblance to their historic roots. Berlin's traditional cooking has always been of the meat-and-two-veg variety. *Eisbein* is the signature local dish, a leathery skinned and extremely fatty pig's trotter, sometimes marinated and usually served with puréed peas. You won't find it on the menu, however, in anything but the most doggedly old-school establishments. More appetising specialities come with the seasons: spring is *Spargelzeit* ('asparagus time'), usually the white stuff served with boiled potatoes

Cinco

In the know
Price categories

We use the following price codes for restaurant listings throughout the guide; they represent the average cost of one main dish.

€ = under €10

€€ = €11-€20

€€€ = €21-€30

€€€€ = over €30

and Hollandaise; in June, little strawberry huts pop up across the city; August is for forest-fresh mushrooms, particularly frilly *Pfifferlinge* (chanterelles); then it's *Kürbiszeit* ('pumpkin time') from November. Proponents of *Neue Deutsche Küche* ('New German Cuisine') make the most of these seasonal offerings, with a focus on fresh, locally sourced produce. You can sample reinterpretations of German standards at **Horváth** (*see p145*) where the award-winning chef Sebastian Frank combines German and Austrian cuisines with flair.

Street Food Thursday *p147*

Berlin's most famous contribution to post-war German cuisine, however, is *Currywurst*, a sliced pork sausage covered in an oleaginous gloop of tomato ketchup with curry powder. Berlin, for some reason, wears its curry-sauce-sausage heritage with pride, although there are rumours that the dish actually originates from Hamburg. (It's best not to bring this up.) Try the traditional version under the railway arches at Prenzlauer Berg's venerable **Konnopke's Imbiss** (*see p115*), or the upmarket organic version – and the city's best chips – at **Witty's** (*see p167*).

The shock of the new

Berliners – for many years deprived of novelty on the culinary front – are wild for every new food trend and hip eatery. Opening nights can see hundreds of people turn up, alerted by Facebook event pages. In recent years Berlin's food crazes have encompassed everything from artisanal ice-cream to ramen, hummus, pulled pork and Korean *bibimbap*. Whatever the latest foodie trend, Berliners want to try it. To see what's next on the menu, visit the Street Food Thursday nights at **Markthalle Neun** (*see p147*), or **Bite Club**'s Friday night events on the Kreuzberg riverside (Hoppetosse by Badeschiff, Eichenstrasse 4, biteclub.de). One food trend that shows no sign of going out of fashion is Berliners' appetite for **brunch**. Lingering over a long, leisurely breakfast is the city's favourite way to start the weekend, and the best eateries go out of their way to offer something special (*see p35* Berlin brunch).

Global flavours

The brevity of Germany's colonial experience means no deep-rooted link with a foreign cuisine. However, with an increasingly cosmopolitan clientele to encourage ethnic variety at street level, Berlin dining has been getting steadily more international.

Turkish food, which arrived with post-war *Gastarbeiter* ('guest workers'), is deeply embedded in the western side of town. Kreuzberg claims to be the place where the doner kebab was invented in the early 1970s, forever associated with **Hasir** (Adalbertstrasse 10, Kreuzberg, 614 2373, www. hasir.de). Every Tuesday and Friday, you can join

---

In the know
Tipping and etiquette

In restaurants, it's customary to tip around ten per cent. Tips are handed directly to the server rather than left on the table. Don't say *danke* ('thank you') as you hand over the cash, unless you want the server to keep the change. In bars, people tend to pay their own way and drink at their own pace – partly because, in many places, bills are only totted up as you leave – but ceremonial rounds of Jägermeister, tequila or vodka are a local nightlife feature. Hardly anywhere shuts before 1am and most bars stay open much later – some until the last customers leave.

Katz Orange *p88*

locals stocking up on delicious fresh produce, snacks and knick-knacks at the sprawling **Türkischer Markt** on Maybachufer (*see p156*). Italian cuisine has also long been well represented (**Osteria No.1**; Kreuzbergstrasse 7, 5779 2999, www.osterian1-berlin.com).

An influx of refugees from South Vietnam in the 1970s and contract workers from North Vietnam in the 1980s has given Berlin a significant Vietnamese population and a surfeit of Vietnamese food: from unappetizing, greasy boxes of noodles at seemingly every street corner to exquisite, freshly prepared *pho* and *bánh mì*. A pioneer of authentic modern Vietnamese cooking in the city, **Si An** (*see p117*) is still going strong. Korean food is likewise well represented at **Ixthys** (*see p174*) and **Yam Yam** (Alte Schönhauser

In the know
Veggie eats

Venture beyond the traditional restaurants and you'll find plenty of eateries serving innovative vegetarian and vegan food for every meal. For brunch and doughnuts, check out **Brammibal's Donuts** (Maybachufer 8, Neukölln, brammibalsdonuts. com); for lunch, try the burgers at **Let It Be** (Treptowerstrasse 90, Neukölln, letitbevegan.de), the clean-eating options at **Daluma** (Weinbergsweg 3, Mitte, daluma.de) or the bowlfuls of goodness at **Holy Flat** (Lenaustrasse 10, Neukölln, www.holy-flat.com). And finally, for dinner, try exquisite Chinese at **Tianfuzius** (Regensburger Strasse 1, Schöneberg, tianfu.de), or the cosmopolitan vegan nosh at **Lucky Leek** (*p116*).

Strasse 6, Mitte, 2463 2486, www.yamyam-berlin.de), where *bibimbap* is king – a bowl of steaming rice, meat, kimchi and a fresh fried egg, all waiting to be mashed into a droolworthy mass of comfort food, topped with lashings of spicy sauce.

There's good-quality Japanese at **Sasaya** (*see p116* and Indonesian at **Mabuhay** (Köthener Strasse 28, Kreuzberg, 265 1867, mabuhay.juisyfood.com). In Charlottenburg, Berlin's Thai community offers up all manner of delicacies alfresco at a hugely popular informal gathering in the Preussen Park (*see p173*). Indian food, however, presents something of a problem. There are places all over town, but standards are generally dire.

Kaffee und Kuchen

Pretty much every street in the city boasts a coffee shop or a bakery, and the tradition of taking a leisurely afternoon break for '*Kaffee und Kuchen*' (coffee and cake) is one of the most appealing aspects of Berlin life. For a quirky twist, try Mitte's **Princess Cheesecake** (*see p88*) where the impossibly rich and decadent creations range from beetroot-flavoured chocolate cheesecake to home-made truffles with Earl Grey-flavoured ganache. If you're after something more old-school, then **Anna Blume** (*see p115*) has a chocolate-box atmosphere, killer cakes and insanely addictive coffee. Fortunately, the watery filter coffee consumed by Berliners for decades has now been replaced by

> ### In the know
> ### Smokers' paradise
>
> Thirty per cent of Berliners smoke and, thanks to a local 2009 ruling protecting bar owners' right to make a living, smokers can continue to ruin their health in the warmth and comfort of most Berlin bars and clubs. Even bars that serve food either have separate smoking sections or pull out the ashtrays as soon as the kitchens close, and in *Kneipen* (traditional pubs) smoking is practically obligatory. If you're tempted yourself – or just want to break the ice with an attractive stranger – asking for '*eine Kippe*' is usually met with good grace and generosity.

Currywurst

so-called 'third-wave coffee', introduced by US and Aussie immigrants. Small-scale roasteries have sprung up all over the city; **Bonanza** (*see p115*) in Prenzlauer Berg was one of the first on the scene and is still hard to beat.

Drink up

Berliners do like a drink, and the city's reputation as an excellent drinking destination is well-deserved. Beer is the main tipple, although local brews such as Berliner Kindl, a party staple, are poor compared to the best of Bavaria or Bohemia. Craft beer – while viewed with some suspicion – is beginning to catch on. Check out the **BRLO Brauhaus** in Gleisdreieck Park (Schöneberger Strasse 16, 0151-7437 4235, www.brlo-brwhouse.de), **Vagabund Brauerei** (*see p122*) or the home brewery in the cellar bar of the **Circus Hostel** (*see p191*).

The capital's changing demographics mean that tiny, elite cocktail bars are also on the increase. Places such as **Buck and Breck** (*see p89*), **Becketts Kopf** (*see p117*) and **Pauly Saal** (*see p28*) are setting the benchmark for avant-garde mixology, but cultured snorts can be found in every part of town at venues such as **Galander Kreuzberg**

💛 Berlin brunch

Breakfast in Berlin is a big deal. Whether you're up bright and early and fancy a leisurely morning meal, or you've been partying all night and need a calorie hit before crashing out, Berlin's brunch culture will see you right. The offer ranges from a simple duo of (excellent) coffee and a pastry, through a traditional German *Frühstuck* of bread rolls (called *Schrippen* in Berlin), cheese and salami, to increasingly elaborate spreads complete with muesli, fruit, yoghurt, cured meats, eggs and authentic dishes from around the globe. Highlights include Aussie comfort food – think lashings of avocado, eggs and unbeatable coffee – at **Silo Coffee** (*see p128*); pastries and crêpes surrounded by freshly cut flowers at **Anna Blume** (*see p115*); a post-clubbing refuel in the fresh air at **Café Schönbrunn** (*see p127*) and hearty portions in a cutesy setting at **1900 Café Bistro** (*see p166*). Other reliable brunch spots include **Barcomi's** and **Café Fleury** in Mitte (*see p87*), **Isla** (*see p159*) in Neukölln and **Café Aroma** (*see p166*) in Schöneberg. For something different, try **La Femme** (Kottbusser Damm 77, 5360 4057, www.lafemme-breakfast. de) in Kreuzberg, which serves traditional Turkish treats such as white cheese, *sucuk* (sausage), olives, eggs and fresh *simit* (a pretzel-shaped sesame-seeded breadstick). But perhaps the go-to spot right now is **Benedict** in Wilmersdorf (*see p172*), which has taken the city's infatuation

with the meal to new heights by serving nothing but breakfast 24 hours a day. Luxury egg dishes and pancakes are the stars of its extensive international menu.

Note that by 11am on a Saturday morning, the whole city seems to be out scouting for brunch; popular spots become jammed, and there's often a wait for tables, followed by incredibly slow service. To avoid such an unpleasant start to your weekend, get to your venue of choice no later than 10.35am, so you can pick your table, place your order and sit back smugly sipping on that first latte-macchiato of the day, watching the frustration of those a bit slower off the mark.

In the know
Service with a smile

While some cities bring panache to waiting tables (Rome), bonhomie (Madrid), or what seems to be a sincere desire to make you have that nice day (San Francisco), traditionally Berlin waiters have specialised in the kind of brusque insouciance that could leave a starving diner choking with rage, particularly on a Saturday at brunch-time when poor service reaches its apotheosis in Berlin. Times are changing, however, and you're now just as likely to be greeted with hospitality, an authoritative rundown of the locally sourced specials and a recommendation for some excellent wine pairings. This is, sort of, how things should be, but it has the unfortunate effect of making you feel that you could be anywhere in the world.

Fear not, old habits die hard; if you stay in Berlin for a few days and eat out a lot, you are more than likely to be barked at or cold-shouldered at least once. How to respond? Don't start looking anxious, wondering what you've done wrong, or getting irate. Maintain a stony expression; if you can, raise an eyebrow. Perhaps mutter loudly to your companion, *'Das Leben ist kein Ponyhof'* (Life's not a pony-stable – apparently a Berlin synonym for luxury). You're not intimidated; you're not impressed. Carry it off, and the waiting staff will soon warm up. If not, and if the service is truly unapologetically bad – don't tip. A Berliner wouldn't.

(*see p142*), **Tier** (Weserstrasse 42, www.tier.bar) and **Cordobar** (*see p90*), the latter being the cognoscenti's wine bar of choice.

Never fear, there are also still plenty of characterful dives and unpretentious *Kneipen* (traditional pubs) – almost one on every corner in some parts of town. Unreconstructed, untouched by changing fashions, with nicotine-stained walls and gruff locals hogging all the bar stools, they have a rough appeal that is the perfect antidote to an overdose of hipster hotspots. The beer is cheap and good too – although you'll have to pay with cash.

In summer, Berliners take their drinking outside: café tables spread out on to the pavements, beer gardens bustle and beach bars spring to life in waterside locations. In fact, enjoying a *Feierabend* (after-work) beer or Club Maté (a fizzy-soda based on the South America stimulant *maté*) on a wooden table outside a *Späti* (late shop) is a fine Berlin custom.

Shopping

Shopping in Berlin can be a frustrating experience. There is no single pedestrian area, no truly instinctive centre of gravity that draws you in. Instead, there are several shopping neighbourhoods in various stages of development, gentrification and corresponding counter-culture.

The heavily trafficked Kurfürstendamm in the West is undoubtedly the most tightly packed with the biggest global players: it's home to the only Apple store in the city, for instance. However, wandering away from the main street in search of 'hidden gems' proves to be a disheartening experience. To find these in Berlin, you need to hop on the U-Bahn and head away from Ku'Damm. But where to go? Fashion-forward, well-paid, bright young things may try Weinmeisterstrasse in Mitte,

Only in Berlin
Ampelmann Shop p90,
Erich Hamann Bittere
Schokoladen p173, Hard
Wax p147, Harry Lehmann p172,
KaDeWe p41, RSVP p92

Best for fashion
Aura p156, DSTM p91, LaLa
Berlin p92, Mykita p92, Voo p147

Best for food & drink
Arminius Markthalle p105,
KaDeWe p41, Markthalle
Neun p147, Thai Park p173

Best street markets
Arkonaplatz Flohmarkt p90,
Flohmarkt am Boxhagener
Platz p130, Mauerpark
Flohmarkt p119, Türkischer
Markt p156, Winterfeldtplatz
Markt p176

Best bookshops
Another Country p142,
Bücherbogen p167,
do you read me?! p91, Marga
Schoeller Bücherstube p169,
Modern Graphics p147,
Saint George's p119

where independent boutiques rub shoulders with
expensive chain stores. Hippies and alternative folk could
be well-served in Bergmannstrasse, Kreuzberg, where
incense burners and boho prints reign supreme.

A mixed bag

Even in the city's most more distinctive areas, Berlin
has a way of pushing against the grain, as the lowbrow
and highbrow, mainstream and avant-garde, designer
chic and street style coexist in striking juxtapositions.
A quirky independent art bookshop might thrive next
to a global megastore, a cheeky sex shop can nestle
comfortably among some of the city's most exclusive
boutiques. Even the influx of big-name international
brands over the past two decades hasn't dampened
the impulse of Berlin's progressives to keep things
interesting: they just move to one side and start a pop-up
kiosk in a former cat sanctuary selling home-made
bibimbap. Or something.

Although malls and international franchises are
increasingly in evidence – a nod either to the broader
smartening-up of the city or to soul-destroying
commercialism, depending on your point of view –

there is still plenty of colourful, home-grown talent and entrepreneurial spirit to discover, with fashion, food and 'lifestyle' leading the way.

Perhaps the best example of the contrasts in the city's shopping scene is the vast **Bikini Berlin** (Budapesterstrasse 38-50, www.bikiniberlin.de), which could be described as a mega-mall for affluent arty hipsters. A minimal, stylish 'experience' featuring more esoteric brands than one would expect to find in the average identikit shopping centre, Bikini Berlin bills itself as a 'concept mall' aimed at the 'urban customer'. For a similar vibe, but in smaller premises, head across town to Mitte's **Soho House** (*see p189*) where **The Store Berlin** (www.thestores.com/berlin) sells luxury items, ranging from fashion, books, plants and cult cosmetics to cold-pressed juices, in an imaginative retail space; there's even a retro hair and beauty salon at the rear. Similarly curated homewares and chic accessories can be found at **Hallesches Haus** (*see p142*) in Kreuzberg.

Bikini Berlin

Shopping by area

Charlottenburg remains the upmarket showpiece it always was. Major department stores and the flagship outlets of familiar international names march westwards from **KaDeWe** on Wittenbergplatz and along the Kurfürstendamm, west Berlin's major shopping avenue. Luxury brands cluster on Fasanenstrasse, while more discreet boutiques, interior design outlets and tasteful bookshops are scattered around the streets between the Ku'damm and Kantstrasse. Knesebeckstrasse, on either side of Savignyplatz, is good for bookshops: try the excellent English-language section at **Marga Schoeller Bücherstube** (*see p169*), which sold anti-Nazi pamphlets in the 1930s and is still going strong; or, for art and architecture, check out **Bücherbogen** (*see p167*).

Heading in the opposite direction, at Potsdamer Platz, there's the big **Arkaden** shopping mall (Alte Potsdamer Strasse 7, potsdamerplatz.de/shopping). Nearby in the Tagesspiegel building, the high-end 'concept' store **Andreas Murkudis** (Potsdamer Strasse 77 & 81E, 680 798 306, www.andreasmurkudis.com) showcases a tasteful spectrum of luxury goods, from Dries van Noten to beautifully crafted, insanely expensive trinkets, baubles and fripperies from home and abroad.

In Mitte, department stores and yet more international brands line Friedrichstrasse, including an elegant branch of **Galeries Lafayette** (Friedrichstrasse 76-78, 209 480, www. galerieslafayette.de), but the area between Alexanderplatz and Rosenthalerplatz fizzles with adventurous and eccentric shops. Shady Mulackstrasse is where the fashion pack list their favourite stores: **Das Neue Schwarz** (*see p92*) for second-hand threads is well worth visiting, as are boutiques such as **Baerck** (no.12, 2404 8994, baerck.

🖤 KaDeWe

Tauentzienstrasse 21-24 (21210, www.kadewe.com). U1, U2, U3 Wittenbergplatz. **Open** *10am-8pm Mon-Fri; 10am-9pm Sat.* **Map** *p162 H9* ⓾ *Department store*

The grand dame of them all, Kaufhaus des Westens (Department Store of the West) to give it its full title, is still the pick of Berlin's malls. Shopping here, or at least gazing at the wares, has been an essential Berliner experience for more than a century. Founded in 1907 by Adolf Jandorf, acquired by Herman Tietz in 1926 and later 'Aryanised' and expropriated by the Nazis, KaDeWe was the only one of Berlin's famous turn-of-the-last-century department stores to survive the war intact; it has been extensively modernised over the last two decades.

KaDeWe stocks an impressive range of high-end designers and has tried to shed its stuffy image by bringing in upbeat, younger labels such as Alice+Olivia and London shoe brand Buffalo. If you're in the market for a new designer handbag, evening gown or Rolex this is still the place to come, but what really distinguishes KaDeWe from your Harrods and Galeries Lafayette is the sixth floor. Here you'll find the quintessential luxury food-hall experience in a city otherwise teeming with budget supermarkets. With counter after counter of delicatessens, butchers, pâtisseries and grocers, and plenty of prepared foods to take away, the olfactory experience as you move between sections

is an experience in itself. The oyster bar is a perfect mid-shop pit stop, and after a visit to the champagne bar, you may need to hand your credit cards over to a more responsible adult. There's something quintessentially 'Charlottenburg' about KaDeWe: a bit stuffy and *bürgerlich* to be sure, but underneath it all, more than a little decadent. Head up another level to reach a cavernous glass-roofed restaurant with a fine view of Wittenbergplatz below.

The bookshop at Urban Spree *p130*

net) and Vivien Westwood haven **Worlds End** (no.26, 8561 0073), each offering up quirky and quality fashion. Local brands, such as **Starstyling** (no.4, 9700 5182, www. starstyling.net) and **Lala Berlin** (*see p92*), design and produce their own gear, much loved by locals in the know. Also in this area you'll find popular street labels (Urban Outfitters, Cos and Adidas), as well as Berlin vintage favourites **Made in Berlin** (Neue Schönhauser Strasse 19, 2123 0601) and **Pick n Weight** (Bergmannstrasse 102, 694 3348, www. picknweight.de). The graffitied, eastern end of Torstrasse has a proliferation of concept stores and big brands selling everything from high-end sneakers to covetable antiques, jewellery, and more minimal and tasteful fashion.

The gentrification of Mitte has been driving less affluent shoppers in the direction of Friedrichshain and Kreuzberg, where a more student (and 'perennial student') population dominates. The Bergmannstrasse neighbourhood in Kreuzberg is where you find second-hand shops, small designer outlets, music stores, bookshops and delis. One of the best bookshops in the city, **Another Country** has been catering to Kreuzbergers

Aura

in German and English for decades, as has the charming, little **Ebert und Weber** nearby (Falckensteinstrasse 44, 6956 5193, www.ebertundweber.de).

Neukölln's shopping scene is rather incoherent; however, the leafy area around Maybachufer conceals a few delights that are worth seeking out if you're in the area. Try **Sing Blackbird** (*see p155*) for chunky knit sweaters and floral dresses, along with a coffee shop for post-rummage refuelling; **Aura** (*see p156*) for traditional silk kimonos, and **Vintage Galore** (*see p157*) for Scandinavian and mid-century furnishings, along with a tastefully curated rack of pre-loved clothing. New shops and cafés are popping up all the time, so this area rewards a wander on a pleasant day. You never know what you might stumble across.

Market analysis

Berlin hosts several interesting flea markets. Sunday's **Mauerpark Flohmarkt** has an eclectic selection but is regarded as somewhat touristy by locals and gets rammed quickly. The **Kunst und Trödel Markt** by Tiergarten station (*see p102*) is a great place for collectors, while the **Flohmarkt am Boxhagener Platz** mixes old furniture and bric-a-brac with work by local artists and T-shirt designers. Markets are also a great place to sample some of the city's foodie trends, from traditional covered produce markets, such as **Arminius Markthalle**, to Sunday's Street Food auf Achse at the

KulturBrauerei (*see p114*), where hipsters snack on Indian *vada pav* and wild game burgers. At the biweekly **Türkischer Markt** on Maybachufer, you can find everything from freshly baked bread to organic cheese and Greek olives, while the **Kollwitzplatz farmers' market** sells a wide range of local artisan produce. And, during weekends in the summer, you will find a delicious Thai food market run by Berlin's Asian community in Wilmersdorf's **Preussenpark**.

Opening hours

Shops generally open at around 10am and are permitted to stay open until 10pm. However, small and traditional stores tend to close around 6pm; most bigger stores and more adventurous smaller retailers stick it out at least until 8pm. Most shops are open on Saturday afternoons, but nearly all are closed on Sunday (unless your trip happens to coincide with one of the city's elusive shopping weekends). Credit and debit cards, PIN machines and contactless payment are less widely used than elsewhere, with most transactions still made in cash.

Another Country *p142*

Entertainment

Berlin's cultural offering rivals anywhere on the planet. During the Cold War, East and West Berlin were both awash with state subsidies for arts institutions, as each side tried to demonstrate the supremacy of its respective ideology. This meant that, after reunification, Berlin had twice as many performance venues as other capitals. Today, the dizzying array of entertainment options – from world-class classical music and avant-garde theatre to arthouse cinema and groundbreaking nightlife – will satisfy even the most demanding culture vulture or party animal.

❤ **Shortlist**

Best classical music & opera
Komische Oper *p77*,
Philharmonie *p110*

Best film screenings
Astor Film Lounge *p169*,
Berlinale *p64*

Best theatre & cabaret
Bar jeder Vernunft *p174*,
Maxim Gorki Theater *p78*

Best alternative nights out
Ballhaus Ost *p119*,
Barbie Deinhoff's *p146*,
Clärchen's Ballhaus *p93*,
Dr. Pong *p119*

Best nightclubs
Berghain *p132*,
Buttons at ://aboutblank *p131*,
Gayhane at SO36 *p149*,
Horse Meat Disco *p76*

Cabaret

Although today's cabaret bears little resemblance to the classic cabaret of the Weimar years, there are some great performers who can re-create an entire era in one night. Don't confuse *Cabaret* with *Varieté*: the latter is a circus-like show, minus the animals but with lots of dancing girls. *Kabarett* is different again: a unique kind of German entertainment with a strong following in Berlin; it's basically political satire sprinkled with songs and sketches, and is likely to be incomprehensible unless you have perfect German and a thorough understanding of local politics. When it comes to *Travestie* – drag revue – Berlin has some of the best on offer, from fabulous to tragic. Venues come in all sizes and styles, from small and dark to huge and glittery. For the more progressive and intelligent drag acts, the **BKA Theater** (*see p143*) is a safe bet.

Classical music & opera

No city in the world can compete with Berlin when it comes to the sheer number of orchestras and opera houses. The German capital boasts enough classical music for two (maybe three) cities, with four high-profile symphony orchestras, a generous handful of chamber orchestras and three state-subsidised opera houses – the

Deutsche Oper (*see p170*), the **Staatsoper Unter den Linden** (*see p78*) and the **Komische Oper**. It's not just quantity, but quality too: the **Berlin Philharmonic** is arguably the finest symphony orchestra in the world.

Film

During the 1920s and '30s, Berlin was a centre for groundbreaking cinema. Pioneering directors Friedrich Wilhelm Murnau and Fritz Lang revolutionised film-making, while the Kurfürstendamm's famously grand film halls, such as the Ufa Palast Am Zoo and the Marmorhaus, offered a swinging good time for fashion-conscious patrons. A few wars and political shifts later, cinema remains an important piece of the city's cultural jigsaw. Though the scene may not quite compare to Berlin of the 1920s, the city's old-school arthouse joints, blockbuster multiplexes, world-class Berlinale and a handful of DIY genre festivals make it hard to say if Berlin's glory days of cinema are long gone or just beginning.

Nowadays, all cinemas seem to have more English-language programming in evidence, but there are also all-English venues run by Yorck cinemas, including the **Babylon Kreuzberg** (*see p148*), plus the **Cinestar IMAX Sony Center** (0451 7030 200, www.cinestar.de).

Bar jeder Vernunft

In the know
What's on

To find out what's on where, check *Zitty* (www.zitty.de) or *Tip* (www.tip-berlin.de), Berlin's two fortnightly listings magazines, or their English-language monthly equivalent *Exberliner* (www.exberliner.com). The LGBT scene is covered by the free monthly *Blu* (www.blu.fm) and *Siegessäule* (www.siegessaeule.de) magazines.

LGBT

Berlin has one of the world's most active queer scenes, but this hasn't appeared out of nowhere; in years past, the city has borne witness to dramatic swings in acceptance and persecution. Today, the city practises a never-again stance towards gay intolerance. Alternative lifestyles of all stripes are considered normal and are even celebrated on giant billboards in U-Bahn stations. You won't need to search hard to uncover Berlin's gay scene: it'll find you in about ten minutes. Venues and events are spread throughout the city, but some areas are still gayer than others, especially Schöneberg, as well as parts of Prenzlauer Berg, Mitte and Kreuzberg.

Nightlife

Berlin's reputation for decadence and nocturnal high jinks stretches all the way back to the 1920s, when the city's legendary cabaret scene and tolerance of homosexuality made it the destination of choice for

Christopher Street Day Parade

In the know
Getting past the bouncers

An increasing number of Berlin clubs operate some sort of door policy, based on the brutal phrase *Gesichtskontrolle* (face control) meaning that bouncers get to decide who gets in and who stays out. To increase your chances, there are a few simple rules to follow in the queue. Be as quiet as possible. Don't be obviously off your face. But don't seem too stiff. Don't take pictures. Don't have this guide in your hand. Use English sparingly. Learn the answer to 'Wie viele?' (How many [people are you])? Zwei, drei, vier, and bear in mind that singles and twos have a better chance than sizeable groups. Some clubs don't like people to try too hard; others will turn punters away who haven't made enough effort. Wear whatever you like but bear in mind that Berliners tend not to dress up in a British sense – short skirts and high heels might be better left at home – unless you're in drag of course.

Europe's party people. During the Cold War, East Berlin had more liberal licensing laws than London, while the western side of town teemed with nihilistic artists and self-exiled musicians, including David Bowie, Iggy Pop and Nick Cave. In the heady post-Wall years, the West Berlin avant-garde collided with party-starved East Berliners to create a DIY rave scene on makeshift dancefloors in abandoned buildings, laying the groundwork for the city's future status as the spiritual home of electronica. The capital is still synonymous with the genre, which is now reinventing itself (again) as a result of an influx of foreign talent.

Berlin still deserves its reputation as one of the world's best party cities; every taste is catered for here, all night long, in every kind of venue, from desperate dives in temporary locations to swanky premises where mirror balls make the world go round. Berliners don't head to clubs until 1am at the earliest, and it's not unusual to start at a party on Friday night and stumble into bed at some point on Sunday afternoon. The real party animals go out during the week too. While this approach is hardcore, the general attitude to clubbing is incredibly laid-back: no dressing up, no planning; Berliners let themselves go with the flow. That said, the club scene is not immune to

Club der Visionaere

ever-increasing gentrification, as developers tussle with locals to reclaim venues in Kreuzberg, Friedrichshain and Prenzlauer Berg for more corporate ends.

Theatre & dance

Berlin's theatre productions are exciting and well attended. The city has five subsidised state theatres – the **Berliner Ensemble** (*see p81*), **Deutsches Theater** (*see p81*), **Maxim Gorki Theater** (*see p78*), **Schaubühne** (*see p170*) and **Volksbühne** (*see p93*) – supplemented by a multitude of flourishing fringe venues. While some performances have English surtitles (most frequently at the Schaubühne), it is equally possible to get a lot out of a show without speaking German, thanks to the visually powerful productions. Berlin also has a dynamic contemporary dance scene that cultivates fresh ideas while continuing to nurture the strong traditions of German dance theatre. The **Staatsballett Berlin** (www.staatsballett-berlin.de) performs from September to June at the state opera houses (*see above*), as well as putting on an experimental season at Berghain (*see p132*) called Shut Up and Dance.

Berlin
Day by Day

Karneval der Kulturen

Itineraries

Berlin is a large and sprawling city with more than its fair share of iconic sights and world-class museums. Many of these are clustered in the centre, but others are more far-flung. Fortunately, Berlin's transport system is efficient and comprehensive, cyclists are well-catered for and walking is a pleasure. Our carefully curated itineraries will help you make the most of your time in Berlin, but you should also be prepared to change your plans on a whim and let the city itself be your guide.

▶ *Budgets include transport, meals and admission prices, but not accommodation and shopping.*

ESSENTIAL WEEKEND

Budget €100-€120 per day.
Getting around If you don't want to walk, either buy a day ticket for public transport (€7) or rent a bike (*see p23* Berlin by bike).

DAY 1

Morning

Sprawling **Tiergarten** park (*see p101*) is the green heart of Berlin. Strolling among the acres of grass, trees and lakes can easily swallow up a sunny day, but more dedicated sightseers should head to the **Siegessäule** (*see p100*) in the centre for magnificent views. From the monument, head down Lichtensteinallee for a hearty breakfast at the delightfully bucolic **Café am Neuen See** (*see p102*), then head east on Strasse des 17 Juni, past the Soviet Memorial, to the **Brandenburger Tor** (*see p72*) – one of the city's most recognisable icons. Just to the north is the equally famous **Reichstag** (*see p103*), seat of the German parliament; a visit to Norman Foster's dome is free, as long as you've booked online in advance. Return to the Brandenburg Gate and continue south on Ebertstrasse as far as the **Denkmal für die ermordeten Juden Europas** (*see p75*), a powerful memorial to victims of the Holocaust.

Afternoon

Decent independent eateries are hard to find around here, so it's worth seeking out **Café Nö!** (*see p74*) for a spot of lunch before continuing down Ebertstrasse to **Potsdamer Platz** (*see p105*),

home to an array of modern malls, cinemas and tower blocks. Get an express lift up to the **Panoramapunkt** observation decks (*see p107*) for another awesome view of the city. Then head east along the remains of the Wall at Niederkirchner Strasse to the infamous Checkpoint Charlie crossing point between East and West Berlin. Today, it's a tacky tourist mess of souvenir shops, kebab joints and coachloads of visitors, but it's still worth visiting the mini-museum at the **Haus am Checkpoint Charlie** (*see p138*). Heading down Friedrichstrasse, make a detour to the **Jüdisches Museum** (*see p140*) to experience Daniel Libeskind's striking and emotive architecture. To the south, boutiques and cafés are now mushrooming in Kreuzberg's Hallesches Tor district; check out **Hallesches Haus** (*see p142*) for a restorative coffee and some window-shopping, then a late-afternoon ramble along the **Landwehrkanal**.

Sony Center

Evening

Now you're perfectly placed to sample the restaurants, cafés and bars of Kreuzkölln. Go high-end at **Eins44** (*see p154*) or **Lode & Stijn** (*see p145*), or get a Lebanese fast-food fix at **Azzam** (*see p152*). Once you're suitably fed, head for **Würgeengel** (*see p147*), an iconic cocktail bar that encapsulates the best of Berlin's nightlife: moody lighting, well-served cocktails and an ever-present haze of smoke. If you want to continue the party, check out the trendy **Prince Charles** club on Prinzenstrasse (*see p148*) or kitsch, queer and welcoming

Barbie Deinhoff's (*see p146*). Or, if you're feeling brave, taxi over to Friedrichshain to try your luck at **Berghain** (*see p132*).

DAY 2

Morning

There's no shortage of breakfast spots around Berlin and indulging in a long and lazy **brunch** is a Berlin experience not to be missed (*see p35*). After a hearty feed, you'll be ready for the **Museumsinsel** (Museum Island; *see p81*), Berlin's UNESCO-listed museum quarter. This is one of the city's most visited areas and it's easy to see why – the group of five major museums makes for an immersive cultural experience. You can't possibly visit them all in one morning, so make your choice between the Pergamonmuseum, with its examples of ancient architecture; the Altes Museum, brimming with antique treasures; the Alte Nationalgalerie for medieval art; the Bode-Museum for sculptures and Byzantine art, and the Neues Museum, with pieces from Ancient Egypt and early history.

Lode & Stijn

Hackesche Höfe

Afternoon

After the morning's cultural overload, wander a few steps north to the **Scheunenviertel** (*see p85*), a historic enclave of shops and cafés, many hidden in a maze-like warren of courtyards or *Höfe*; the most famous are the Jugendstil **Hackesche Höfe** (*see p86*). Refuel at **Moggs** (*see p88*), which serves up the hugest, juiciest salt-beef sandwiches this side of Lower Manhattan. Mitte's classy boutiques attract fashionistas to the area around Mulackstrasse and Alte Schönhauser Strasse; check out the likes of **Das Neue Schwarze** (*see p92*), **Lala Berlin** (*see p92*) and **DSTM** (*see p91*) for the definitive Berlin black, structured look. This district is also a gallery heartland; along **Auguststrasse** are some of the coolest art spots in town. Enjoy coffee and cake at **Barcomi's** (*see p86*) before sauntering south to Alexanderplatz, the former hub of East Berlin during the GDR era. Remnants of the brutalist architecture of the day remain – most notably in the shape of the **Fernsehturm** (*see p94*), completed in 1969. It's worth braving the queues for a ride up to the observation deck and an early evening drink in the revolving café.

Evening

For dinner, head two stops north on the U8 to Rosenthaler Platz to check out the restaurants around Torstrasse: sample quality locavore dining at **Das Lokal** (*see p88*), Vietnamese *banh mí* at **Côcô** (*see p87*) or simple Middle Eastern fare at **Yarok** (*see p89*). There are plenty of bars here too, where you can round off the night in a blur of cocktails and dancing; for a selection, *see p89*. If you'd rather skip the bar hopping and hardcore partying (we don't blame you), you're well-placed to experience Berlin's rich cultural offering, with opera at the world-renowned **Komische Oper** (*see p77*), cutting-edge theatre at **Maxim Gorki Theater** (*see p78*) and the **Sophiensaale** (*see p93*), or circus acts and shimmying feather boas at **Chamäleon** (*see p93*).

Komische Oper

Fernsehturm

FAMILY DAY OUT

Budget €200-€250 for a family of four.
Getting around Children under six travel free on public transport. Cycling is also an option.

Morning

Finding somewhere child-friendly for breakfast is never a problem in Berlin, especially around Prenzlauer Berg, and Kreuzberg. Seek out one of the city's *Kindercafés*, which are especially designed for families. **Kindercafe Milchbart** (Paul-Robeson-Strasse 6, 6630 7755, www.milchbart.net) in Prenzlauer Berg has its own climbing area, sandbox and ball pond, plus excellent coffee and healthy eats. After breakfast, you could attempt a museum. The **Bode-Museum** (*see p83*) is particularly good for families as it houses an interactive children's museum aimed at four- to ten-year-olds. Nearby **Monbijou Park** on Oranienburger Strasse – just over the pedestrian bridge from the Bode Museum – has playgrounds and, in summer, a great paddling pool. Alternatively, dinosaur fanatics will enjoy the fossils and multimedia displays at the **Museum für Naturkunde** (*see p79*). Teens might prefer to head to the **Computerspielemuseum** (*see p127*) on Karl-Marx-Allee. Afterwards, they can release some excess energy at the **Raw Tempel** (Revaler Strasse 99, Friedrichshain), a sports and arts complex housed in a dilapidated set of old factories that includes **Der Kegel** climbing centre (www.derkegel.de) and the **Skatehalle** skateboarding centre (www.skatehalle-berlin.de).

Afternoon

When you start feeling peckish, take the U7 to south-west Kreuzberg for a wide choice of food options. Try **Café Kreuzzwerg** (Hornstrasse 23, 9786 7609, www.cafe-kreuzzwerg.de) or **Café Blume**

Museum für Naturkunde

(Fontanestrasse 32, 6449 0778, www.blumeberlin.de) close to **Volkspark Hasenheide**. The park has an adventure playground, crazy golf course and small zoo. Also in this area is the huge supervised indoor playground **Jolo** (Am Tempelhofer Berg 7D, 6120 2796, www.jolo-berlin.de), where facilities include an inflatable mountain, mini bumper cars and a snack bar. And, to the south, is the vast expanse of **Tempelhofer Feld** (*see p158*), perfect for safe cycling, kite-flying and picnics. Once the kids have let off steam, make your way to the **Haus am Checkpoint Charlie** (*see p138*), which displays the old cars and balloons that people used to circumvent the Wall. There are fine views from the tethered balloon nearby. Another option is to visit the **Deutsches Technikmuseum Berlin** (*see p139*) for vintage locomotives and cars, computers and gadgets, plus fantastic hands-on experiments. After that you're one stop on the U2 from Potsdamer

Deutsches Technikmuseum

Platz, where family-friendly attractions include the **aquarium** (*see p94*), **Legoland Discovery Centre** and the **Panoramapunkt** observation deck (*see p107*).

Evening

Head back to Kreuzberg for dinner. Kids eat for free on Sundays at **Italian Osteria No.1** (Kreuzbergstrasse 7, 5779 2999, www.osterian1-berlin.com) and there's more family-friendly fare at **Tomasa Villa Kreuzberg** (Kreuzbergstrasse 62, 8100 9885, www. tomasa.de). For dessert, seek out some ice-cream at **Isabel's Eiscafé** (Böckstrasse 51, 6981 6832, www.eiscafe-isabel. berlin/) or **Fräulein Frost** (*see p155*). If you're ready for a child-free evening, there are a number of English-speaking babysitting agencies: **Babysitter-Express Berlin** (4000 3400, www.babysitter-express.de) operates a 24-hour hotline for all your childcare emergencies and **Kinderinsel** (4171 6928, www.kinderinsel.de/en) offers round-the-clock childcare for kids up to 14.

Tempelhofer Feld

BUDGET BREAK

Budget €40-€50.
Getting around Buy a day pass for public transport (€7) or hire a bike (€10).

Morning

Silo Coffee in Friedrichshain (*see p128*) serves hearty breakfasts for less than a tenner. From here, you can stroll through the street art and market stalls of the **RAW Gelände** to **East Side Gallery** (*see p126*), where artists have decorated a stretch of the Berlin Wall. Enjoy views up and down the River Spree before crossing into Kreuzberg. Continue east along the river, perhaps stopping in summer for a dip at the **Badeschiff** (*see p149*) en route to **Treptower Park** (*see p149*). Check out the impressive **Soviet Memorial** (*see p150*) at the park's southern end.

Afternoon

A bike will come in handy for whizzing up to Neukölln for lunch. At **Azzam** (*see p152*), a bowl of houmous the size of your head (plus pitta and veg) is under €4. If you're here on a Tuesday, Friday or Saturday, head for the Maybachufer to people-watch and nab a bargain at the **Türkischer Markt** (*see p156*). Time for some sightseeing? In Mitte, the **Denkmal für die ermordeten Juden Europas** (*see p75*) and the **Brandenburger Tor** (*see p72*) are both free to visit. Alternatively, head north on the S-Bahn to Nordbahnhof to visit the **Gedenkstätte Berliner Mauer** (*see p120*) and learn about the political and physical division of the city.

Evening

The best way to spend a summer evening is strolling along one of Berlin's many waterways, sipping cold beer from a *Spätkauf*. On the Spree near Monbijou Park, you can watch the salsa dancing and see the **Museumsinsel** (*see p81*) at sunset. Or head to the **Landwehrkanal**, where the cobblestone Admiralbrücke draws street musicians and a vibrant crowd. From here, you have your pick of some cheap and cheerful restaurants – try pizza at **Il Casolare** or ramen at **Cocolo** (for both, *see p144*). There's plenty of unpretentious watering holes, too, such as the charming faux-nautical **Ankerklause** (*see p152*). In less clement weather, check *Index* (indexberlin.de) for listings of free gallery openings. And, if you want to go partying, head to cosy club **Süss war Gestern** (*see p132*): admission is free before 11pm and drinks are dangerously cheap.

Türkischer Markt

Diary

The German capital has long eschewed high-profile, glitzy events in favour of homegrown, local efforts. In fact, part of the city's dishevelled charm is the resourcefulness of its inhabitants, their willingness to take to the streets and create their own low-budget fun. May Day kicks off the summer season with a typical Berlin combination of street parties and demonstrations. The end of the year is also marked in customary Berlin style – with fireworks recklessly launched from hilltops and cars.

However, despite its counter-culture reputation, Berlin has been steadily gaining international recognition in certain spheres, especially for music (of all genres), contemporary art and fashion. With the prestigious Berlin International Film Festival sprinkling a little stardust over the wintry city each February, it may finally be time for Berlin to dust off its black tie and heels.

Spring

Even if the canals haven't totally thawed out yet, sun-starved Berliners come out in droves, determined to enjoy their coffee alfresco, coat or not. In April, the Japanese **Kirschblütenfest** is a particular highlight. By May, Berlin is in full swing, with the riotous **May Day** and, later, the buzzing **Karneval der Kulturen** taking over the streets of Kreuzberg. All in all, late spring hits Berlin's sweet spot: not too hot, not too cold, not too crowded – local kids don't get out of school until July.

Late Mar MaerzMusik – Festival für Zeitfragen
www.berlinerfestspiele.de
A holdover from the more culture-conscious days of the old East Germany, this ten-day contemporary music festival invites international avant-garde composers and musicians to present new works.

Late Apr Gallery Weekend
www.gallery-weekend-berlin.de
Around 50 galleries time their openings for the last weekend in April, making for an arty extravaganza attended by leading dealers and ordinary art-lovers.

Late Apr Kirschblütenfest
www.hanamifest.org
Taking place just on Berlin's border with Brandenburg, this one-day Hanami Cherry Blossom Festival celebrates Japan's generous gift to Berlin upon the city's reunification. Over 70 stands offer Japanese goodies, from calligraphy to regional specialities, as well as the chance for a leisurely walk around the Teltow canal, which once divided East and West Germany.

Late Apr/May ILA Berlin Air Show
www.ila-berlin.de.
This popular biennial event – the next is in 2020 – is held at Schönefeld airport over six days. It features around 1,000 exhibitors from 40 countries, with aircraft of all kinds and a serious focus on space travel.

1 May May Day
An annual event since 1987, when Autonomen engaged in violent clashes with police. The riots have quietened in recent years, but Kreuzberg is still very lively on 1 May, especially at Spreewaldplatz near Kotti. During the day, there are lots of street parties and music, as well as protests. However, as night draws in, alcohol-fuelled misadventures spoil the atmosphere. Be sure to withdraw cash the night before (ATMs shut down on the day) and to make solid plans with friends, as mobile service is erratic, too.

May Theatertreffen Berlin
www.berlinerfestspiele.de
A jury picks out ten of the most innovative and controversial new theatre productions from companies across Germany, Austria and Switzerland, and the winners come to Berlin to perform their pieces over two weeks in May.

Late May Deutschland Pokal-Endspiel
https://ticketportal.dfb.de
The domestic football cup final has been taking place at the Olympiastadion every year since 1985. It regularly attracts some 65,000 fans, and tickets are very hard to come by.

❤ May/June Karneval der Kulturen

www.karneval-berlin.de
Inspired by London's Notting Hill Carnival and intended as a celebration of Berlin's ethnic and cultural diversity, this long holiday weekend (always Pentecost) centres on a 'multi-kulti' parade (on the Sunday) involving dozens of floats, hundreds of musicians and thousands of spectators. The parade and festival snake from the Hallesches Tor area to Hermannplatz.

Summer

Summer is when Berlin really turns on the charm, though you won't have it all to yourself. Expect gorgeous days by the Spree and lots of company. However, the city is so spread out that the crowds are never overwhelming. The street festivals are a highlight, too: among the best are the **Fête de le Musique**, **Christopher Street Day Parade** and **Tanz im August**. The huge number of free outdoor activities makes summer a great time for budget travellers, though accommodation prices are slightly higher from June to August. Don't forget your swimming costume to make the most of the lakes and outdoor pools.

21 June Fête de la Musique

www.fetedelamusique.de
A regular summer solstice happening since 1995, this music extravaganza of bands and DJs takes place across the city. The selection is mixed, with everything from heavy metal to *Schlager*.

Late June 48 Stunden Neukölln

http://48-stunden-neukoelln.de
For one weekend, under-the-radar artists transform studios, cafés and even apartment buildings into temporary exhibition spaces in Berlin's most hyped neighbourhood. The casual entry requirements mean the art on display ranges from the weird and wonderful to the utterly dire. Best encountered with beers and an open mind.

June/July Berlin Philharmonie at the Waldbühne

www.waldbuehne-berlin.de
The Philharmonie ends its season with an open-air concert that sells out months in advance. Over 20,000 Berliners light the atmospheric 'forest theatre' with candles once darkness falls.

July & late Jan Berlin Fashion Week

www.fashion-week-berlin.com
OK, so it's not quite Paris, but Berlin's twice-yearly style shindig is gradually becoming a serious event

Deutsch-Amerikanisches Volksfest p62

on the fashion calendar. In recent years, there's been a focus on young talent and 'green fashion', which can be seen at the Ethical Fashion Show and at the Greenshowroom.

July Classic Open Air
www.classicopenair.de
Big names usually open this concert series held over five days in one of Berlin's most beautiful squares.

Late July Lesbisch-Schwules Stadtfest
www.regenbogenfonds.de
The Lesbian & Gay Street Fair takes over Schöneberg every year, filling several blocks in West Berlin's gay quarter. Participating bars, clubs, food stands and musical acts make this a dizzying, non-stop event that also serves as a kick-off for the Christopher Street Day Parade (*see below*).

❤ Sat in late July Christopher Street Day Parade
www.csd-berlin.de
Originally organised to commemorate the 1969 riots outside the Stonewall Bar on Christopher Street in New York, this fun and flamboyant parade has become one of the summer's most enjoyable and inclusive street parties. Hundreds of thousands of people march for and celebrate the rights of LGBT people each year. Check the website for details of the route.

July/Aug Deutsch-Amerikanisches Volksfest
www.deutsch-amerikanisches-volksfest.de
Established by the US forces stationed in West Berlin, the German-American Festival lasts about three weeks and offers a tacky but popular mix of carnival rides, cowboys doing lasso tricks, candy floss, hot dogs and Yankee beer.

Aug Tanz im August
www.tanzimaugust.de
This three-week event is Germany's leading modern dance festival, with big-name participants.

Aug Internationales Berliner Bierfestival
www.bierfestival-berlin.de
Describing itself as 'the world's longest beer garden', with a 2011 Guinness World Record to prove it, this two-day festival has been running for nearly 20 years, showcasing hundreds of beers from over 80 countries and bringing conviviality to the city's premier Stalinist boulevard.

Aug Young.euro.classic
www.young-euro-classic.de
This summer concert programme brings together youth orchestras from around Europe for two weeks.

❤ Last Sat in Aug Lange Nacht der Museen
www.lange-nacht-der-museen.de
Around 100 museums, collections, archives and exhibition halls stay open into the early hours of the morning, with special events, concerts, readings, lectures and performances. A ticket gets you free travel on special shuttle buses and regular public transport. Lange Nacht der Museen is the final night of Berlin's MuseumsSommer, in which museums around the city host special open-air events throughout July and August.

Autumn

Summer weather can continue well into September and early October, with some lovely sunny days, peaking around the **Berlin Marathon**, but as November draws near, the climate becomes increasingly damp and cold – although the fog along the canals can be quite atmospheric. Skip

Festival of Lights

Berlin's half-hearted attempt at Oktoberfest and enjoy, instead, a string of excellent cultural events, from **Berlin Art Week** and the **International Literaturfest** to the **Festival of Lights**. Hotel prices dip in autumn, before rising again towards Christmas.

Sept Musikfest Berlin
www.berlinerfestspiele.de
This major classical music festival, held over the space of three weeks, presents more than 70 works by 25 composers. Orchestras, instrumental and vocal ensembles, and numerous soloists take part, with many from abroad (Sweden, Denmark, Israel, the UK and the United States in recent years).

Sept Internationales Literaturfestival Berlin
www.literaturfestival.com
A major literary event, with readings, symposiums and discussions over ten days, drawing well-known authors and rising stars from around the world.

Last Sun in Sept Berlin Marathon
www.bmw-berlin-marathon.com
Fewer than 300 people took part in the inaugural Berlin Marathon in 1974; now, it's one of the biggest and most popular road races in the world with more than 40,000 runners, plus a million spectators lining the route to cheer them on.

Late Sept Berlin Art Week
www.berlinartweek.de
Berlin Art Week has become the highlight of the contemporary art calendar in the city since the inaugural event in 2012. Around 50 participating institutions put on events, art fairs (notably ABC Contemporary and Positions Berlin) and wildly popular opening nights. Even the bigger venues, such as Tempelhof Airport and the Hamburger Bahnhof, struggle to handle the swarms of art scenesters at peak times.

3 Oct Tag der Deutschen Einheit
The Day of German Unity is a public holiday commemorating the day, back in 1990, when two Germanies became one. Head to the Brandenburg Gate to party with up to one million other revellers.

Mid Oct Festival of Lights
www.festival-of-lights.de
For ten days every year, Berlin's world-famous sights and

♥ Berlinale

Various venues (259 200, www. berlinale.de). **Tickets** *€7-€16; €100 festival pass.* **Date** *mid Feb.*

For more than 60 years, the Berlinale (or Internationale Filmfestspiele Berlin, to use its official title) has been the city's biggest cultural event, as well as one of the world's three most prominent film festivals.

Born out of the Cold War, the Berlinale developed from a propaganda showcase, supported by the Allies, into a genuine meeting place – and frequent collision point – for East and West. Whether it was the 1959 French boycott over Stanley Kubrick's indictment of war, *Paths of Glory*, the jury revolt over the pro-Vietnamese film *OK* in 1970, or the 1979 Eastern Bloc walk-out over the depiction of Vietnamese people in *The Deer Hunter*, the festival's drama was never confined to the screens. The years following the fall of the Berlin Wall were particularly exciting: the mood and energy of the festival reflected the joy and chaos of the changing city. The future direction of the Berlinale will again be up for grabs once Carlo Chatrian takes over from long-term festival director Dieter Kosslick in 2019.

Although Potsdamer Platz is the focus of the festival, screenings take place around the city, including at Alexanderplatz, in the Zoo Palast cinema in Tiergarten and in a renovated crematorium (silent green Kulturquartier) in Wedding. In this way, the Berlinale offers the chance not only to watch undiscovered

movies and rub shoulders with fellow film buffs and industry leaders, but to experience Berlin's unique architectural and cultural heritage. In recent years, the festival has taken on more of the glamour and celebrity of its two major rivals, Cannes and Venice. What remains the same, however, is the chance to see arguably the widest and most eclectic movie mix of any film festival anywhere. The films are presented in nine sections, of which the following are the most significant.

International Competition

Films compete for the festival's most prestigious awards – the Golden and Silver Bears – and the winners are announced at the closing night gala. A rise in celebrity attendance at the festival saw a much-criticised shift towards conservative, US-centric films in recent years, with the festival performing a balancing act between maintaining its authentic, experimental feel while accepting a degree of commercial success. However, critics were left politely bewildered and, in some cases, openly hostile, when the judges announced the 2018 winner of the Golden Bear to be the intimate, unsettling *Touch Me Not* by avant-garde Romanian director Adina Pintilie, while the crowd-pleasing *Isle of Dogs* (Wes Anderson) took silver – a timely reminder, perhaps, of the festival's enduring maverick values.

International Forum of Young Cinema

Some devotees claim this is the real Berlin festival, and the place where discoveries are made. Born out of the revolt that dissolved the Competition in 1970, the Forum has no format or genre restrictions, and provides a platform for challenging, eclectic fare that you won't see elsewhere.

Panorama
Originally intended to showcase films that fell outside the guidelines of the Competition, Panorama shines a spotlight on world independent arthouse movies, gay and lesbian works and political films.

Perspektive Deutsches Kino
Perspektive reflects the festival's focus on the next generation of German cinema. It is a big audience favourite, helped by the fact that all films are shown with English subtitles. If you think German cinema has a bad rep, this is where to break down the stereotypes.

Retrospective
Perhaps the festival's best bet for sheer movie-going pleasure, the Retrospective often concentrates on the mainstream, but it's an opportunity to experience classics and rarities on the big screen. Themes have ranged from great directors, such as Louis Buñuel, Fritz Lang and Ingmar Bergman, to subjects including 1950s glamour girls, Weimar cinema, science fiction and even Nazi entertainment films.

Buying tickets
Films are usually shown three times. Tickets range in price from €8 to €20 and can be bought up to three days in advance (four days for Competition repeats) at the main ticket office in the Potsdamer Platz Arkaden (Alte Potsdamer Strasse, Tiergarten, 259 2000) as well as at cinemas Kino International (Karl-Marx-Allee 33) and Haus der Berliner Festspiele (Schaperstrasse 24). Other official partners are announced before the festival. Tickets are also available online, but on the day of screening they can only be bought at the theatre box office; last-minute tickets are often available. Queues for advance tickets can be long and online tickets go fast, so plan well ahead. From January onwards, check for updates and programme information at www.berlinale.de.

Berlinale bear

monuments become the canvas for spectacular light and video projections. The illuminations are switched on at 7pm nightly.

❤ Early Nov JazzFest Berlin

www.berlinerfestspiele.de
A fixture since 1964, JazzFest Berlin is one of the oldest and most prestigious in Europe, showcasing a wide range of jazz from an array of internationally renowned artists; past guests have included Miles Davis and Duke Ellington. Curator and jazz player Nadin Deventer took over as artistic director in 2018.

Nov Berliner Märchentage

www.berliner-maerchentage.de
The fortnight-long Berlin Fairytale Festival celebrates tales from around the world, with some 400 storytelling and music events taking place in a carnival atmosphere, for children and adults. The central theme varies each year.

Winter

There's plenty to admire about Berlin in winter. The cold weather, dark nights and frozen canals highlight Berlin's austere architecture and make the prospect of spending hours in the city's compelling museums all the more appealing. If loud noises and home-made fireworks aren't your thing, skip **Silvester** (New Year's Eve) and come earlier in December for **Christmas markets**, *Glühwein* and a lux day at the spa (see **Vabali** *p105* and **Stadtbad Neukölln** *p160*). In February, the world-class **Berlinale** (*see p64*) brings international cinema and its attendant glamour to town.

Dec Christmas markets

www.weihnachtsmarkt-deutschland.de
Traditional markets spring up across Berlin during the Christmas season, offering toys, mulled wine and gingerbread. This is one of the biggest. There's another good one in Spandau (*see p179*).

31 Dec Silvester

Given Berliners' enthusiasm for tossing firecrackers out of windows, New Year's Eve is always going to be vivid, noisy and hazardous. Thousands celebrate at the Brandenburger Tor. Thousands more trek up the Teufelsberg in the Grunewald or head to Viktoriapark in Kreuzberg to watch the fireworks across the city. Be careful out there!

Jan Grüne Woche

www.gruenewoche.de
The best thing about this ten-day show dedicated to food, agriculture and horticulture is the opportunity to sample food and drink from the far corners of Germany and across the planet.

Mid Jan Ultraschall Berlin – Festival für Neue Musik

ultraschallberlin.de
Ultrasound Berlin focuses on new music played in high-profile venues by some of the world's leading specialist ensembles. Concerts are broadcast live, and there are talks by composers and other events.

❤ Late Jan/early Feb Transmediale

www.transmediale.de
One of the world's largest international festivals for media art and digital culture, with exhibitions and screenings from artists working in video, TV, computer animation, internet and other visual media.

DIARY

66

Berlin
by Area

Alexanderplatz

Mitte

For decades, Mitte – meaning 'middle' or 'centre' – floundered in a no-man's-land between East and West. But now, Mitte is right back in the swing of things. It contains many of Berlin's biggest sights: the Brandenburg Gate (Brandenburger Tor), the TV Tower (Fernsehturm) and the magnificent UNESCO World Heritage Site of Museum Island (Museumsinsel), which is in the midst of an epic overhaul, scheduled to be fully completed by 2025. But there's much more to this area than ticking off the sights – galleries abound, as do cool shops. As for nightlife, take your pick from fine dining at the likes of Borchardt and Grill Royal to the bar scene that stretches down Torstrasse, and the late-night kebab mecca of Rosenthalerplatz.

Best museums
Humboldt Forum *p83*,
Museum für Naturkunde
p79, Neues Museum *p84*,
Pergamonmuseum *p85*

Best brunch
Barcomi's *p86*, Commonground
p87, Café Fleury *p87*

Best blow-out dining
Borchardt *p74*, Grill Royal *p80*,
Das Lokal *p88*

Best souvenirs
Ampelmann Shop *p90*,
Arkonaplatz Flohmarkt *p90*,
RSVP *p92*

Best fashion boutiques
DSTM *p91*, LaLa Berlin *p92*,
Das Neue Schwarz *p92*, Wood
Wood *p92*

Best landmarks
Brandenburger Tor *p72*,
Holocaust Memorial *p75*,
Fernsehturm *p94*

Best cultural venues
Komische Oper *p77*, Maxim Gorki
Theater *p78*, Sophiensaele *p93*

Best nights out
Bar 3 *p89*, Chamäleon *p93*,
Clärchen's Ballhaus *p93*, Kim
Bar *p90*

Unter den Linden & around

Unter der Linden runs east
from the **Brandenburger Tor**
(*see p72*) at Pariser Platz to the
Museumsinsel. Originally laid
out to connect the city centre
with the king's hunting grounds
of Tiergarten, the street takes its
name from the lime trees (*Linden*)
that shade the central walkway.
Its grand 18th- and 19th-century
buildings were reduced to rubble
during and after World War II, but
the majority have been restored or
replaced with imposing embassies,
banks and cultural institutions.

To the south of Pariser Platz
is the vast **Holocaust Memorial**

(Denkmal für die ermordeten
Juden Europas; *see p75*).

Sights & museums

Deutsche Bank KunstHalle
*Unter den Linden 13-15 (202 0930,
www.deutsche-bank-kunsthalle.
de). U6 Französische Strasse.* **Open**
10am-8pm daily **Admission** *€4;
€3 reductions; free under-12s.
Free to all Mon.* **Map** *p70 N7.*
Deutsche Bank took over the
management of this space from
the Guggenheim in April 2013 and
now holds four shows a year, with
guest curators invited to build
exhibitions from the banks's vast
corporate art collection.

➔ **Getting around**
With five U-Bahn lines, one S-Bahn that bisects the district and a multitude
of trams heading north, east and west from Alexanderplatz, you're spoilt
for public transport options in Mitte. 'Der Alex' is the central hub and most
visitors to Berlin will at least change connections here. Plenty of regional
trains leave from Alexanderplatz too, heading to Potsdam, Spreewald
and other popular day-trip destinations. For a picturesque walk, get off
the S-Bahn at Hackescher Markt and walk over the beautifully restored
Friedrichsbrücke for a stunning introduction to Museum Island.

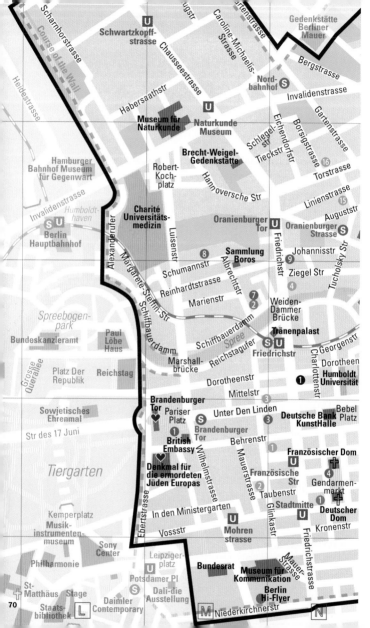

Scharnhorststrasse

Course of the Wall

Heidestrasse

U Schwartzkopff-strasse

Chausseestrasse

Caroline-Michaelis-Strasse

Augustrasse

Gedenkstätte Berliner Mauer

Bergstrasse

Habersaathstr

Nord-bahnhof **S**

Invalidenstrasse

Gartenstrasse

Eichendorffstr

Borsigstrasse

Gartenstrasse

U

Museum für Naturkunde

Naturkunde Museum

Schlegelstr

Tieckstr

16

Torstrasse

Hamburger Bahnhof Museum für Gegenwart

Robert-Koch-platz

Brecht-Weigel-Gedenkstätte

Hannoversche Str

Linienstrasse

15

Auguststr

Invalidenstrasse

Humboldt-haven

S U Berlin Hauptbahnhof

Charité Universitäts-medizin

Alexanderufer

Luisenstr

Oranienburger Tor **U**

Oranienburger Strasse **S**

Friedrichstr

Johannisstr

9

Tucholsky Str

Margarete-Steffin-Str

8

Sammlung Boros

Albrechtstr

Ziegel Str

4

Schumannstr

Reinhardtstrasse

Schiffbauerdamm

Marienstr

7

2

Weiden-Dammer Brücke

Spreebogenpark

Paul Löbe Haus

Schiffbauerdamm

Spree

Tränenpalast

Bundeskanzleramt

Grosse Queraallee

Platz Der Republik

Reichstag

Marshall-brücke

Reichstagufer

Georgenstr

S U Friedrichstr

Dorotheen

Charlottenstr

Humboldt Universität **1**

Dorotheenstr

Mittelstr

Sowjetisches Ehrenmal

Str des 17 Juni

Tiergarten

Brandenburger Tor ♥ Pariser Platz

S Brandenburger Tor

3

Unter Den Linden

3

Behrenstr

Deutsche Bank KunstHalle

Bebel Platz

Wilhelmstrasse

1

British Embassy

Französischer Dom ✝

U

Mauerstrasse

Denkmal für die ermordeten Jüden Europas ♥

Französische Str

4

Gendarmen-markt

2

Taubenstr

1

Deutscher Dom ✝

Kemperplatz

Ebertstrasse

In den Ministergarten

U

Glinkastr

Stadtmitte

U

Musik-instrumentenmuseum

Sony Center

Vossstr

Mohren strasse

Kronenstr

Friedrichstrasse

Philharmonie

Leipziger-platz

U Potsdamer Pl

Bundesrat

Museum für Kommunikation

Mauer Strasse

St-Matthäus **L** Stage

Staats-bibliothek

Daimler Contemporary

Dali-die Ausstellung

M Niederkirchnerstr

Berlin Hi-Flyer

N

70

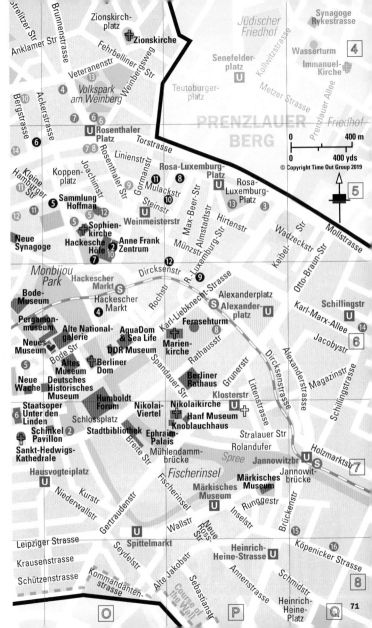

Anklamer Str

Strelitzer Str

Brunnenstrasse

Zionskirch-
platz

Zionskirche

Fehrbelliner Str

Weinbergsweg

Jüdischer
Friedhof

Synagoge
Rykestrasse

Senefelder-
platz
U

Kollwitzstrasse

Wasserturm

Immanuel-
Kirche

4

Veteranenstr

13

Volkspark
am Weinberg

Teutoburger-
platz
U

Metzer Strasse

Prenzlauer Allee

Prenzlauer
Friedhof

Ackerstrasse

4

Bergstrasse

10

7

6

6

**Rosenthaler
Platz**
U

Torstrasse

PRENZLAUER
BERG

0   400 m

14

6

7 8

Linienstrasse

Rosenthaler Str

Kleine Hamburger Str

11

Koppen-
platz

Joachimstr

Gormanstr

Mulackstr

**Rosa-Luxemburg-
Platz**

8

U

Rosa-
Luxemburg-
Platz

0   400 yds

© Copyright Time Out Group 2019

5

11

**Sammlung
Hoffman**

9

11

Steinstr

10

Max-Beer-Str

Almstadtstr

Hirtenstr

13

3

5

12

12

Weinmeisterstr

**Sophien-
kirche**

Münzstrasse

R.-Luxemburg-Str

Wadzeckstr-Str

Keibelstr

Str

Otto-Braun-Str

Mollstrasse

5

**Neue
Synagoge**

**Hackesche
Höfe**

2

**Anne Frank
Zentrum**

7

10

12

Dircksenstr

9

Monbijou
Park

**Hackescher
Markt**
S

**Bode-
Museum**

Hackescher
Markt

Rochstr

Karl-Liebknecht-Strasse

Alexanderplatz
S
**Alexander-
platz**
U

Karl-Marx-Allee

Schillingstr
U

14

**Pergamon-
museum**

**Alte National-
galerie**

4

Fernsehturm

8

Jacobystr

6

**Neues
Museum**

5

Bode Str

**AquaDom
& Sea Life
DDR Museum**

**Marien-
kirche**

Rathausstr

Magazinstr

Schillingstrasse

**Altes
Museum**

**Berliner
Dom**

**Neue
Wache**

**Deutsches
Historisches
Museum**

Spandauer Str

**Berliner
Rathaus**

Grunerstr

Littenstrasse

Alexanderstrasse

Dircksenstrasse

**Staatsoper
Unter den
Linden**

6

**Humboldt
Forum**

Schlossplatz

**Nikolai-
Viertel**

Nikolaikirche
U
Hanf Museum

Klosterstr

**Schinkel
Pavillon**

2

Stadtbibliothek

Knoblauchhaus

Stralauer Str

Holzmarktstr

7

**Sankt-Hedwigs-
Kathedrale**

**Ephraim-
Palais**

Breite Str

Rolandufer

Jannowitzbr
U S

Jannowit-
brücke

Hausvogteiplatz
U

Niederwallstr

Kurstr

Gertraudenstr

Fischerinsel

Mühlendamm-
brücke

Spree

Fischerinsel

**Märkisches
Museum**

Brückenstr

15

Spittelmarkt
U

Wallstr

Neue Ross Str

**Märkisches
Museum**

Runggestr

Inselstr

Köpenicker Strasse

16

Leipziger Strasse

Seydelstr

Alte Jakobstr

**Heinrich-
Heine-Strasse**
U

Annenstrasse

Schmidstr

Krausenstrasse

Schützenstrasse

Kommandanten-
strasse

Course of
the Wall

Sebastianstr

Heinrich-
Heine-
Platz

8

O

P

Q

71

💜 Brandenburger Tor

*Pariser Platz. S-Bahn
Brandenburger Tor.* **Map** *p70 M7.*

Constructed in 1791 to a design
by Carl Gotthard Langhans
and modelled on the Propylaea
gateway into ancient Athens,
the Brandenburg Gate was built
as a triumphal arch celebrating
Prussia's capital city. It was
initially called the Friedenstor
(Gate of Peace) and is the only
city gate remaining from Berlin's
original 18. (Today, only a few
U-Bahn station names recall
the other city gates, such as
Frankfurter Tor or Schlesisches
Tor). The Quadriga statue, a four-
horse chariot driven by Victory
and designed by Johann Gottfried
Schadow, sits on top of the gate.
It has had an eventful life. When
Napoleon conquered Berlin in
1806, he carted the Quadriga off
to Paris and held it hostage until
his defeat in 1814. The Tor was
badly damaged during World
War II and, during subsequent
renovations, the GDR removed the

Prussian Iron Cross and turned
the Quadriga round so that the
chariot faced west. The current
Quadriga is actually a 1958 copy
of the 18th-century original. The
Brandenburg Gate was stranded in
no-man's-land between East and
West Berlin for 30 years, and from
its vantage point on top of the gate,
the statue had a front row seat
for some of the most significant
moments in reunification
history. The Quadriga watched
on when Ronald Reagan called
on Mr Gorbachev to 'Tear down
this wall!'. It was there too
when, on 22 December 1989,
the Brandenburger Tor border
crossing was reopened, and
Helmut Kohl, the West German
chancellor, walked through to be
greeted by Hans Modrow, the East
German prime minister, just prior
to Germany's reunification. Since
then both gate and Quadriga
have been given facelifts. The
Iron Cross has been replaced, and
the Quadriga turned back to face
into Mitte once again.

Deutscher Dom

Gendarmenmarkt, entrance in Markgrafenstrasse (2273 0431). U2, U6 Stadtmitte. **Open** *May-Sept 10am-7pm Tue-Sun. Oct-Apr 10am-6pm Tue-Sun. Guided tours every half hour 11am-5pm; call first for English- or French-speaking guide.* **Admission** *free.* **Map** *p70 N7.*

The neoclassical domed tower of this church – and the identical tower of the Französischer Dom on the other side of the square – were built in 1780-85 by Carl von Gontard for Frederick the Great, in imitation of Santa Maria in Montesanto and Santa Maria del Miracoli in Rome. The Deutscher Dom was intended for Berlin's Lutheran community. The dome is topped by a 7-m (23-ft) gilded statue representing Virtue. Badly damaged by Allied bombing in the war, the church and tower burned down in 1943, and were restored in the 1980s and '90s.

Inside is a permanent exhibition on the history of Germany's parliamentary system, from the 1848 revolution through the suspension of parliamentary politics by the Nazis, up to the present day. Visitors are encouraged to consider the role of parliaments throughout the modern world, but there are no translations, so to get much out of this without a guided tour your German must be up to scratch.

Deutsches Historisches Museum

Zeughaus, Unter den Linden 2 (203 040, www.dhm.de). U6 Französische Strasse. **Open** *10am-6pm daily.* **Admission** *€8; €4 reductions; free under-18s.* **Map** *p70 O6.*

The permanent exhibition in the Zeughaus provides an exhaustive blast through German history from 100 BC to the present day, divided chronologically into significant

Deutsches Historisches Museum

eras. The museum originally had trouble raising the funds to buy historical objects, but there's enough here now for the exhibits to work on their own, without the need for an overarching narrative. German nationalism becomes the focus once you enter the 19th century, and, later on, more than one room is dedicated to the Nazi era. The DHM has succeeded admirably in looking the past straight in the eye, although the attempt to be impartial means that it's sometimes factual to the extreme. Temporary exhibitions are housed in the gorgeous IM Pei building.

Französischer Dom & Hugenottenmuseum

Gendarmenmarkt (229 1760, www.franzoesischer-dom.de). U2, U6 Stadtmitte. **Open** *see the website.* **Admission** *Church free. Tower €3; €1 reductions. No cards.* **Map** *p70 N7.*

Built in the early 18th century for Berlin's 6,000-plus-strong French Protestant community, the church (known as the Französischen

Friedrichstadtkirche) was later given a Baroque domed tower, as was the Deutscher Dom across the square. The tower, with its fine views over Mitte, is purely decorative and unconsecrated – and not part of the modest church, which has a separate entrance at the western end.

An exhibition on the history of the French Protestants in France and Berlin-Brandenburg is displayed within the building. The museum chronicles the religious persecution suffered by Calvinists (note the bust of Calvin on the outside of the church) and their subsequent immigration to Berlin after 1685, at the behest of the Hohenzollerns. The development of the Huguenot community is also detailed, with paintings, documents and artefacts. One part of the museum is devoted to the church's history, particularly the effects of World War II – it was bombed during a Sunday service in 1944 and remained a ruin until the mid 1980s. The tower and museum were closed for extensive renovation work in 2017-18.

Schinkel Pavillon

Oberwallstrasse 1 (2088 6444, www.schinkelpavillon.de). U2 Hausvogteiplatz. **Open** *noon-6pm Thur-Sun.* **Admission** *€4; reductions €3.* **Map** *p70 O7.*
This gallery space is in the gardens of the Kronprinzenpalais, which itself claims to be the world's first contemporary art institution: the palace displayed work by Berlin's expressionists from 1918 until the Nazis closed it down for showing 'degenerate' art. Today, the octagonal pavilion with its wall-to-ceiling glass, designed to GDR specifications in 1969, happily shows all manner of installation, sculpture and performance art, cheerily degenerate or not. Philippe Parreno, Douglas Gordon and James Franco have all appeared.

Restaurants & cafés

❤ Borchardt €€€-€€€€
Französische Strasse 47 (8188 6262). U6 Französische Strasse. **Open** *11.30am-late daily.* **Map** *p70 N7* ❶ *Brasserie*
The original Borchardt opened next door at no.48 in the late 19th century. It became the place for politicians and society folk, until it was destroyed in World War II. Now, Roland Mary and Marina Richter have reconstructed a highly fashionable, Maxim's-inspired bistro. People come not for the respectable French food, but for the clannish atmosphere, where you can often spot a film star or politico. Ideal if you fancy a dozen oysters and a fillet of pike-perch or beef after a cultural evening nearby.

Café Nö! €-€€
Glinkastrasse 23 (201 0871, www.cafe-noe.de). U6 Französische Strasse. **Open** *noon-1am Mon-Fri.* **Map** *p70 M7* ❷ *Wine bar*
This unassuming but right-on wine bar with simple and wholesome meals is owned by a former GDR rock musician now continuing his family's gastronomy

💙 Holocaust Memorial (Denkmal für die ermordeten Juden Europas)

Cora-Berliner-Strasse 1 (2639 4336, www.holocaust-denkmal.de). U2, S1, S2, S25 Potsdamer Platz. **Open** *Memorial 24hrs daily. Information centre Apr-Sept 10am-8pm Tue-Sun. Oct-Mar 10am-7pm Tue-Sun.* **Admission** *free.* **Map** *p70 M7.*

No debate about the intersection of history, architecture and the form of Berlin's reunified cityscape lumbered on for so long or conjured so much controversy as the one that engendered this grid of concrete blocks.

The Memorial to the Murdered Jews of Europe by Peter Eisenman was eventually unveiled in 2005 after more than a decade of arguments and redesigns. It consists of a 'field' of 2,711 'stelae', arranged in undulating rows on 19,704sq m (212,000sq ft) of ground, with an attendant information centre. Each of the concrete slabs has its own foundation, and they tilt at differing angles. Ranging in height from 20 cm to 4.7 m, the slabs are as individual as headstones. The effect is (no doubt deliberately) reminiscent of the packed graves in Prague's Old Jewish Cemetery. There's no vantage point or overview; to fully engage with the structure you need to walk into it. It's haunting in places, especially on overcast days and near the middle of the monument, where it's easy to feel a sense of confinement as you lose sight of the outside world;

other visitors to the monument are seen in glimpses as they pass between the stelae, only to quickly disappear. Early criticism often focused on the monument's lack of specificity – there are no stars of David here, no obvious symbolism or recognition of German culpability – but it has since won grudging recognition from many former critics.

The underground information centre is like a secular crypt, containing a sombre presentation of facts and figures about the Holocaust's victims.

▶ *On the other side of Ebertstrasse is a monument to the Nazi's homosexual victims.*

tradition. Given the mostly bland or overpriced restaurants in the neighbourhood, this is a genuine pearl. Snacks include the shaved Swiss cheese tête de moine and anchovy crostini; more substantial fare includes Alsatian *Flammkuchen*, and *Maultaschen* (ravioli) with spinach.

Einstein Unter den Linden
€€-€€€
*Unter den Linden (2043 632, einstein-udl.com). U6 Französische Strasse. **Open** 7am-late Mon-Fri; 8am-late Sat, Sun. **Map** p70 M7* ③
Austro-German
Although it remains the typical Viennese coffeehouse, new management has breathed life into this wood-panelled classic. Known as the meeting place for politicians, Einstein has been open for breakfast, lunch and *Apfelstrudel* for the past 20 years. Now you can also expect a formidable wine and dinner menu, a testament to classic Austrian cuisine, with a nod and wink to a younger and more contemporary foodie crowd.

Bars & pubs
Newton Bar
*Charlottenstrasse 57 (2029 5421, www.newton-bar.de). U6 Französische Strasse. **Open** 11am-late daily. **Map** p70 N7* ①
Homage seems to be Berlin's preferred method for naming bars, and here iconoclastic fashion photographer Helmut Newton is immortalised. For those unfamiliar with his pictures of statuesque models, an entire wall of this large bar is dedicated to a series of his black and white nudes. Stick to the classics, martinis or a good single malt, settle into the cosy seating and watch the world go by from the heated terrace with a view on to Gendarmenmarkt.

Shops & services
Friedrichstrasse is arguably the city's glitziest shopping street, lined with luxury brands, upmarket department stores and high-end malls, including **Quartier 205** at nos.66-70, **Quartier 206** at nos.71-74 and **Galeries Lafayette** at no.75 (www.galerieslafayette.de).

Entertainment
Use the River Spree entrance to the Deutsches Historisches Museum (*see p73*) to reach the **Zeughaus Cinema**.

Akademie der Künste
*Pariser Platz 4 (200 571 000, www.adk.de). U55, S1, S2, S25 Brandenburger Tor. **Box office** 10am-7pm daily. **Tickets** €4-€13. **Map** p70 M7* ① *Live shows*
Founded by Prince Friedrich III in 1696, this is one of the oldest cultural institutions in Berlin. By 1938, the Nazis had forced virtually all its prominent members into exile. It was re-established in West Berlin in 1954 to serve as 'a community of exceptional artists' from around the world. Post-reunification, it moved into a new building at its pre-war address on Pariser Platz, but some events are still held at its Tiergarten address (Hanseatenweg 10). Events include performances of 20th-century compositions, jazz concerts, poetry readings, film screenings and art exhibitions.

Horse Meat Disco
*Bauakademie, Schinkelplatz (no phone, www.horsemeatdiscoberlin. com). U2 Hausvogteiplatz. **Open** varies. **Admission** €10. No cards. **Map** p70 O7* ② *LGBT club*
It may have been born in London's Vauxhall, but Horse Meat Disco has matured in Berlin. Resident DJs call it 'the queer party for everyone', though, as with many sex-themed

Komische Oper

MITTE

clubs, it attracts a lot of gay men. Whoever is there, it's a fantastic party, inspired by the heyday of New York City nightlife.

💗 Komische Oper
Behrenstrasse 55-57 (202 600, www.komische-oper-berlin.de). U6 Französische Strasse. **Box office** *Unter den Linden 41 (4799 7400); 11am-7pm Mon-Sat; 1-4pm Sun.* **Tickets** *€12-€79.* **Map** *p70 N7* ❸
Opera
Founded in 1947, the Komische Oper made its reputation by breaking with the old operatic tradition of 'costumed concerts' – singers standing around on stage – and instead emphasising 'opera as theatre', with real acting skill demanded of its young ensemble. It has the smallest budget of the big three and prides itself on contemporary, even controversial, productions and an outreach programme that includes Turkish subtitling. It doesn't shy away from sex and violence either, with a notorious version of Mozart's *Die Entführung aus dem Serail* that used real prostitutes in the cast, who were graphically murdered on stage. Hungarian conductor Henrik Nánási concluded his tenure at the end of 2018 and is due to be

succeeded by Ainãrs Rubikis. The Staatsballett Berlin also performs here. Discounted tickets are sold just before performances.

Konzerthaus
Gendarmenmarkt 2 (2030 92101, www.konzerthaus.de). U6 Französische Strasse. **Box office** *noon-7pm Mon-Sat; noon-4pm Sun.* **Tickets** *€21-€52.* **Map** *p70 N7* ❹
Classical music
Formerly the Schauspielhaus am Gendarmenmarkt, this 1821 architectural gem by Schinkel was all but destroyed during the war. Lovingly restored, it reopened

77

in 1984 with three main concert spaces. Organ recitals in the large hall are a treat, played on the massive 5,811-pipe Jehmlich organ. The Konzerthausorchester is based here, and the Rundfunk-Sinfonieorchester Berlin and the Staatskapelle Berlin also play here.

♥ Maxim Gorki Theater
*Am Festungsgraben 2 (2022 1115, www.gorki.de). U6, S1, S2, S25, S3, S5, S7, S9 Friedrichstrasse. **Box office** noon-6.30pm Mon-Sat; 4-6.30pm Sun. **Tickets** €10-€30. **Map** p70 N6* ⑤ *Theatre*
Shermin Langhoff and Jens Hilje have been leading the theatre towards ever more socially inclusive and challenging heights since they took over the artistic directorship in 2013. Expect new interpretations of classical and modern dramas, as well as adaptations from films and novels, with the result that the atmosphere alone is often enough to transcend the language barrier.

Staatsoper Unter den Linden
*Unter den Linden 7 (203 540, tickets 2035 4555, www.staatsoper-berlin.de). U6 Französische Strasse. **Box office** 11am-7pm daily. **Tickets** varies. **Map** p70 N7* ⑥ *Opera*
After a four-year, €240-million refurbishment that took seven years and €400 million to complete, the Staatsoper reopened on home turf in 2017. Originally founded as Prussia's Royal Court Opera for Frederick the Great in 1742 and designed by Knobelsdorff along the lines of a Greek temple, the building was destroyed in World War II but faithfully rebuilt in 1955. The reopening drew lackluster praise from critics, but its new acoustic-boosting raised ceiling provides optimum conditions for listening to the house orchestra,

the Staatskapelle Berlin. Founded in 1570, this is one of the world's finest opera orchestras and has Daniel Barenboim as conductor for life. His presence ensures that performances are of the highest musical quality, even if they have sometimes been overshadowed by peculiar staging. The Staatsballett Berlin also performs here.

North of Unter den Linden

The continuation of Friedrichstrasse north of Unter den Linden is less appealing and lively than its southern stretch, but there are a few sights and cultural venues here that make a detour worthwhile. For details of the **Hamburger Bahnhof**, *see p104*.

Sights & museums

Brecht-Weigel-Gedenkstätte
*Chausseestrasse 125 (200 571 844, www.adk.de/de/archiv/gedenkstaetten). U6 Oranienburger Tor. **Open** Guided tours (every 30 mins) 10-11.30am, 2-3.30pm Tue; 10-11.30am Wed; 10-11.30am, 5-6.30pm Thur; 10-11.30am Fri; 10am-3.30pm Sat; 11am-6pm Sun; and by appointment. **Admission** €5; €2.50 reductions. No cards. **Map** p70 M5.*
Brecht's home from 1948 until his death in 1956 has been preserved exactly as he left it. Tours of the house (phone in advance for an English tour) give interesting insights into the life and reading habits of the playwright. The window at which he worked overlooks the grave of Hegel in the neighbouring cemetery. Brecht's wife, actress Helene Weigel, continued living here until her death in 1971. The Brecht archives are kept upstairs.

Sammlung Boros

❤ Museum für Naturkunde

Invalidenstrasse 43 (8891 408591, www.museumfuernaturkunde. berlin). U6 Naturkundemuseum. **Open** *9.30am-6pm Tue-Fri; 10am-6pm Sat, Sun.* **Admission** *€8; €5 reductions.* **Map** *p70 M5.*
Berlin's renovated Natural History Museum is a real trove. The biggest (literally) draw is the skeleton of a Brachiosaurus dinosaur, which weighed 50 tons at death and is as high as a four-storey house. 'Oliver' – as the dinosaur is nicknamed – is one of the world's largest known land animals and was discovered in the early 1900s. Don't miss the creepy *Forschungssammlungen* (research collections), which show off some of the museum's store of over a million pickled animals suspended in jars of alcohol. Berlin's most famous polar bear, Knut, who died in 2011, is now stuffed and on display.

Sammlung Boros

Reinhardtstrasse 20 (no phone, www.sammlung-boros.de). U6 Oranienburger Tor. **Open** *by appointment.* **Admission** *€15; €9 reductions. No cards.* **Map** *p70 M6.*
More akin to a museum than an actual gallery, this concrete World War II bunker has been transformed into a 3,000sqm (32,290sqft) space containing the formidable collection of advertising mogul Christian Boros and his wife Karen. Works on view include contemporary greats such as Olafur Eliasson and Sarah Lucas, as well as a healthy selection of contemporary local and international names that have caught Boros's beady eye. Tours are on weekends by appointment only; book well in advance through the website.

Tränenpalast

Reichtagsufer 17 (4677 77911, www. hdg.de/traenenpalast). **Open** *9am-7pm Tue-Fri; 10am-6pm Sat, Sun.* **Admission** *free.* **Map** *p70 N6.*
Immediately after the construction of the Berlin Wall, the GDR erected a check-in hall at Friedrichstrasse railway station in 1962. On the border between East and West, the hall was soon renamed the *Tränenpalast*, or Palace of Tears, as it was here that families and friends on opposing sides of the wall were forced to separate. In autumn 2011, the building reopened as a museum commemorating the division of Berlin. Visit the restored inspection rooms to experience the oppressive atmosphere.

Museum für Naturkunde

The meat is sourced from local suppliers as well as from Argentina, Ireland and Australia. The walls are adorned with rather striking soft-porn art from the owner's collection. Reservations essential.

Shops & services

Dussmann das KulturKaufhaus

Friedrichstrasse 90 (2025 1111, www.kulturkaufhaus.de). U6, S1, S2, S5, S7, S25, S75 Friedrichstrasse. **Open** *9am-midnight Mon-Fri; 9am-11.30pm Sat.* **Map** *p70 N6* ❶ *Books & music*

Intended as a 'cultural department store', this spacious five-floor retailer has books, magazines, CDs and DVDs. You can borrow reading glasses (€10 deposit) or a portable CD player (€50 deposit) for the time you're in the store. The huge English-language section has an excellent selection of cookbooks and travel literature among novels and non-fiction. The well-hidden 'vertical garden,' designed by French botanist Patrick Blanc, houses thousands of tropical plants on a single 270sqm (2,900sqft) wall. There's also a café-restaurant serving afternoon tea, coffee and small plates.

Restaurants & cafés

♥ Grill Royal €€€-€€€€

Friedrichstrasse 105B (2887 9288, www.grillroyal.com). U6, S1, S2, S5, S7, S25, S75 Friedrichstrasse. **Open** *6pm-1am daily.* **Map** *p70 N6* ❹ *Steakhouse*

One of the city's best-known venues, nestled on the riverside, Grill Royal is a stylish, friendly and profoundly meaty experience. Not for vegetarians or those on a diet or budget, Grill is as compelling for its people-watching potential as it is for its (stoutly priced) steaks, seafood and accoutrements.

Bars & pubs

Ständige Vertretung

Schiffbauerdamm 8 (282 3965, www.staev.de). U6, S1, S2, S5, S7, S25, S75 Friedrichstrasse. **Open** *10.30am-1am daily.* **Map** *p70 M6* ❷

The knick-knack-filled Ständige commemorates the still-controversial decision to move the German capital from Bonn to Berlin after reunification. Ständige Vertretung – 'permanent representation' – was the name West and East Germany used to describe the special consulates they kept in each other's countries, not wanting to legitimise the other by calling it an embassy. Due to the pub's proximity to the government quarter, you get the odd politician popping in for some draught Kölsch. There's a lovely terrace by the river in summer, and you can get a bite to eat too.

Entertainment

Berliner Ensemble
Bertolt-Brecht-Platz 1 (2840 8155, www.berliner-ensemble. de). U6, S1, S2, S25, S3, S5, S7, S9 Friedrichstrasse. **Box office** *10am-6.30pm Mon-Sat.* **Tickets** *€5-€30; €9 reductions.* **Map** *p70 M6* **7** *Theatre*
Probably Berlin's most famous theatre, thanks mainly to its historical association with Bertolt Brecht. Under current artistic director Claus Peymann, it is regarded by Germans as a little too comfortable and touristy, a place where older, formerly radical directors go to work. You can still see the late Heiner Müller's 20-year-old staging of *The Resistable Rise of Arturo Ui*, along with productions by Robert Wilson and Peter Stein.

Deutsches Theater
Schumannstrasse 13A (2844 1221, tickets 2844 1225, www. deutschestheater.de). U6, S1, S2, S25, S3, S5, S7, S9 Friedrichstrasse. **Box office** *11am-6.30pm Mon-Sat; 3-6.30pm Sun.* **Tickets** *€5-€48; €9 reductions.* **Map** *p70 M5* **8** *Theatre*
Of all the theatres in Berlin, the Deutsches Theater behaves most like a state theatre in any other German city, offering a *Spielplan* of new interpretations of works by Goethe and Schiller alongside Shakespeare, Aeschylus and a smattering of new plays. Productions vary enormously, from intensely exciting and innovative to more stately fare.

Friedrichstadtpalast
Friedrichstrasse 107 (2326 2326, www.palast.berlin). U6, S1, S2, S25, S3, S5, S7, S9 Friedrichstrasse. **Box office** *10am-6.30pm daily.* **Tickets** *€19-€117.* **Map** *p70 N5* **9** *Cabaret*
An East Berlin institution in a building that was originally designed to be the opera house in Damascus, this is the city's biggest revue theatre. Since reunification, it's mainly featured big Vegas-style musical revues – with Vegas-style prices to match. It's usually packed with coachloads of German tourists.

Museumsinsel

At the eastern end of Unter den Linden is the Museumsinsel, the island in the Spree where Berlin was born. The island is a UNESCO World Heritage Site thanks to its five major museums, all of which are subject to a massive and ongoing renovation programme, masterminded by British architect David Chipperfield. It is also the site of the bombastic **Berliner Dom** and the reconstructed Stadtschloss, which is due to open as the **Humboldt Forum** in late 2019.

In the know
Museum passes

If you want to visit all five museums on the island, get a MuseumsInsel combined ticket (€18, €9 reductions), valid for one day and available both online and from ticket desks inside any of the participating museums. If you're planning a longer stay, consider the Museum Pass Berlin (see *p24*). For other Information and offers, see www.museumsportal-berlin.de/en

Sights & museums

Alte Nationalgalerie

Bodestrasse 1-3 (266 424242, www. smb.museum/ang). U6, S1, S2, S5, S7, S25, S75 Friedrichstrasse, or S5, S7, S75 Hackescher Markt. **Open** *10am-6pm Tue, Wed, Fri-Sun; 10am-8pm Thur.* **Admission** *€8; €4 reductions, or Museumsinsel ticket (see p81).* **Map** *p70 O6.*

With its ceiling and wall paintings, fabric wallpapers and marble staircase, the Old National Gallery is a sparkling home to one of the largest collections of 19th-century art and sculpture in Germany. Friedrich Stüler was commissioned to design the building to house the collection of wealthy industrialist JHW Wagener in 1861, who donated it to the Prussian state. The 440 paintings and 80 sculptures span the years from Goethe to the early modern period, with Romantic German artists such as Adolph Menzel, Caspar David Friedrich, Max Liebermann and Carl Spitzweg well represented. There are also some first-rate works from Manet, Monet and Rodin. Although the gallery is worth a visit, don't expect to see any kind of definitive German national collection.

Altes Museum

Am Lustgarten (266 424242, www. smb.museum/am). U6, S1, S2, S5, S7, S25, S75 Friedrichstrasse, or S5, S7, S75 Hackescher Markt. **Open** *10am-6pm Tue, Wed, Fri-Sun; 10am-8pm Thur.* **Admission** *€10; €5 reductions, or Museumsinsel ticket (see p81).* **Map** *p70 O6.*

Opened as the Royal Museum in 1830, the Old Museum was originally the home for all the art treasures on Museumsinsel. It was designed by Schinkel and is considered one of his finest buildings, with a particularly magnificent entrance rotunda, where vast neon letters declare that 'All Art Has Been Contemporary'. The Egyptian galleries are now housed in the Neues Museum round the corner (*see p84*), but this building showcases other ancient

Altes Museum

civilisations, with an excellent look at the Etruscans and Romans on the top floor. The main floor exhibits the collection of classical antiquities, including a world-class selection of Greek art; pride of place goes to the superlative third-century bronze, *The Praying Boy*.

Berliner Dom

Am Lustgarten (2026 9136, guided tours 2026 9119, www.berliner-dom.de). U6, S1, S2, S5, S7, S25, S75 Friedrichstrasse, or S5, S7, S75 Hackescher Markt. **Open** *Apr-Sept 9am-7pm daily. Oct-Mar 9am-7pm daily.* **Admission** *€7; €4 reductions; free under-18s.* **Map** *p70 O6.*

The dramatic Berlin Cathedral celebrated its centenary in 2005. Built in Italian Renaissance style, it was destroyed during World War II and remained a ruin until 1973, when extensive restoration work began. It has always looked fine from the outside, but now that the internal work is complete, it is fully restored to its former glory. Crammed with detail and containing dozens of statues of eminent German Protestants, its lush 19th-century interior is hardly the perfect acoustic space for the frequent concerts that are held here (even on the colossal organ), but it's worth a visit to see the crypt containing around 90 sarcophagi of notables from the Hohenzollern dynasty, or to clamber up for splendid views from the cupola. Call to book a guided tour.

Bode-Museum

Monbijoubrücke (266 424242, www.smb.museum/bm). U6, S1, S2, S5, S7, S25, S75 Friedrichstrasse, or S5, S7, S75 Hackescher Markt. **Open** *10am-6pm Tue, Wed, Fri-Sun; 10am-8pm Thur.* **Admission** *€12; €6 reductions, or Museumsinsel ticket (see p81).* **Map** *p70 N6.*

Built by Berlin architect Ernst Eberhard von Ihne in 1904, the Bode-Museum was originally intended by Wilhelm von Bode to be a home for art from the beginnings of Christendom; it now contains the Byzantine Collection, Sculpture Collection and the Numismatic Collection. The neo-Baroque great dome, the basilica hall and the glorious cupola were carefully restored in the early years of the new millennium to keep up with modern curatorial standards, but they retain their magnificence. Most impressively, despite having one of the world's largest sculpture collections and more than half a million pieces in the coin collection, the museum somehow retains a totally uncluttered feel, and the sculptures stand free from off-putting glass cases. Highlights include the wall-length Apse Mosaic from AD 545 and the 14th-century Mannheim High Altar.

❤ Humboldt Forum

Stadtschloss, Unter den Linden 3 (265 9500, www.humboldtforum.com). U2 Hausvogteiplatz or U6 Französische Strasse. **Map** *p70 O7.*

Eagerly anticipated, the Humboldt Forum is the cultural centre that will sit like a jewel inside the new Berliner Stadtschloss. Opening in stages from late 2019, the forum promises to bring together diverse cultures and perspectives and to seek new insights into topical issues around globalisation. The exhibition spaces will host the state's collection of artefacts from Oceania, Central America, Africa and the Far East, which were previously displayed at the ethnology and Asian art museums in Dahlem (see *p181*). Look out for masks and effigies from New Guinea, and a remarkable collection of original canoes and boats. There are also superb carvings from Benin and the Congo,

💜 Neues Museum

Bodestrasse 1 (266 424242, www. smb.museum/nm). U6, S1, S2, S5, S7, S25, S75 Friedrichstrasse, or S5, S7, S75 Hackescher Markt. **Open** *10am-6pm Tue, Wed, Fri-Sun; 10am-8pm Thur. Entry by timed ticket.* **Admission** *€12; €6 reductions, or Museumsinsel ticket (see p81).* **Map** *p70 O6.*

Designed by Friedrich August Stüler in the mid-19th century, the Neues Museum was left a vacant wreck for years, following bomb damage in World War II. Reconstruction began in the GDR in the late 1980s, only to be abandoned when Germany was reunified. The job of rebuilding the Neues Museum finally went to architect David Chipperfield, whose design was awarded the European Union Prize for Contemporary Architecture in 2011. It beautifully blends architectural elements of old and new by accentuating the original design with modern elements used to restore structural continuity.

The museum reopened in 2009 and houses the Egyptian Museum & Papyrus Collection, the Museum of Prehistory & Early History and artefacts from the Collection of Classical Antiquities. The most famous object is the bust of the Egyptian queen Nefertiti (which Germany refuses to return to Egypt despite repeated requests). The Prehistory and Early History galleries, which trace the evolution of *Homo sapiens* from 1,000,000 BC to the Bronze Age, have the skull of a Neanderthal from Le

Moustier and reproductions (and some originals) of Heinrich Schliemann's famous treasure from ancient Troy, including works in ceramic and gold, as well as weaponry. The famed 'Berlin Golden Hat' is the most notable piece in the room dedicated to the Bronze Age. Look out, too, for the sixth-century BC grave of a girl buried with a gold coin in her mouth. Information is available in English. Admission is within a half-hour ticketed time slot, so book online to skip the queues.

Pergamonmuseum

beaded artefacts from Cameroon and a host of archaeological objects and fine artworks from India, Japan, China and Korea, dating from the early Stone Age to the present. In addition to the museum exhibits, a new exhibition entitled 'Berlin and the World' will explore the city's relationship to global issues of migration, war, religion and culture.

❤ Pergamonmuseum

*Bodestrasse 1-3 (266 424242, www. smb.museum/pm). U6, S1, S2, S5, S7, S25, S75 Friedrichstrasse, or S5, S7, S75 Hackescher Markt. **Open** 10am-6pm Mon-Wed, Fri-Sun; 10am-8pm Thur. **Admission** €12; €6 reductions, or Museumsinsel ticket (see p81). **Map** p70 N6.*
One of the world's major archaeological museums, the Pergamon should not be missed, although protracted and ongoing renovations may affect the visitor experience until 2023. The museum comprises the **Antikensammlung** (Collection of Classical Antiquities) and the **Vorderasiatisches Museum** (Museum of Near Eastern Antiquities) and, among its many treasures, contains

three unmissable exhibits. The star attraction is the Hellenistic Pergamon Altar, dating from 170-159 BC; huge as it is, the museum's partial reconstruction is only a third of the original's size. In an adjoining room, and even more architecturally impressive, is the towering Roman Market Gate of Miletus (29m/95ft wide and almost 17m/ 56ft high), erected in AD 120. This leads through to the third of the big attractions: the extraordinary blue- and ochre-tiled Gate of Ishtar and the Babylonian Processional Street, dating from the reign of King Nebuchadnezzar (605-562 BC). There are plenty of other astonishing things to see, including some stunning Assyrian reliefs.

The Pergamon is also home to the **Museum für Islamische Kunst** (Museum of Islamic Art), which takes up some 14 rooms in the southern wing. This wide-ranging collection includes applied arts, crafts, books and architectural details from the eighth to the 19th centuries. Entrance to this museum is included in the overall admission price, as is an excellent audio guide.

▶ *The cost and timescale of the museum's renovation programme have both increased, meaning that the Pergamon Altar is now likely to remain closed until 2023.*

Scheunenviertel

The Scheunenviertel stretches around the north bank of the River Spree from Friedrichstrasse to Hackescher Markt. Originally the out-of-town site for highly flammable hay barns (*Scheunen*), it became the centre of Berlin's immigrant community, including many Jews from Eastern Europe. Following the fall of the Wall, the dilapidated buildings were a magnet for squatters who opened make-shift studios and other cultural spaces. These have now been gentrified into galleries, boutiques and cafés, making this one of Berlin's most rewarding quarters for a ramble.

Sights & museums

Hackesche Höfe
Oranienburger Strasse at Rosenthaler Strasse. S5, S7, S75 Hackescher Markt. **Map** *p70 O5.*
Built in 1906-07, these are the most famous of the Scheunenviertel's characteristic courtyards (*Höfe*). A complex of nine interlinking Jugendstil quadrangles with elegant ceramic façades, the *Höfe* miraculously survived two world

wars but fell into disrepair before being restored in the mid 1990s using the old plans. Today, they house a tourist-friendly collection of shops, galleries, cafés and entertainment venues.

Neue Synagoge
Centrum Judaicum, Oranienburger Strasse 28-30 (8802 8316, www. centrumjudaicum.de). S1, S2, S25 Oranienburger Strasse. **Open** *see the website for details.* **Admission** *see the website for details. No cards.* **Map** *p70 N5.*
Built in 1857-66 as the Berlin Jewish community's showpiece, it was the New Synagogue that was attacked during Kristallnacht in 1938, but not too badly damaged – Allied bombs did far more harm in 1945. The façade remained intact and the Moorish dome has been rebuilt. Inside is a permanent exhibition about Jewish life in Berlin and a glassed-in area protecting the ruins of the sanctuary. Tours are available, both of the synagogue and the surrounding area, but book ahead. For more on the Jewish experience, visit the **Anne Frank Zentrum** (Rosenthaler Strasse 39, 2888 65610, www.annefrank.de).

Restaurants & cafés
Also check out the Store Kitchen and Cecconi's at **Soho House** (*see p189*).

♥ Barcomi's €
Sophie-Gips-Höfe, Sophienstrasse 21 (2859 8363, www.barcomis. de). U8 Weinmeisterstrasse. **Open** *9am-9pm Mon-Sat; 10am-9pm Sun.* **Map** *p70 O5* ⑤ *Café*
Berlin's very own domestic goddess, Cynthia Barcomi, opened her first café in Kreuzberg back in 1997 – a different age in reunified Berlin years. The American expat brought her nation's sweet treats to Berlin, doling out blueberry pancakes and whoopee pies as well

as bagels. She now supplies baked goods all over town and has two bestselling cookbooks under her belt. The café is situated in a quiet courtyard near Hackescher Markt, and locals flock to the outdoor tables to escape the tourist hubbub. **Other location** Bergmannstrasse 21, Kreuzberg (694 8138).

❤ Café Fleury €
Weinbergsweg 20 (4403 4144). U8 Rosenthaler Platz. **Open** *8am-8pm Mon-Sat; 9.30am-8pm Sun.* **No cards. Map** *p70 O4* ⑥ *Café*
This wildly popular French café at the bottom of the hill up to Prenzlauer Berg provides the perfect perch from which to people-watch over a buttery croissant and café au lait. A variety of cakes, tarts, salads and baguettes are offered for lunch.

CôCô €
Rosenthalerstrasse 2 (5547 5188, www.banhmi-coco.de). U8 Rosenthaler Platz. **Open** *11am-10pm Mon-Thur; 11am-11pm Fri, Sat; noon-10pm Sun.* **No cards. Map** *p70 O5* ⑦ *Vietnamese*
There's been a *banh mi* explosion in Berlin. Contending for the title of Perfect Sandwich, this Vietnamese

In the know
Stolpersteine

Walking around Berlin, you may stumble across a brass-plated cobblestone with writing engraved on it – this is a Stolpersteine (literally 'stumbling block'), set down to remember a victim of the Holocaust in front of their house. Remarkably, they are all the work of artist Gunter Hemnig, who casts and installs each one. Since 1992, he's put in over 40,000 of them across Europe, with close to 3,000 in Berlin alone, the majority commemorating Jewish victims, but also Roma, homosexuals and victims of euthanasia.

speciality combines fatty pâté and roast pork slices, offset by coriander and zingy pickled daikon and carrot, all in an airy-light baguette (rice flour is used to combat the humidity in Vietnam). CôCô's choice of sandwich fillings includes *banh mi thit nuong* (with lemongrass meatballs) and *banh mi chay* (with tofu), as well as the classic variety – all are made to order at the bar. If the sun's out, take your sandwich to the nearby Weinbergpark and munch in peace on the hillside.

❤ Commonground €
Rosenthalerstrasse 1 (no phone, www.commongrnd.de). U8 Rosenthaler Platz. **Open** *7.30am-midnight Mon-Thur; 7.30am-2am Fri; 8.30am-2am Sat; 8.30am-midnight Sun.* **No cards. Map** *p70 O5* ⑧ *Café*
Run by the team behind Friedrichshain's immensely popular Silo Coffee, Commonground is situated inside the ground floor of the Circus Hotel. Bigger than it looks from the outside, the café features comfy armchairs, an outdoor terrace and the quality coffee, snacks and craft cocktails you'd expect. Step in for one of the best brunch menus in Berlin.

District Mot €-€€
Rosenthaler Strasse 62 (2008 9284, www.districtmot.com) U8 Rosenthaler Platz. **Open** *noon-midnight daily.* **Map** *p70 O5* ⑨ *Vietnamese*
Immensely fun, with a fabulous venue that makes you feel you're in downtown Saigon, District Mot serves up a street-food menu with aplomb. The bao burger has won Berlin's best burger award more than once, and as long as you don't mind sitting on a plastic stool and using toilet paper as a napkin, there's more than enough on the menu to satisfy the hungriest visitor. If you're feeling a bit more

grown up, the Chen Che in a courtyard just over the road, offers clay-pot Vietnamese kitchen in a calm tea-house style environment.

Katz Orange €€€
Bergstrasse 22 (983 208 430, www. katzorange.com). U8 Rosenthaler Platz. **Open** *6pm-late daily.* **Map** *p70 N4* ⑩ *Modern German*
Set off the street in a handsome 19th-century red-brick ex-brewery, Katz Orange is a grown-up restaurant for locavore dining with an excellent late-night cocktail bar attached. The restaurant takes pains to source local produce from trusted farmers and suppliers to create a short menu of seasonal dishes. A beautiful dining experience with a Berlin flavour.

❤ Das Lokal €€-€€€
Linienstrasse 160 (2844 9500, www.lokal-berlin.blogspot.co.uk). S1, S2, S25 Oranienburger Strasse. **Open** *5pm-late daily.* **Map** *p70 N5* ⑪ *Modern German*
Das Lokal comes from fine heritage: it opened while the much-loved Kantine was being redesigned alongside David Chipperfield's studio. The weekly changing seasonal menu might feature starters of pigeon with chestnuts, mussels in broth or asparagus croquettes – all designed to demonstrate the superior flavour of well-sourced produce. It's also an oasis for offal dishes and for game, which is plentiful in Berlin's surrounding forests.

Mogg €-€€
Auguststrasse 11-13 (0176 6496 1344, www.moggmogg.com). U6 Oranienburger Tor. **Open** *11am-10pm Mon-Fri; 10am-10pm Sat, Sun.* **Map** *p70 N5* ⑫ *Deli*
This New York-style deli is a lunchtime hotspot for local galleristas, where all the necessaries are pitch-perfect: the pickles pack a hefty crunch; fresh

coleslaw is just the right side of creamy-sour; and the toasted rye bread reveals a fluffy interior. Yet all play second fiddle to the thick wodge of smoky goodness that is their pastrami meat. The menu features classics such as the Reuben, topped with melted 'Swiss' cheese, sauerkraut and a special dressing, plus matzo ball soup and cream cheese bagels.

Nola's am Weinberg €€
Veteranenstrasse 9 (4404 0766, www.nola.de). U8 Rosenthaler Platz. **Open** *10am-1am daily.* **Map** *p70 O4* ⑬ *Swiss*
This former park pavilion has a fabulous terrace overlooking the park slope, as well as a bar and dining room. Expect artery-hardening Swiss fare, such as venison goulash with mushrooms and spinach noodles, or cheese and spinach rösti topped with a fried egg. On Sundays, they do a magnificently generous brunch buffet.

Noto €€-€€€
Torstrasse 173 (2009 5387, www. noto-berlin.com). U8 Rosenthaler Platz. **Open** *6pm-midnight daily.* **Map** *p70 N5* ⑭ *Modern German*
Noto exemplifies contemporary Berlin dining: a laid-back setting, with the chef-owner cooking traditional German produce made modern through creative techniques. The succinct menu changes weekly, zipping from cocoa and pumpkin ravioli in a rabbit ragoût to the signature dish of veal spare ribs in an Asian-style sweet marinade.

Princess Cheesecake €
Tucholskystrasse 37 (2809 2760, www.princess-cheesecake.de). U6 Oranienburger Tor. **Open** *10am-8pm daily.* **Map** *p70 N5* ⑮ *Café*
A perfect pit stop during a day's Auguststrasse gallery-hopping,

Commonground

Princess Cheesecake is where you can try the venerable 'Kaffee und Kuchen' tradition – Germany's equivalent of afternoon tea. Decor takes equally from minimalism as it does from the baroque, and the cakes are accordingly clean-lined but opulent in flavour. Try a classic baked cheesecake or one of the more adventurous numbers such as 'Mi Cariño Suave', laden with candied almonds and toffee and topped with quark cream. **Other location** Knesebeckerstrasse 32, Charlottenburg (8862 5870).

Yarok Berlin €
Torstrasse 195 (9562 8703, www.yarok-restaurant.de). U6 Oranienburger Tor, U8 Rosenthaler Platz. **Open** *2-11pm daily.* **No cards**. *Map p70 N5* **16** *Middle Eastern*
This *Imbiss* sets the bar high. Serving some of the finest Middle-Easten *Tellers* (plates) in the city, Yarok – meaning 'green' in Hebrew – offers up yummy falafel, silky houmous, spectacular minced-beef kebab and zingy juices, all at great prices.

Bars & pubs

🖤 Bar 3
Weydingerstrasse 20 (2804 6973). U2 Rosa-Luxemburg-Platz. **Open** *9pm-late Tue-Sat.* **No cards**. *Map p70 P5* **3**
Located in a backstreet off Torstrasse, this cosy bar is a favourite of Mitte media types and art stars. With a large horseshoe-shaped bar dominating the room, it's bar stools or standing only, as this place seriously packs out with a slick, bespectacled clientele and the occasional actor or celebrity. The house wine is very good. Or try the Kölsch beer from Cologne – tradition dictates that it's served in a tiny glass, constantly refilled by the barman until you abandon it half-full or lay a beer mat over the top.

Buck and Breck
Brunnenstrasse 177 (www. buckandbreck.com). U8 Rosenthaler Platz. **Open** *7pm-late winter; 8pm-late summer.* **Map p70 O4** **4**

A tiny little speakeasy hidden away behind a plain door, Buck and Breck is not such a well-kept secret these days, but still a very pleasant place to drink. Ring the doorbell to enter the one-room bar where mixologists whip up astounding creations with the seriousness of scientists. With only room for 20 or so guests, this is an intimate experience and less hipstery than you might expect. Smoking is allowed inside, but cell phones aren't.

Cordobar

Grosse Hamburger Strasse 32 (2758 1215, www.cordobar.net). S1, S2, S25 Oranienburger Strasse, U8 Rosenthaler Platz. **Open** *7pm-2am Tue-Sat.* **Map** *p70 O5* **5**
The Parisian-wine-bar-with-small-plates model has become extremely popular in recent years, and Mitte finally has an excellent example. The Cordobar is owned by Austrian sommelier Willi Shlögl and friends (including film director Jan-Ole Gerster), so the list focuses on southern German and Austrian wines, with many unsulphured 'natural' bottles. Hot and cold dishes, such as blood-sausage pizza or smoked eel with brussels sprouts, are also available.

♥ Kim Bar

Brunnenstrasse 10 (no phone, www. kim-bar.com). U8 Rosenthaler Platz. **Open** *8pm-late Tue-Sat.* **No cards. Map** *p70 O4* **6**
A veteran of the Mitte scene, Kim has been a favourite with twentysomething art-scenesters since it opened in 2007, although its ramshackle atmosphere and charm have received a bit of a sprucing up in recent years. The entrance is low-key: look for an all-glass façade and crowds of people sporting billowy monochrome clothing. Cheap drinks and a rotating roster of neighbourhood DJs add to the don't-give-a-damn aesthetic.

Mein Haus am See

Brunnenstrasse 197-198 (2759 0873, www.mein-haus-am-see.club). U8 Rosenthaler Platz. **Open** *9am-late daily.* **No cards. Map** *p70 O4* **7**
This hugely popular split-level joint is situated a stone's throw from busy Rosenthaler Platz and is a great alternative to the tired Sankt Oberholz. The owners' slightly vapid claim is that 'it's not a bar, it's not a club, it's something sexier in between', but it's certainly hard to categorise. There are exhibitions, readings, DJs and it almost never closes, so whether you want another beer, a sobering coffee or a panino at 4.30am, this is the place to come. Excellent breakfasts too.

Shops & services

♥ Ampelmann Shop

Rosenthaler Strasse 40-41 (4404 8801, www.ampelmann.de). S5, S7, S75 Hackescher Markt. **Open** *9.30am-8pm Mon-Thur; 9.30am-9pm Fri, Sat; 1-6pm Sun.* **Map** *p70 O5* **2** *Gifts & souvenirs*
You'll find a huge variety of stuff emblazoned with the old East's enduring symbol, the jaunty red and green traffic-light men (*see opposite* In the know). As you can see from the number of shops dotted around the city, they've become unofficial city mascots and have even started colonising West Berlin road crossings too.

♥ Arkonaplatz Flohmarkt

Arkonaplatz (786 9764, www. troedelmarkt-arkonaplatz.de). U8 Bernauer Strasse. **Open** *10am-4pm Sun.* **Map** *p70 O4* **3** *Market*
A broad array of retro gear – ranging from vinyl to clothing, books to trinkets, bikes to coffee tables – all available here at moderate prices. The golden rule of flea markets applies at Arkonaplatz: the best stuff gets snapped up early.

Buchhandlung Walther König

*Burgstrasse 27 (2576 0980, www.
buchhandlung-walther-koenig.
de). S5, S7, S75 Hackescher Markt.
Open 10am-8am Mon-Sat. **Map** p70
O6* **④** *Books*
Cologne-based Walther König
is Germany's top art publisher,
with several branches dotted
throughout Europe; it also
stocks the bookshops at Berlin's
museums. This flagship store
by Museumsinsel heaves with
beautifully reproduced catalogues
and a comprehensive range of
critical-theory literature. These
books would make a handsome gift
for the art-lover in your life.

do you read me?!

*Auguststrasse 28 (6954 9695, www.
doyoureadme.de). U8 Rosenthaler
Platz, or S1, S2, S25 Oranienburger
Strasse. **Open** 10am-7.30pm Mon-
Sat. **Map** p70 O5* **⑤** *Books*
On Mitte's main art drag, this
small shop's shelves heave with
glossy picks of global fashion,
style, art and design print media.
The magazines are attractively
presented, and there's a small
selection of books in the back.

♥ DSTM

*Torstrasse 161 (4920 3750, www.
dstm.co). U8 Rosenthaler Platz.
Open noon-8pm Mon-Fri; 1-8pm
Sat. **Map** p70 N5* **⑥** *Fashion*
There's plenty of young Berlin
designers cutting their teeth at
boutiques around the city, but
Canadian-born Jen Gilpin's label,
Don't Shoot The Messenger, is
the definitive city look. Local
influences can be read from all
over: shades of Marlene Dietrich's
austere raunchiness and even
the complex fastenings of fetish-
ware are apparent in the billowy
clothing, made mostly in fine black
silk and leather. Angular cutouts
offer glimpses of flesh, and sleek
shapes are conjured by inventive
draping that proves Gilpin's skilled
technique.

Fun Factory

*Oranienburger Strasse 92 (2804
6366, www.funfactory.com). S5, S7,
S75 Hackescher Markt. **Open** noon-
8pm Mon-Thur; 11am-9pm Fri, Sat.
Map p70 O5* **⑦** *Sex shop*
Berlin's temple to adult toys
lies slap-bang in the middle
of Hackescher Markt's central
shopping area. With an interior
designed by American futurist
Karim Rashid, the two-floor shop
caters to a mixed gay/straight crowd
of all stripes. Staff are extremely
helpful if advice is needed.

In the know
Ampelmännchen

Wondering why the pedestrian traffic
lights have much jauntier little red
and green men than in other cities?
Both are wearing hats, and the
green man has a very purposeful
stride. They are *Ampelmännchen*, a
hangover from East Germany, which
had different traffic lights from West
Germany. In the euphoria following
the collapse of Communism, the
Ampelmännchen started to die
out and be replaced by their more
straight-laced western counterparts –
until *Ostalgie* struck and a campaign
was launched to bring them back.
Due to their marketability as
souvenirs, you can now see them on
both sides of the reunified city.

♥ LaLa Berlin

Alte Schönhauser Strasse 3 (2009 5363, www.lalaberlin.com). U2 Rosa-Luxemburg-Platz. **Open** *11am-7pm Mon-Sat.* **Map** *p70 P5* ❽ *Fashion*

Iranian-born Leyla Piedayesh knocks out stylish and cosy knitwear at her Mitte boutique. She's got a shop in Copenhagen too and has become well known across the Atlantic, not least due to famous fans such as Claudia Schiffer, Cameron Diaz and Jessica Alba.

Mykita

Rosa-Luxemburg-Strasse 6 (6730 8715, www.mykita.com). U2, U5, U8, S5, S7, S75 Alexanderplatz. **Open** *11am-7pm Mon-Fri; 11am-6pm Sat.* **Map** *p70 P6* ❾ *Accessories*

This Berlin-based glasses label has been a mainstay for fashion-conscious locals since 2004, but the brand has hit the big time since some of its more experimental frames were picked up by the likes of Lady Gaga. The handmade prescription frames and sunglasses are presented on stark, industrial shelving in this beautifully lit, ultra-minimalist store.

♥ Das Neue Schwarz

Mulackstrasse 38 (2787 4467, www.dasneueschwarz.de). U2 Rosa-Luxemburg-Platz, U8 Weinmeisterstrasse. **Open** *noon-8pm Mon-Sat.* **Map** *p70 P5* ❿ *Fashion*

Mulackstrasse is full of expensive designer boutiques, so Das Neue Schwarz ('the new black') is a great alternative for those looking for a (relative) bargain. The hand-selected stock offers almost-new designer pieces from past seasons, most still with tags. There's stuff for both boys and girls: chunky Céline handbags, flashy Bernard Willhelm bomber jackets, Chloé wedges and

do you read me?!

Dries Van Noten suits, to name just a few.

♥ RSVP

Mulackstrasse 14 & 26 (3195 6410, www.rsvp-berlin.de). U8 Weinmeisterstrasse. **Open** *11am-7pm Mon-Sat.* **Map** *p70 O5* ⓫ *Gifts & souvenirs*

This small but beautiful boutique is the perfect pit stop if you're looking for a gift or have a passion for some of the world's most beautiful notebooks. Expect stationery for the aesthete: art deco scissors, exotic erasers, weighty Rivoli writing paper, Polish notebooks and Koh-I-Noor mechanical pencils. It's just gorgeous.

♥ Wood Wood

Rochstrasse 4 (2804 7877, www.woodwood.dk). U8 Weinmeisterstrasse. **Open** *noon-8pm Mon-Fri; noon-7pm Sat.* **Map** *p70 P5* ⓬ *Fashion*

An avant-garde design collective from Copenhagen, Wood Wood offers beautiful, angular and sometimes outrageous street fashion, sneakers and accessories by Japanese (or co-opted by Japan) designers, such as Sonia Rykiel, Comme des Garçons and White Mountaineering. Almost half the stock is Wood Wood's own, an explosion of prints, stitching and bright colours tempered by clean, classic cuts.

Entertainment

❤ Chamäleon
Hackesche Höfe, Rosenthaler Strasse 40-41 (tickets 400 0590, www.chamaeleonberlin.de). S3, S5, S7, S9 Hackescher Markt. **Box office** *noon-6pm Mon, Sun; noon-8pm Tue-Fri; noon-9.30pm Sat. Performances from 6pm daily.* **Tickets** *€37-€57.* **Map** *p70 O5* ❿ *Cabaret*
This beautiful old theatre with a touch of decadence is located in the courtyards of the Hackesche Höfe. The focus is on contemporary circus performances that combine stunning acrobatics with musical theatre.

❤ Clärchen's Ballhaus
Auguststrasse 24 (282 9295, www.ballhaus.de). S1, S2, S25 Oranienburger Strasse. **Open** *11am-late daily.* **Admission** *€5-€9. No cards.* **Map** *p70 N5* ⓫ *Club*
In the heart of Mitte, this determinedly un-hip dance hall gives the techno clubs a run for their money in terms of popularity and downright fun. Clärchen's Ballhaus has been frequented by fleet-footed Berliners since it was established by Clara Haberman in 1913. Today, its often cheesy playlists and vintage surroundings attract everyone from students to 75-year-old Ballhaus veterans. It's not unusual to see a geriatric

Fred Astaire type teaching a young pink-haired artist how to tango or foxtrot. The Ballhaus has two dance floors: a ground-floor space and the smaller Spiegelsaal (Mirror Salon) upstairs, where huge cracked mirrors, chandeliers, ornate mouldings and candlelight transport guests straight back to the 1920s.

❤ Sophiensaele
Sophienstrasse 18 (283 5266, www.sophiensaele.com). U8 Weinmeisterstrasse. **Tickets** *€15; €10 reductions.* **Map** *p70 O5* ⓬ *Theatre*
Hidden on a quiet side road near Hackescher Markt and set back behind a little courtyard, Sophiensaele is easy to miss. Here, over four floors, you're likely to see some of the most cutting-edge performances in Berlin in some of the most atmospheric performance spaces the city has to offer.

Volksbühne
Linienstrasse 227 (2406 5777, www.volksbuehne-berlin.de). U2 Rosa-Luxemburg-Platz. **Box office** *11am-7pm Mon-Sat.* **Tickets** *€6-€36; €6-€18 reductions.* **Map** *p70 P5* ⓭ *Theatre*
Built in 1914, the Volksbühne is Berlin's most imposing theatre; its austere exterior was well suited to the regime of artistic director Frank Castorf, whose productions seemed to enrage as much as delight. However, the appointment of Chris Dercon, former director of the Tate Modern in London, resulted in the theatre being occupied by protesters who worried that it would lose its avant-garde touch to commercialism and gentrification; in April 2018, Dercon stepped down. It's not yet clear how the theatre will proceed, but it continues to put on 'theatre by the people, for the people.'

Alexanderplatz & around

Remodelled in the 1970s by Erich Hönecker to reflect the glories of socialism, Alexanderplatz is a huge soulless space dominated by the impressive golf-ball-on-a-knitting-needle that is the **Fernsehturm** (Television Tower). Other notable buildings include the **Marienkirche** and the red-brick **Berliner Rathaus**. For a vague impression of what this part of the city might have looked like before Allied bombers and the GDR did their work, take a stroll around the **Nikolaiviertel**, just to the south, where the area's few undamaged historic buildings were reconstructed around the city's oldest church, the **Nikolaikirche** (dating from 1220).

Sights & museums

AquaDom & Sea Life
Spandauer Strasse 3 (992 800, www.visitsealife.com/berlin). S5, S7, S75 Hackescher Markt. **Open** *10am-7pm daily.* **Admission** *€17.50; €12.50 reductions.* **Map** *p70 O6.*
Billed as two attractions in one, both involving lots of water and plenty of fish. Sea Life leads you through 13 themed aquaria offering fish in different habitats. The AquaDom is the world's largest free-standing aquarium – a space age tuboid that looks like it might have just landed from some alien planet. A lift takes you up through the middle of this giant cylindrical fishtank – a million litres of saltwater that is home to 2,500 colourful creatures and is enfolded by the atrium of the Radisson Blu hotel. Unfortunately, only the staff are allowed to scuba-dive through the tank to feed the fish.

DDR Museum
Karl Liebknecht Strasse 1 (847 123 731, www.ddr-museum.de). S5, S7, S75 Hackescher Markt. **Open** *10am-8pm Mon-Fri, Sun; 10am-10pm Sat.* **Admission** *€9.80; €6 reductions; free under-6s.* **Map** *p68 O6.*
Bright blue neon signage and a Trabant in the window welcome you into 'one of Europe's most interactive museums!' This is *Ostalgie* in action. Touchscreens, sound effects and even the 'DDR Game' mean that the more distasteful aspects of East German life are cheerfully glossed over. The museum is essentially a collection of GDR memorabilia, from travel tickets to Palast der Republik serviettes. Climb inside the Trabi or sit on a GDR couch in a GDR living room where you can watch GDR TV. Even the much-feared Stasi get the interactive family treatment too – you can pretend to be a Stasi officer and listen in on a bugged flat. Take it all with a large pinch of salt.

❤ Fernsehturm
Panoramastrasse 1A (no phone, www.tv-turm.de). U2, U5, U8, S5, S7, S75 Alexanderplatz. **Open** *Mar-Oct 9am-midnight daily. Nov-Feb 10am-midnight daily.* **Admission** *€15.50; €9.50 reductions; free under-4s.* **Map** *p70 P6.*
Built in the late 1960s at a time when relations between East and West Berlin were at their lowest ebb, the 365-m (1,198-ft) Television Tower – its ball-on-spike shape visible all over the city – was intended as an assertion of communist dynamism and modernity, while at the same time providing a transmission tower to compete with the powerful television signals emanating from the West. The design by Herbert Henselmann was inspired by the launch of Sputnik, the first artificial satellite, in October 1957.

Henselmann's tower would have a tapering shaft, to represent a rocket soaring into the sky; and at the very top would be a bright, socialist-red sphere to represent a satellite.

Construction began in 1965, and the Fernsehturm finally opened on 7 October 1969 – the 20th anniversary of the founding of the GDR. It marked the very centre of the city in the manner of a medieval church tower, allowed the second GDR TV station to commence broadcasting, and advertised the thrusting triumph of socialism in a form visible for miles around, in particular all over West Berlin. Communist authorities were, however, displeased to note a particular phenomenon: when the sun shone on the tower, reflections on the ball formed the shape of a cross. Berliners dubbed this phenomenon 'the Pope's revenge'. Nevertheless, the authorities were proud enough of their tower to make it one of the central symbols of the East German capital, and today it is one of Berlin's most popular graphic images.

Take an ear-popping trip in the lift to the observation platform at 203m (668ft): a great way to orient yourself early on a visit to Berlin. When the weather is clear, the view is unbeatable by night or day – particularly looking westwards, where you can take in the whole of the Tiergarten and surrounding area. If heights make you hungry, take a twirl in the revolving restaurant, which offers an even better view. There are usually queues to get up there, however.

Hanf Museum
Mühlendamm 5 (242 4827, www. hanfmuseum.de). U2, U5, U8, S5, S7, S75 Alexanderplatz. **Open** *10am-8pm Tue-Fri; noon-8pm Sat, Sun.* **Admission** *€4.50, €3 reductions; free under-10s. No cards.* **Map** *p70 P7.*

The world's largest hemp museum aims to teach the visitor about the uses of the plant throughout history, as well as touching on the controversy surrounding it. The café (doubling as a video and reading room) serves cakes made with hemp, as well as those without it.

Marienkirche
Karl-Liebknecht-Strasse 8 (2475 9510, www.marienkirche-berlin.de). U2, U5, U8, S5, S7, S75 Alexanderplatz. **Open** *10am-6pm daily.* **Admission** *free.* **Map** *p70 P6.*

Construction of the Marienkirche began in 1270, making it one of Berlin's few remaining medieval buildings. Just inside the door is a wonderful 'Dance of Death' fresco dating from 1485, and the 18th-century Walther organ here is considered his masterpiece. Marienkirche hit the headlines in 1989 when the East German civil rights movement chose it for one of their first sit-ins, since churches were among the few places where people could congregate without state permission.

Märkisches Museum
Am Köllnischen Park 5 (240 020 171, www.stadtmuseum. de/maerkisches-museum). U2 Märkisches Museum. **Open** *10am-6pm Tue-Sun.* **Admission** *€5; €3 reductions. Free 1st Wed of mth.* **Map** *p70 P7.*

One of Berlin's state museums, the Märkisches Museum presents a host of artefacts related to the culture and history of the city; different sections examine themes such as Berlin as a newspaper city, women in Berlin's history, city guilds, intellectual Berlin and the military. There are models of the city at different times, and some good paintings, including works by members of the Brücke group. Note that the museum will be closed for at least three years from 2020, with renovations also affecting the nearby Marinehaus. Upon reopening, the two buildings will be at the heart of a new museum and creative quarter centred on Köllnischen Park.

Bars & pubs

Besenkammer

Rathausstrasse 1 (242 4083). U2, U5, U8, S5, S7, S75 Alexanderplatz. **Open** *24hrs daily.* **No cards.** **Map** *p70 P6* ⑧

The oldest gay pub in the city, Besenkammer ('broom closet') is a tiny place under the S-Bahn tracks at Alexanderplatz, and it virtually never closes. It's probably not a bar you'd spend a whole night in, but well-worth the trip for the queer history: it was a refuge for gay men in the GDR, and, in 1973, gay activist Michael Eggert met here with sympathisers from the West. Their discussion inspired movements that would radically change views on sexuality in East Germany.

Entertainment

Kino International

Karl-Marx-Allee 33, Mitte (2475 6011, www.yorck.de). U5 Schillingstrasse. **Tickets** *€7-€9.50. No cards.* **Map** *p70 Q6* ⑭ *Cinema*

The monumental post-Stalinist architecture of Kino International belies a modest 551-seat auditorium, but the real reason to come here is for the lobby, with its crystal chandeliers and upholstered seating. A first-class example of 1960s GDR chic, it overtook the Colosseum as East Berlin's premier cinema, and became a common venue for Communist Party functions and socialist shindigs.

▶ *Kino International is also the home of the gay and lesbian Club International, which shows LGBT films every Monday ('Mongay') at 10pm.*

KitKatClub

Köpenicker Strasse 76 (no phone, www.kitkatclub.org). U8 Heinrich-Heine-Strasse. **Open** *11pm-late Mon, Fri, Sat.* **Admission** *€10-€15. No cards.* **Map** *p70 Q7* ⑮ *Club*

This legendary sex and techno club for all is a labyrinthine complex of half a dozen dancefloors, a dubious swimming pool and a grimy dungeon mock-operating room. Saturday nights feature the club's flagship CarneBall Bizarre, with the Afterhour event to follow throughout Sunday. For pure polysexual hedonism, look out for cult party Gegen (http://gegenberlin.com) every two months. Most parties have a fetish dress code – except Electric Mondays – so if you arrive wearing jeans you'll have to leave them in the cloakroom and dance in your knickers.

Tresor

Köpenicker Strasse 70 (no phone, www.tresorberlin.de). U8 Heinrich-Heine-Strasse. **Open** *11pm-late Mon; midnight-late Wed-Sat.* **Admission** *€5-€12. No cards.* **Map** *p70 Q8* ⑯ *Club*

Berlin's original techno club is housed in what was formerly the main central-heating power station for East Berlin. The colossal location is breathtaking, but only a tiny portion of the vast space is in use; plans to create a huge centre of alternative art and culture have resulted so far in the Ohm performance space next door and large-scale experimental music festivals, such as **Berlin Atonal** (www.berlin-atonal.com). The experience of the basement floor is one you'll not forget; a black hole occasionally punctuated by flashing strobes with some of the loudest, hardest techno it's humanly possible to hear.

Tiergarten & Around

A slightly uncertain mish-mash of districts plus the grand green park that gives the area its name, Tiergarten straddles the centre of Berlin; it's home to dozens of embassies as well as the iconic Reichstag parliament building. Tiergarten was once hemmed in on the east by the Wall, but these days it's right at the heart of things again, stretching from the futuristic Hauptbahnhof in the north to the Zoo in the south-west.

South of the park is Potsdamer Platz, Berlin's rejuvenated commercial centre, as well as the museums and venues of the Kulturforum – including the spectacular modernist Philharmonie concert hall.

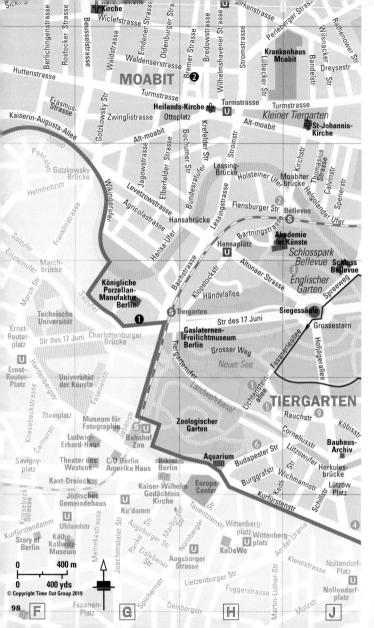

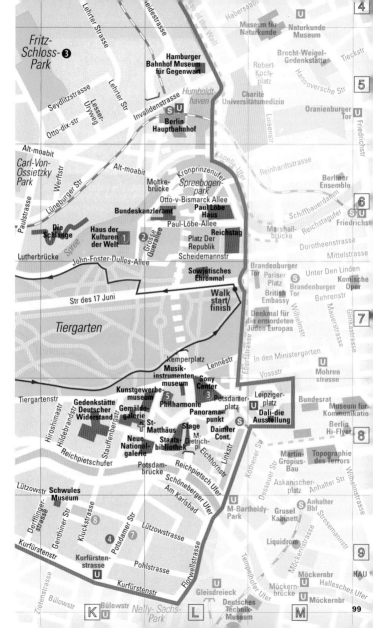

TIERGARTEN & AROUND

Best architecture
Haus der Kulturen der Welt *p104*,
Philharmonie *p110*,
Reichstag *p103*

Best viewpoints
Panoramapunkt *p107*, Reichstag
p103, Siegessäule *p100*

Best blow-out dinner
Cinco *p108*, Hugos *p108*

Best places to unwind
Café am Neuen See *p102*,
Vabali Spa *p105*

Best art museums
Gemäldegalerie *p106*,
Hamburger Bahnhof *p104*

Best family day out
Zoologischer Garten &
Aquarium *p108*

The park & the government district

A hunting ground for the Prussian electors since the 16th century, **Tiergarten** (*see right*) was opened to the public in the 18th century. It was badly damaged during World War II and, in the desperate winter of 1945-46, almost all the surviving trees were cut down for firewood. But, today, joggers, nature lovers, gay cruisers and picnickers pour into the park in fair weather.

In the centre of the park is the **Siegessäule** (Victory Column; climb to the top for fine views), with the landscaped **Englischer Garten** just to the north. The park's main thoroughfare, Strasse des 17 Juni (the date of the East Berlin workers' strike of 1953), is one of the few pieces of Hitler's plan for 'Germania' that actually got built – a grand east-west axis linking Unter den Linden to Neu-Westend. Towards its eastern end stands the **Sowjetisches Ehrenmal** (Soviet Memorial), built out of granite and

marble from the ruins of Hitler's Neue Reichskanzlei; it was once the only piece of Soviet property in West Berlin.

At the north-eastern corner of the park stands the **Reichstag** (*see p103*), crowned by Norman Foster's glass cupola, and a cluster of government buildings that were built after reunification around a bend in the River Spree; the most notable is the **Bundeskanzleramt** (Federal Chancellery). Nearby, the 1957 **Haus der Kulturen der Welt** (House of World Cultures) is an impressive piece of modern architecture and well-loved arts institution.

Sights & museums

❤ Siegessäule

*Strasse des 17 Juni (391 2961). S5, S7, S75 Bellevue. **Open** Summer 9.30am-6.30pm Mon-Fri; 9.30am-7pm Sat, Sun. Winter 10am-5pm Mon-Fri; 10am-5.30pm Sat, Sun. **Admission** €3; €2.50 reductions; free under-5s. No cards. **Map** p98 J7.*

→ Getting around

Once you're inside the Tiergarten, you're about as far as it gets from U-Bahn and S-Bahn lines in Berlin. Practically, this means at most a 20-minute walk, since the park is ringed with stations, including the famous Berlin Zoo station on its western edge. If you do get footsore, don't despair: there are often cycle rickshaws waiting by the Siegessäule. Potsdamer Platz is served by U2, S1, S2 and S25 lines. Berlin Hauptbahnhof is the main hub in Moabit.

🖤 A stroll through the Tiergarten

U55, S1, S2, S25 Brandenburger Tor. **Map** *p98 L7.*

Make like a Berliner and stretch your legs with a stroll, jog or cycle through Berlin's most famous park. This 5-km (3-mile) circuit will return you to your starting point ready for your next adventure within an hour or so.

Start with the **Brandenburger Tor** at your back. Cross the road, heading west, up the right-hand side of **Strasse des 17 Juni**. This wide thoroughfare is regularly pedestrianised for national holidays, important football games and concerts, but you should beware cyclists zooming down the cycle lanes. On your right, you'll see the **Sowjetisches Ehrenmal**, complete with tanks. 100 m further on, carefully cross the busy road then turn north-west into the park, following the paths but bearing right until you reach the banks of the River Spree. Follow the river, then, at the **Lutherbrücke** (Luther's bridge), turn left back into the park following the Spreeweg until you reach the **Siegessäule**. Wave hello to 'Gold-Else' (as Berliners call the statue) and then cross over, entering the southern half of the Tiergarten for the first time. Continue south-west from the Siegessäule, following the broad path known as Fasanerieallee as far as a little bridge over a stream. On sunny days, you'll pass fields of sunbathers and happy picnickers. If you've worked up an appetite, cross the bridge and immediately turn right towards **Café am Neuen See**. If not, then follow the stream

east. You'll soon meet a bigger path known as the Grosser Weg. Keep bearing right until you meet another bridge. Cross it and keep on going. Soon you'll hear the traffic on Tiergartenstrasse just ahead. Now take the turning left onto the **Luiseninsel**, a small island where you'll find a statue of Queen Luise, wife of Frederick William III of Prussia, among beautiful flowers in spring and summer. Leave the island via the **Ahornsteig** (maple path) and continue on without deviating. On your right, you'll see an open meadow full of the strange rocks of the **Global Stone Project**, a private and somewhat eccentric peace initiative. Finally, reaching the end of the Ahornsteig, turn left and then immediately right to find yourself back at the Brandenburger Tor.

Tiergarten's biggest monument was built in 1871-73, to commemorate Prussian campaigns against Denmark (1864), Austria (1866) and France (1870-71). Originally positioned in front of the Reichstag, it was moved by Hitler to form a centrepiece for the east–west axis connecting western Berlin with the palaces and ministries of Mitte. On top of the column is a gilded goddess of victory by Friedrich Drake; captured French cannons and cannonballs, sawn in half and gilded, decorate the column itself. It's an arduous 285 steps up to the viewing platform.

Restaurants & cafés

♥ Café am Neuen See €-€€
Lichtensteinallee 2 (254 4930, www.cafeamneuensee.de). S5, S7, S75 Tiergarten. **Open** *9am-late daily.* **No cards.** **Map** *p98 H8* ❶ *Brasserie*

Hidden away by a small lake in the western part of the Tiergarten, this café, beer garden and brasserie rolled into one is among Berlin's most idyllic spots. In summer, there are rowing boats for hire, and it's a fun and buzzy place to while away an afternoon, eating excellent stone-baked pizza washed down with big jugs of Pilsner – or, unusually for Berlin, cider. With a warm welcome for children, this is the perfect spot for families to grab a table during a ramble through the Tiergarten.

In the know
Gaslaternen-Freilichtmuseum Berlin

A charming little oddity right by the Tiergarten S-Bahn station, this open-air gas-lamp museum has over 90 examples of historic streetlights, all lovingly restored. Take a turn through here at night and bask in their historic glow (*map p98 H7*).

Konditorei Buchwald €
Bartningallee 29 (391 5931, www. konditorei-buchwald.de). S5, S7, S75 Bellevue. **Open** *9am-7pm daily.* **No cards.** **Map** *p98 J6* ❷ *Café*

One Berlin institution (afternoon coffee and cake) celebrated by another: Buchwald, which has been pumping out the sugar and caffeine fix in style for over 160 years. The premises are charming and old-fashioned. The cakes, particularly the *Baumkuchen*, are legendary. Arrive early afternoon, grab a table and savour the history.

Teehaus im Englischen Garten €€
Altonaer Strasse 2 (3948 0400, www.teehaus-tiergarten.com). S5, S7, S75 Bellevue. **Open** *noon-11pm Tue-Sat; 10am-11pm Sun.* **No cards.** **Map** *p98 J7* ❸ *German*

This 1950s garden in the north-west of the Tiergarten was designed to commemorate Anglo-German relations during the blockade of Berlin and is filled with trees donated by George VI. The thatched tea house serves seasonal specialities, such as venison stew or goose leg with dumplings.

Shops & services

Kunst und Trödelmarkt
Strasse des 17 Juni 110-114 (2655 0096, www.berliner-troedelmarkt. de). U2 Ernst-Reuter-Platz, or S5, S7, S75 Tiergarten. **Open** *10am-5pm Sat, Sun.* **Map** *p98 G7* ❶ *Market*

This second-hand market lies on the stretch of road west of Tiergarten S-Bahn station. You'll find good-quality, early 20th-century objects (with prices to match) alongside a jumble of vintage clothing, old furniture, records and books. Full of interesting stuff, and with a cast of eccentric locals to practise your haggling on, the market isn't a bad

💙 Reichstag

Platz der Republik 1 (227 32152, www.bundestag.de/en/). U55, S1, S2, S25 Brandenburger Tor. **Open** *8am-midnight daily (last entry 9.45pm).* **Admission** *free.* **Map** *p98 L6.*

The imposing Reichstag was controversial from the beginning. Architect Paul Wallot struggled to find a style that would symbolise German national identity at a time – 1884-94, shortly after unification – when no such style or identity existed. The scene of Weimar squabblings, it was then badly damaged by fire on 17 February 1933; an incident for which the Nazis blamed Dutchman Marius van der Lubbe, a Communist, and which they used as an excuse to begin their seizure of power. The Reichstag remained a burnt-out ruin during the Third Reich and was then stranded for decades beside the Wall. But following its celebrated renovation by Lord Foster in the 1990s, the Reichstag finally became a fitting home for the Bundestag (Federal Parliament). Foster conceived of it as a 'dialogue between old and new': graffiti scrawled by Russian soldiers in 1945 was left on view, and there was no attempt to deny the building's turbulent history.

No dome appeared on Foster's original plans, but the German government insisted upon one as a sop to conservatives. Foster, in turn, demanded that unlike the structure's original dome (damaged in the war and demolished in the 1950s), the new dome must be open to visitors as a symbol of political transparency; due to the materials used, it ended up costing even more than a replica would have done. A lift whisks you up to the roof; from here, ramps lead to the top of the dome, from where there are fine views of the city. At the centre is a funnel of mirrors, angled so as to shed light on the workings of democracy below, but also lending an almost funhouse effect to the dome. An excellent (free) audio guide points out all the surrounding landmarks.

A trip to the top of this open, playful and defiantly democratic space is a must. Book in advance by filling in an online form at visite. bundestag.de and suggesting three possible time-slots at least three working days in advance.

Haus der Kulturen der Welt

place to bring children, who enjoy hunting among the *Trödel* for treasures.

Entertainment

💙 Haus der Kulturen der Welt

John-Foster-Dulles-Allee 10 (3978 7175, www.hkw.de). U55 Bundestag or S3, S5, S7, S75 Hauptbahnhof. **Open** *10am-7pm daily; event times vary.* **Admission** *varies.* **Map** *p98 K6* ❶ *Cultural venue*

Set up in 1989 to promote the arts of developing countries, the 'House of World Cultures' features a lively programme of concerts, exhibitions and symposia centred around global cultural questions. Housed in Hugh Stubbins' oyster-like building, erected in 1957 as America's contribution to the Interbau Exhibition, this is a treasured Berlin cultural institution. There's a decent café on the premises.

Tipi am Kanzleramt

Grosse Querallee (3906 6550, www.tipi-am-kanzleramt.de). Bus 100, 248. **Box office** *noon-6.30pm Mon-Fri; 3-5.30pm Sat, Sun. Performances 8pm most days.* **Tickets** *€30-€62.* **Map** *p98 K6* ❷ *Cabaret*

A circus tent in the Tiergarten, near the Federal Chancellery, hosts cool international performers presenting various comedy, dance and cabaret shows. Fare is similar to Bar jeder Vernunft, except everything's twice the size.

North of the park

Bordered by canals and the River Spree, Moabit is a little pocket of working-class Berlin that has found itself unnervingly close to the action in recent years. New cafés and bars have sprung up in the streets around the **Arminiusmarkthalle**, and development continues apace around the hulking **Berlin Hauptbahnhof**.

Sights & museums

💙 Hamburger Bahnhof – Museum für Gegenwart

Invalidenstrasse 50-51 (3978 3439, www.smb.museum/en/museums-institutions/hamburger-bahnhof/home.html). U55, S5, S7, S75 Hauptbahnhof. **Open** *10am-6pm Tue, Wed, Fri-Sun; 10am-8pm Thur.* **Admission** *(incl temporary exhibitions) €10; €5 reductions.* **Map** *p98 L5.*

This contemporary art museum opened in 1997 within a vast, grand neoclassical former train station. Outside is a stunning fluorescent light installation by Dan Flavin. Inside, the biggest draw is the controversial Friedrich Christian Flick Collection: some 2,000 works from around 150 artists (mainly from the late 20th century), with key pieces by Bruce Nauman and Martin Kipperberger. Flick, from a steel family whose fortune was earned partly from Nazi-era slave labour, paid for the refurbishment of the adjacent Rieckhalle to warehouse the (many large-scale) works, which are doled out in temporary, themed exhibitions.

Shops & services

Arminiusmarkthalle

Arminiusstrasse 2-4 (www. arminiusmarkthalle.com). U9 Turmstrasse. **Open** *10am-10pm Mon-Fri; 10am-6pm Sat.* **Map** *p98 H5* ❷ *Market*
Opened in 1898, the Arminiusmarkthalle has been selling Berliners their groceries for well over 100 years. Inside this traditionally built market hall, you'll find stands selling everything from cheese and wine to fresh fish and flowers. There are also are some fine *Imbisse*, where you can grab lunch or dinner, including a Peruvian *picanteria* and pisco bar. Overall, a highly recommended spot to wander, pick up some *Feinkosten* and people-watch.

❤ Vabali Spa

Seydlitzstrasse 6 (911 4860, www.vabali.de). U55, S5, S7, S75, Hauptbahnhof. **Open** *9am-midnight daily.* **Admission** *from €21.50.* **Map** *p98 K5* ❸ *Spa*
The perfect place to relax or detox from a night on the tiles, Vabali has proved a huge hit with Berliners. Set over a spectacular 20,000 square metres, with indoor and outdoor pools, 11 saunas and steam rooms, jacuzzi, treatment rooms, a restaurant and gardens, Vabali's worth the ticket price. And with robes and towels for hire and swimming costumes surplus to requirements, you can just rock up on a whim.

Potsdamer Platz & south of the park

In the 1920s, Potsdamer Platz was one of the Europe's busiest city squares, but it was bombed flat in World War II and, during the Cold War, became a grim no-man's-land bisected by the Wall. The area was redeveloped at the turn of the millennium as the commercial centrepiece of the reunified city. The soaring glass-and-steel **Sony Center** contains a number of attractions, including the **Legoland Discover Center** (301 0400, www.legolanddiscoverycentre. de/berlin-en), a great rainy day destination for kids.

Immediately to the west are a slew of embassies and the **Kulturforum**, one of the city's major concentrations of museums, galleries and arts institutions, including the **Philharmonie** (*see p110*) and the **Gemäldegalerie**. A short walk away is the **Zoologischer Garten & Aquarium** and the hub of West Berlin around Bahnhof Zoo.

Sights & museums

Bauhaus Archiv – Museum für Gestaltung

Klingelhöferstrasse 13-14 (254 0020, www.bauhaus.de). U1, U2, U3, U4 Nollendorfplatz. **Open** *see the website for details.* **Map** *p98 J8.*
Walter Gropius, founder of the Bauhaus school, designed this elegant white building that now

houses this absorbing design museum. The permanent exhibition presents a selection of furniture, ceramics, prints, sculptures, photographs and sketches created in the Bauhaus workshop between 1919 and 1933, when the school was closed down by the Nazis. There are also first-rate temporary exhibitions from the extensive archive. An interesting gift shop sells design icons. The museum celebrates the Bauhaus centenary in 2019.

Daimler Contemporary

Haus Huth, Alte Potsdamer Strasse 5 (2594 1420, www.art.daimler. com). U2, S1, S2, S25 Potsdamer Platz. **Open** *11am-6pm daily.* **Admission** *free.* **Map** *p98 L8.*
As you'd expect, Daimler's art collection is serious stuff. It sticks to the 20th century, specifically abstract and geometric art; the collection numbers around 1,800 works from artists such as Josef Albers, Max Bill, Walter de Maria, Jeff Koons and Andy Warhol. Daimler hosts one (free) guided tour per month, delving deep into the themes of the current collection; check the website for details.

In the know
Tagesspiegel art and design

Stop by the former *Tagesspiegel* newspaper complex on Potsdamer Strasse to visit two excellent commercial art galleries: **BlainSouthern** (644 931 510, www. blainsouthern.com) and **Galerie Guido W Baudach** (3199 8101, www. guidowbaudach.com). The building also houses **Andreas Murkudis** (680 798 306, www.andreasmurkudis. com), a design concept store selling immaculately displayed clothes among items of contemporary furniture and homewares.

Gedenkstätte Deutscher Widerstand

Stauffenbergstrasse 13-14 (2699 5000, www.gdw-berlin.de). U2, S1, S2, S25 Potsdamer Platz. **Open** *9am-6pm Mon-Wed, Fri; 9am-8pm Thur; 10am-6pm Sat, Sun. Guided tours 3pm Sun.* **Admission** *free.* **Map** *p98 K8.*
The Memorial to the German Resistance chronicles the German resistance to National Socialism. The building is part of a complex known as the Bendlerblock, owned by the German military from its construction in 1911 until 1945. At the back is a memorial to the conspirators killed on this site during the attempt to assassinate Hitler on 20 July 1944. Regular guided tours are in German only, but you can book an English tour four weeks in advance.

♥ Gemäldegalerie

Matthäikirchplatz (266 424242, www.smb.museum/gg). U2, S1, S2, S25 Potsdamer Platz. **Open** *10am-6pm Tue, Wed, Fri; 10am-8pm Thur; 11am-6pm Sat, Sun.* **Admission** *€10; €5 reductions.* **Map** *p98 K8.*
The Picture Gallery is a first-rate early European collection with many fine Italian, Spanish and English works on display, but the real highlights are the superb Dutch and Flemish pieces. Fans of Rembrandt can indulge themselves with around 20 paintings, the best of which include a portrait of preacher and merchant Cornelis Claesz Anslo and his wife, and an electric Samson confronting his father-in-law. Two of Franz Hals' finest works are here – the wild, fluid, almost impressionistic *Malle Babbe* (Mad Babette) and the detailed portrait of the one-year-old Catharina Hooft and her nurse. Other highlights include a couple of unflinching portraits by Robert Campin (early 15th century), a version of Botticelli's *Venus Rising*,

and Corregio's brilliant *Leda with the Swan*. Look out too for a pair of Lucas Cranach Venus and Cupid paintings and his *Fountain of Youth*. Pick up the excellent (free) English-language audio guide.

Kunstgewerbemuseum
Matthäikirchplatz (266 424242, www.smb.museum/kgm). U2, S1, S2, S25 Potsdamer Platz. **Open** *10am-6pm Tue-Fri; 11am-6pm Sat, Sun.* **Admission** *€8; €4 reductions.* **Map** *p98 L8.*
The Museum of Decorative Arts reopened in late 2014 after an extensive two-year revamp. There are some lovely items in its collection of European arts and crafts, stretching from the Middle Ages through Renaissance, Baroque and rococo to Jugendstil and art deco. Additional features include an impressive fashion gallery, covering 150 years of fashion history, and the design collection in the basement.

Museum für Film und Fernsehen
Sony Center, Potsdamer Strasse 2 (300 9030, www.deutsche-kinemathek.de). U2, S1, S2, S25 Potsdamer Platz. **Open** *10am-6pm Tue, Wed, Fri-Sun; 10am-8pm Thur.* **Admission** *€7; €4.50 reductions; free to all 4-8pm Thur. No cards.* **Map** *p98 L8.*
Since 1963, the Deutsche Kinemathek has been amassing films, memorabilia, documentation and antique film apparatus. In 2000, all this stuff found a home in this roomy, well-designed exhibition space set over two floors in the Sony Center. Striking exhibits include the two-storey-high video wall of disasters from Fritz Lang's adventure films and a morgue-like space devoted to films from the Third Reich. On a lighter note, there's a collection of 'claymation' figures from Ray Harryhausen films, such as *Jason*

and the Argonauts. But the main attraction is the Marlene Dietrich collection of personal effects, home movies and designer clothes. Exhibitions are often linked with film programming at the **Arsenal** cinema (*see p109*) downstairs.

Neue Nationalgalerie
Potsdamer Strasse 50 (266 424242, www.smb.museum/nng). U2, S1, S2, S25 Potsdamer Platz. **Closed** *until 2020.* **Map** *p98 L8.*
The New National Gallery, a stark glass-and-steel pavilion designed in the 1960s by Mies van der Rohe, was built to house German and international artworks from the 20th century. The collection features key pieces by Kirchner, Picasso, Gris and Léger. The Neue Sachlichkeit is well represented by paintings from George Grosz and Otto Dix, while the Bauhaus contribution includes work from Paul Klee and Wassily Kandinsky. The gallery is currently closed for a major renovation (the first in its history), masterminded by David Chipperfield under the guiding principle 'as much Mies as possible'. It should reopen in summer 2020.

❤ Panoramapunkt
Kollhoff Tower, Potsdamer Platz 1, entrance on Alte Potsdamer Strasse (2593 7080, www.panoramapunkt.de). U2, S1, S2, S25 Potsdamer Platz. **Open** *Summer 10am-8pm daily. Winter 10am-6pm daily.* **Admission** *€7.50; €6 reductions. No cards.* **Map** *p98 L8.*
What's billed as 'the fastest elevator in Europe' shoots up to the 100-m-high (328-ft) viewing platform in the Kollhoff Tower. The building's north-east corner is precisely at the point where the borders of Tiergarten, Mitte and Kreuzberg all meet – and also on what was the line of the Wall. From this vantage point, you can peer through railings and

the neighbouring postmodern high-rises at the landmarks of new Berlin. There are good views to the south and west; looking north, the DB Tower gets in the way.

Schwules Museum
Lützowstrasse 73 (6959 9050, www. schwulesmuseum.de). U1, U2, U3, U4 Nollendorfplatz. **Open** *2-6pm Mon, Wed, Fri, Sun; 2-8pm Thur; 2-7pm Sat.* **Admission** *€7.50; €4 reductions. No cards.* **Map** *p98 K9.*
The Gay Museum opened in 1985 in Kreuzberg but has since moved to this location. It is still one of very few in the world dedicated to homosexual life and survives mostly thanks to private donations and bequests. The museum puts on regular exhibitions and shows an impressive collection of visual art, while the library and archives contain 8,000 books (500 in English), 3,000 international periodicals, photos and posters, plus TV, film and audio footage, all available to borrow.

❤ Zoologischer Garten & Aquarium
Hardenbergplatz 8 (254 010, www. zoo-berlin.de). U2, U9, S5, S7, S75 Zoologischer Garten. **Open** *Zoo from 9am daily; closing times vary throughout the year. Aquarium 9am-6pm daily.* **Admission** *Single attraction €15.50; €8-€10.50 reductions. Combined admission €21; €10.50-€15.50 reductions.* **Map** *p98 H8.*
Germany's oldest zoo was opened in 1841 to designs by Martin Lichtenstein and Peter Joseph Lenné. With almost 14,000 creatures, it's one of the world's largest and most important zoos, with more endangered species in its collection than any zoo in Europe except Antwerp. It's beautifully landscaped, with lots of architectural oddities, and there are plenty of places for a coffee, beer or snack.

Restaurants & cafés

Café Einstein €€
Kurfürstenstrasse 58 (2639 1919, www.cafeeinstein.com). U1, U2, U3, U4 Nollendorfplatz. **Open** *8am-midnight daily.* **Map** *p98 J9* ④ *Austrian*
For a taste of Old World decadence, visit this Nollendorfplatz institution. It's set in a neo-Renaissance villa built in the 1870s by a wealthy industrialist; red leather banquettes, parquet flooring and the crack of wooden chairs all contribute to the historic Viennese café experience. You could come for a bracing breakfast of herb omelette with feta cheese and spinach, or, in the afternoon, enjoy a classic apple strudel and a *Wiener Melange* (a creamy Austrian coffee), all served with a flourish by the charming uniformed waiters.

❤ Cinco €€€€
Das Stue Hotel, Drakestrasse 1 (311 7220, www.5-cinco.com). S5, S7, S75 Tiergarten. **Open** *6.30-10pm Tue-Sat.* **Map** *p98 H8* ⑤ *Spanish*
Chef Paco Pérez gained another Michelin star (his fifth) within Cinco's first year of opening. He supposedly keeps a camera trained on the kitchen 24/7, so he can quality-control all the way from Spain. The menu combines Catalan traditional cooking and the inventive plating of Spain's *nueva cocina*. Try the button mushroom royale with squid tartare and truffle or the pigeon, corn, mole and huitlacoche. Booking advised.

❤ Hugos €€€€
Hotel InterContinental Berlin, Budapester Strasse 2 (2602 1263, www.hugos-restaurant.de). U2, U9, S5, S7, S75 Zoologischer Garten. **Open** *6.30-10.30pm Tue-Sat.* **Map** *p98 H8* ⑥ *Fine dining*
One of Berlin's best restaurants right now, and with the awards to prove it. Chef Thomas Kammeier

TIERGARTEN & AROUND

juxtaposes classic French technique – the silver Christofle cheese trolley is a sight to behold – with New German flair. With tasting menus and wine pairings, expect dishes such as imperial caviar with pickled gherkin, shallot crumble and bonito jelly, or Australian roast beef with turnips, watercress and pear cabbage. Vegetarian menu available.

Joseph-Roth-Diele €
*Potsdamer Strasse 75 (2636 9884, www.joseph-roth-diele. de). U1 Kurfürstenstrasse. **Open** 10am-midnight Mon-Fri.* **No cards.** *Map p98 K9* ➐ *German*
A traditional Berlin book café, just a short stroll south of Potsdamer Platz, which pays homage to the life and work of interwar Jewish writer Joseph Roth. It's an amiable place, decorated in ochre tones and with comfortable seating, offering tea, coffee, wine, beer, snacks and great-value lunch specials such as meatloaf with mash.

Kin Dee €€€
*Lützowstrasse 81 (215 5294, www.kindeeberlin.com). U1 Kurfürstenstrasse. **Open** from 6pm Tue-Sat Map p98 K9* ➑ *Thai*
In 2017, Kin Dee took over from Berlin-Thai institution Edd's. Part of the gastronomic network around Grill Royal, Kin Dee is proving a deserving successor. Head chef and owner Dalad crosses culinary boundaries, serving creative Thai cuisine with a focus on fresh, high-quality ingredients. Offering set menus of small plates, excellent vegetarian options and a well-chosen wine list, Kin Dee has gone down a storm.

Nordic Embassies Canteen €
*Rauchstrasse 1 (305 0500, www. nordicembassies.org). U2, U9, S5, S7, S75 Zoologischer Garten. **Open** 1-3pm Mon-Fri.* **No cards.** *Map p98 J8* ➒ *Scandinavian*

The striking Nordic embassy complex, clad in maplewood and glass, houses an excellent lunch secret. The canteens of Berlin's civic buildings are all open to the public, so after 1pm you can tuck into the excellent subsidised food provided for the Scandinavian diplomats. The choice of a meat, fish and vegetarian dish changes daily.

Entertainment

Arsenal
*Sony Center, Potsdamer Strasse 2 (2695 5100, www.arsenal-berlin. de). U2, S1, S2, S25 Potsdamer Platz. **Tickets** €8; €3 reductions. No cards. **Map** p98 L8* ➌ *Cinema*
Berlin's own cinematheque offers a brazenly eclectic programme that ranges from classic Hollywood to contemporary Middle Eastern cinema, Russian art films to Italian horror movies, niche documentaries to retrospectives of cinema's leading lights. There are plenty of English-language films and some foreign-language films with English subtitles.

▶ *The Arsenal is one of the core venues for the Berlin International Film Festival (see p64 Berlinale).*

Wintergarten Varieté
*Potsdamer Strasse 96 (588 433, www.wintergarten-berlin.de). U1 Kurfürstenstrasse. **Box office** 11am-8pm Mon-Sat; 11.30am-6pm Sun. **Tickets** vary. Map p98 K9* ➍ *Cabaret*
Prussia meets Disney with shows that are slick, professional and a little boring. Excellent acrobats and magicians, but some questionable comedy acts.

❤ Philharmonie

Herbert-von-Karajan Strasse 1 (2548 8301, www.berliner-philharmoniker.de). U2, S1, S2, S25 Potsdamer Platz. **Box office** *open 3-6pm Mon-Fri; 11am-2pm Sat, Sun.* **Tickets** *€10-€242.* **Map** *p98 L8* ⑤

Berlin's most famous concert hall, home to the world-renowned Berlin Philharmonic Orchestra, is also its most architecturally daring: a marvellously puckish piece of organic modernism. Designed by Hans Scharoun, the golden building with its distinctive vaulting roof opened in 1963. Its reputation for superb acoustics is accurate, but it does depend on where you sit. Behind the orchestra, the acoustics leave much to be desired, but in front (where seats are much more expensive), the sound is heavenly. The same rules apply in the smaller Kammermusiksaal, which opened in 1987.

The **Berliner Philharmoniker** was founded in 1882 by 54 musicians keen to break away from the penurious Benjamin Bilse, in whose orchestra they played. It has been led by some of the world's greatest conductors, as well as by composers including Peter Tchaikovsky, Edvard Grieg, Richard Strauss and Gustav Mahler. Its greatest fame came under the baton of Herbert von Karajan (1955-89), who was succeeded by Claudio Abbado. From 2002 to 2018 it was under the leadership of Sir Simon Rattle who attracted younger audiences to the Philharmonie and showcased contemporary composers,

such as Thomas Adès and Marc Anthony Turnage. In 2019, the baton passes to the media-shy Kirill Petrenko, a choice that has been praised in Berlin and in wider classical music circles. Petrenko's relative anonymity and refusal to be interviewed has made him a fascinating enigma for the press, and his arrival is eagerly anticipated.

The Berlin Phil gives about 100 performances in the city during its August to June season, plus 20 to 30 concerts around the world. Some tickets are available at a discount immediately before performances, although it is notoriously difficult to snap one up.

Prenzlauer Berg & Mitte North

Prenzlauer Berg has been visibly transformed by Berlin's history. From 19th-century roots as a working-class district, it's become the most desirable neighbourhood for hip young families; the bijou children's clothing shops speak nothing of its previous life as a centre of GDR dissidence or post-Wall bohemia. Even if there aren't many major museums or sights to visit, the area still has fine examples of late 19th-century civic architecture, Berlin's biggest flea market at the Mauerpark and lots of great shopping. A blend of old and new, sleekly modern and charmingly quaint, Prenzlauer Berg is ideal for a weekend's exploring.

Following the S-Bahn ring westwards takes you across commercial Gesundbrunnen to reach working-class Wedding, the neighbourhood perennially touted as the next big thing. Wedding has never quite lived up to the hype, and nor does it seem to want to, but once you move away from the built-up concrete centre around the S-Bahn, the neighbourhood becomes friendlier and greener, sparsely dotted with cafés and bars.

Prenzlauer Berg

The district's focal point is leafy **Kollwitzplatz**. The square is lined with bars, cafés and restaurants, and hosts an organic market on Thursdays. Knaackstrasse, heading south-east from Kollwitzplatz, brings you to one of the district's main landmarks, the **Wasserturm**. This water tower, constructed by English architect Henry Gill in 1852-75, provided running water for the first time in Germany. During the war, the Nazis used its basement as a prison and torture chamber; a plaque commemorates their victims. The tower has since been converted into swanky apartments.

Opposite the Wasserturm on Rykestrasse is the **Synagoge Rykestrasse**, a neo-romanesque turn-of-the-century structure that was badly damaged during Kristallnacht in 1938. After undergoing renovation in 1953, it was the only working synagogue in East Berlin. Now it stands

→ Getting around

From the U2, which crosses Alexanderplatz, you can exit onto Eberswalder Strasse, which is about midway between Mauerpark and Kollwitzplatz. From there it's easy to walk to most places in Prenzlauer Berg in about ten or 15 minutes. The area is also well served by the M1 tramline. Bernauer Strasse U-Bahn (U8) and Berlin Nordbahnhof (S-Bahn) are best for reaching Gedenkstätte Berliner Mauer, but the area is also served by the M5, M8, M10 and M12 trams. Wedding and Gesundbrunnen are both accessible on the Ringbahn. Cycling isn't advised in this area due to the heavy traffic on the main streets.

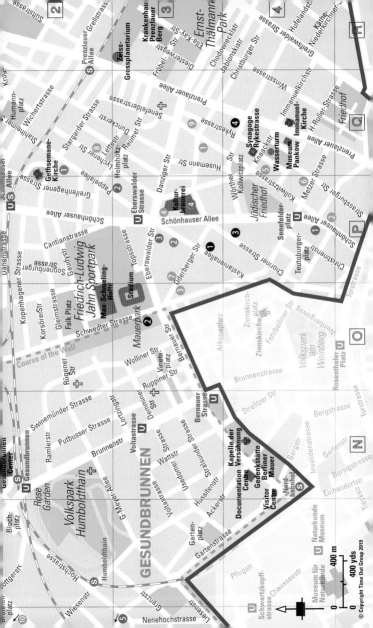

peacefully in gentrified surrounds. Nearby, to the south-west of Kollwitzplatz, is the **Jüdischer Friedhof**, Berlin's oldest Jewish cemetery; it's fairly gloomy due to its closely packed stones and canopy of trees. To learn more about the district's history, look in at the **Museum Pankow** (Prenzlauer Allee 227, 902 953 917).

Moving on clockwise to the other side of Kollwitzplatz, Knaackstrasse extends north-west to the vast complex of the **Kulturbrauerei**, an old brewery that now houses a concert space, galleries, artists' studios, a market, a cinema and a museum. West from here, the area around Kastanienallee has plenty of good bars, shops and restaurants, including the **Prater** pub and beer garden (*see p118*). To the north-west, Eberswalder Strasse skirts the base of the **Mauerpark** (www.mauerpark.info). The site of an old train station, this area became a 'death strip' when the Wall went up, with a viewing platform for West Berliners to look into the East. It was turned into a community space in the 1990s, with two large sports halls, a graffiti-daubed section of the Wall and a home for the popular Sunday flea market which attracts bargain hunters, circus performers and assorted hippy types. Situated just south of Schönhauser Allee S-Bahn on Stargarder Strasse is the striking neo-Gothic **Gethsemanekirche** (445 7745, www.ekpn.de), built in August Orth's typical red-brick style – he also built the Zionskirche. It served as an important meeting place for GDR dissidents in the late 1980s. A statue outside commemorates their sacrifice.

East of here, on the other side of Prenzlauer Allee, is **Ernst-Thälmann-Park**, named after the leader of the pre-1933 German Communist Party. In its north-west corner stands the renovated **Zeiss-Grossplanetarium**, a fantastic GDR space that once celebrated Soviet cosmonauts. On the Greifswalder Strasse side of the park is a bombastic 1980s statue of Ernst Thälmann himself, raising a Communist fist. The statue was built with an amusing contemporary feature: a heated nose to melt any accumulating snow.

Sights & museums

❤ Museum in der Kulturbrauerei
*Kulturbrauerei, Knaackstrasse 97 (4677 77911, www.hdg.de/berlin). U2 Eberswalderstrasse. **Open** 10am-6pm Tue, Wed, Fri-Sun; 10am-8pm Thur. **Admission** free. **Map** p113 P3.*
'Everyday Life in the GDR' is a fascinating permanent exhibition here, featuring hundreds of objects that show the contradictory nature of Communist life. Examples of leisure time include a Trabi roof-mounted tent, a mocked-up GDR living room and clothing customised to break the drab uniformity.

Zeiss-Grossplanetarium
*Prenzlauer Allee 80 (4218 4510, www.planetarium.berlin). S8, S9, S41, S42, S85 Prenzlauer Allee. **Open** 9am-3pm Mon-Fri; 10am-4pm Sat. **Admission** €8; €6 reductions. **Map** p113 R3.*
This vast planetarium was constructed in 1987 as part of the city's 750th anniversary; at the time, its Cosmorama projector was one of the most advanced in Europe. Now, following renovation, it's described as one of the world's best star theatres, with illumination systems projecting onto a black velvet dome. There are a number of different shows that explore space and our planet, so check the listings.

Bonanza

The Barn speciality coffee roastery is a shrine to the coffee bean. Owner Ralf Rüller has even made headlines for his serious approach: when he opened this second, more spacious branch (the original is in Mitte), customers were bemused by the industrial bollard set in the doorway. Ralf was taking a rather humourless stand against the area's 'yummy mummy' invasion by banning prams (and laptops and dogs), so there are no distractions from appreciation of the finished product. Try the pour-over Hario V60 for an alternative cupping method. **Other locations** Auguststrasse 58, Mitte ; Café Kranzler, Kurfürstendamm 18.

❤ Bonanza €
*Oderberger Strasse 35 (0171 563 0795 mobile, www.bonanzacoffee. de). U2 Eberswalder Strasse. **Open** 8.30am-6pm Mon-Fri; 10am-6pm Sat, Sun. **No cards**. **Map** p113 O3* ③ *Café*
Bonanza serves some of the best coffee in Berlin. The proprietors are concerned with every detail, from relationships with suppliers to roasting the beans in-house and getting the right steam temperature. The bar is dominated by a highly sensitive handmade Synesso Cyncra machine, and seating is minimal. The flat white is smooth and divine. The cake selection is small – pretty much just carrot cake and brownies – but high grade.

Konnopke's Imbiss €
*Schönhauser Allee 44B, under U-Bahn tracks (442 7765, www.konnopke-imbiss.de). U2 Eberswalder Strasse. **Open** 10am-8pm Mon-Fri; 11.30am-8pm Sat. **No cards**. **Map** p113 P3* ④ *Imbiss*
This venerable sausage stand (refurbished a few years ago) has been under the same family management since 1930. After

Restaurants & cafés

The **Kulturbrauerei** hosts a Sunday food market, Street Food auf Achse (www. streetfoodaufachse.de), where you can try the latest taste trends.

Anna Blume €
*Kollwitzstrasse 83 (4404 8749, www.cafe-anna-blume.de). U2 Eberswalder Strasse. **Open** 8am-midnight daily; kitchen until 10pm. **Map** p113 Q3* ① *Café*
This café-cum-florist is named after a poem by Kurt Schwitters. There are expensive but high-quality pastries, plus sweet and savoury crêpes, soups and hot dishes. The terrace is lovely in summer, and the interior, not surprisingly, smells of flowers.

❤ The Barn €
*Schönhauser Allee 8 (no phone, www.thebarn.de). U2 Senefelderplatz; U8 Rosenthaler Platz. **Open** 8.30am-6pm Mon-Fri; 10am-6pm Sat, Sun. **No cards**. **Map** p113 P4* ② *Café*

coming up with a secret recipe for ketchup (not available after the Wall was erected), it was the first place to offer *Currywurst* in East Berlin and still serves probably the most famous – if not the best – *Currywurst* in the city. Expect a queue.

Lucky Leek €€-€€€

Kollwitzstrasse 54 (6640 8710, www.lucky-leek.com). U2 Senefelderplatz. **Open** *6-10pm Wed-Sun.* **No cards.** **Map** *p113 Q4* **5** *Vegan*

Chef Josita Hartanto started out at Charlottenburg's haute-cuisine La Mano Verde and has since carved out quite a following for her inventive vegan food. She's pushed the boundaries through clever plating and textural contrast, with dishes such as filo-spinach pockets of seitan with macadamia dumpling and brussel-sprout praline. For the full effect, opt for the five-course menu with a wine pairing.

MontRaw €€

Strassburger Strasse 33, (2578 2707, www.montraw.com) U2 Senefelderplatz or U8 Rosenthaler Platz. **Open** *8.30am-6pm Mon-Fri; 10am-6pm Sat, Sun.* **Map** *p113 P4* **6** *Middle Eastern*

Becketts Kopf

Promising Middle Eastern recipes with a Mediterranean interpretation, MontRaw is about as far as you can get from houmous and kebabs. Fresh, clean fusion flavours are served by a friendly, knowledgeable team in exquisite surroundings. Chef Ben Barabi serves us 'new Israeli food with a twist' inspired by the recipes of his childhood. Try the charred octopus served on a lentil puree with salsa verde and Jerusalem artichoke. The menu is small but carefully chosen, the wine-list reasonably priced. A smash hit since it opened in 2018; you're advised to book ahead.

Oderquelle €€

Oderbergerstrasse 27 (4400 8080, www.oderquelle.de). U2 Eberswalder Strasse. **Open** *6pm-late Mon-Sat; noon-late Sun.* **Map** *p113 P3* **7** *Austrian/German*

This simple yet cosy Prenzlauer Berg classic might be a tad more expensive than its rivals, but that's because it's better than them. The menu is short but changes regularly. Typical dishes are goose leg stuffed with vegetables on red-wine risotto or vegetable strudel in tomato sauce. It's particularly nice in summer, when you can sit outside and watch the world go by.

Sasaya €€

Lychener Strasse 50 (4471 7721, www.sasaya-berlin.de). U2 Eberswalder Strasse. **Open** *noon-3pm, 6-11.30pm Mon, Thur-Sun.* **No cards.** **Map** *p113 Q2* **8** *Japanese*

The lack of fresh fish available in Berlin poses a challenge for Japanese restaurants; there are scores of pan-Asian places serving 'discount' sushi, but the real thing is hard to come by. An authentic menu and a bustling atmosphere have kept Sasaya a long-term favourite. The sashimi is eye-poppingly fresh, but there are also fine cooked dishes, such as

grilled horse mackerel and *kakuni* (braised pork belly). For a real taste of the ocean, try one of the dressed seaweed salads. Booking is essential.

Si An €

Rykestrasse 36 (4050 5775, www. sian-berlin.de). U2 Senefelderplatz, or tram M2, M10. **Open** *noon-midnight daily.* **No cards.** **Map** *p113 Q3* ❾ *Vietnamese*

Si An was one of the first Viet restaurants to really up the ante on decor while making an effort to cook everything fresh. There are various *phos* and usually some sort of combination of curry, rice and meats, heaped with fresh herbs and vegetables. The approach has clearly paid off, as it now has a mini-empire of restaurants including Saigon street-food specialist District Mot (*see p87*) and tea house Chen Che.

Bars & pubs

Becketts Kopf

Pappelallee 64 (4403 5880, www. becketts-kopf.de). U2 Eberswalder Strasse. **Open** *8pm-late daily.* **No cards.** **Map** *p113 Q2* ❶

This long-running cocktail bar is an oasis of fine drink in rather sparsely served Prenzlauer Berg.

It follows the classic 'speakeasy' model: enter via an unmarked door and find yourself in rooms draped in red velvet. Settle back on the chesterfield sofas and enjoy the fresh air of the no-smoking room – a relative rarity in Berlin's bar scene. Try the Aviation, a paean to the classier days of air travel: a florid mix of gin, violet, maraschino and lemon. A grizzled portrait of playwright Samuel Beckett (not averse to a drink himself) keeps watch over proceedings.

Shops & services

Fein & Ripp

Kastanienallee 91-92 (4403 3250, www.feinundripp.de). U2 Eberswalder Strasse. **Open** *noon-7pm Mon-Sat.* **Map** *p113 P3* ❶ *Fashion*

A curious shop, which started out selling old stock discovered in a Swabian clothes factory – primarily cotton underwear in all shapes and sizes, from the 1920s to the '70s. They've now expanded into brands that continue traditional production methods: Frye's heavy leather prison boots, which come 'distressed', and Pike Brothers' stiff blue denim jeans. Unfortunately, dressing like a Depression-era hobo doesn't come cheap these days.

❤ Prater Biergarten

*Kastanienallee 7-9 (448 5688, www.pratergarten.de). U2 Eberswalder Strasse. **Open** 6pm-late Mon-Sat; noon-late Sun. **No cards.** Map p113 P3* ❷

In the mid 16th century, brewing beer during the summer was outlawed in Bavaria due to the drink's rapid deterioration in the heat and the risk of fire spreading from the brewery kettles. Instead, brewers were encouraged to build cellars next to the River Isar in which to store beer for summer drinking. They discovered that if they planted lines of chestnut trees over these cellars, it kept the beer cooler and fresher for longer. After that, it was only second nature for drinkers to want to linger with a cool beer under their shady boughs, and thus the Bavarian tradition of the *Biergarten* was born. Refrigeration has technically done away with the need for beer gardens, but their popularity throughout Germany shows no sign of diminishing: enjoying a foaming *Stein* and a plate of *Wurst* in the open air is the essence of Southern German conviviality and hospitality.

Beer gardens in Berlin are generally open from April to September and are popular meeting spots after work or on a sunny weekend. These are places to hang loose and drink copious amounts of beer in good company. Prater Garten has been doing Berliners a brisk service since 1852. The enthusiastic beer-swilling, big wooden tables and platefuls of *Bratwurst* and

Bretzeln (pretzels) might make you feel as though you've been teleported down south to Munich. There's an indoor bar with a traditional German restaurant, but in summer you'll want to grab a house-brewed Pils and join the all-day buzz outdoors under the chestnut trees. Brunch is served from 10am to 4pm at the weekend, but, as is the case with all true beer gardens, you're also permitted to bring food from home to enjoy with beer bought on the premises: check out the sumptuous picnics laid out by locals. Prater opens early on sunny days, so be prepared to jostle for elbow room by noon even on weekdays.

▶ *There's also an open-air theatre here where productions by the Volksbühne (People's Theatre; see p93) are performed.*

♥ Mauerpark Flohmarkt

Bernauer Strasse 63-64 (0176 2925 0021 mobile). U8 Bernauer Strasse. Open 10am-6pm Sun. Map p113 O3 ❷ *Market*

One of the biggest and busiest flea markets in Berlin sells everything from local designer clothes to cardboard boxes of black-market CDs. Students and residents hawk their things here; even if the market's massive popularity has meant prices creeping higher, you can still stumble upon a trove of rare records or vintage clothing.

Onkel Philipp's Spielzeugwerkstatt

Choriner Strasse 35 (449 0491, www.onkel-philipp. de). U2 Senefelderplatz. Open 9.30am-6.30pm Tue, Wed, Fri; 11am-8pm Thur; 11am-4pm Sat. Map p113 P4 ❸ *Toys*

Here's one for kids, both big and small: a toy-repair shop that's an Aladdin's cave of aged playthings, wooden toys, puzzles, trains, puppets and more. If you ask nicely, owner Philipp Schünemann lets you view his private GDR toy collection, a remote control unveiling a special surprise.

Saint George's

Wörther Strasse 27 (8179 8333, www.saintgeorgesbookshop.com). U2 Senefelderplatz; tram M2. Open 11am-8pm Mon-Fri; 11am-7pm Sat. Map p113 Q4 ❹ *Books*

Founded by Paul and Daniel Gurner, twin brothers from England, Saint George's harks back to the heyday of London's Charing Cross Road. It's a sweet spot, where leather sofas coax readers to peruse at leisure. Housing around 10,000 English-language books, including plenty of biographies and contemporary fiction, it's also reliable for second-hand books in good condition.

Entertainment

8MM

Schönhauser Allee 177B (4050 0624, www.8mmbar.com). U2 Senefelderplatz. Open 9pm-late daily. No cards. Map p113 P4 ❶ *Club*

Sometimes the 4/4 techno beat can seem inescapable in Berlin, so head to this one-room dive bar for an alternative. Weekends get raucous with DJs playing a mix of punk and new-wave staples, and the occasional touring band member getting behind the decks for a concert after-party. Drinks are very reasonably priced, making it just the place for your umpteenth nightcap.

♥ Ballhaus Ost

Pappelallee 15 (4403 9168, www.ballhausost.de). U2 Eberswalderstrasse. Tickets €15; €8 reductions. No cards. Map p113 P3 ❷ *Theatre*

This somewhat dilapidated ex-ballroom hosts art, performance art, dance and concerts, with undiscovered talents performing alongside more established, internationally known artists. There's also a lounge and bar populated by a very cool crowd.

♥ Dr. Pong

Eberswalder Strasse 21 (no phone, www.drpong.net). U2 Eberswalder Strasse. Open 8pm-late Mon-Sat; 7pm-late Sun. No cards. Map p113 P3 ❸ *Club*

Bring your table-tennis bat (or hire one for a €5 deposit) and prepare for drunken ping-pong carnage. The action doesn't start until around midnight, but then you can expect 30 or so players – some good, some bad – to surround the table in one almighty round-the-world session. There's a bar and, bizarrely, Twiglets for nourishment. Note that the opening hours are unreliable.

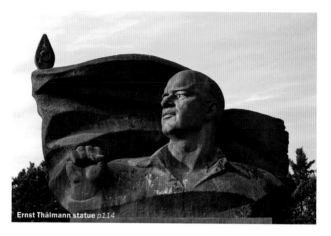

Ernst Thälmann statue *p114*

Kulturbrauerei

Schönhauser Allee 36 (4435 2170, www.kultur brauerei.de). U2 Eberswalder Strasse. **Open** *varies.* **Admission** *€5-€30.* **Map** *p113 P3* ❹ *Live music*

With its assortment of venues, outdoor bars and barbecues, this cultural centre housed in an enormous former brewery can resemble a cross between a medieval fairground and a school disco. The two spaces operated by the Kulturbrauerei proper are Maschinehaus and the larger Kesselhaus, where concerts vary from reggae to Frank Zappa cover bands. There's an emphasis on German acts too.

Wedding & Gesundbrunnen

These working-class industrial districts, formerly on the western side of the Wall, are now politically part of Mitte, though few visitors venture very far into their largely grim streets. The big draw to the area is the **Gedenkstätte Berliner Mauer** (Berlin Wall Memorial). Elsewhere, **Volkspark Humbolthain** and **Plötzensee**, Berlin's only inner-city lake (*see p182* Berlin's bathing lakes), provide welcome relief from the graffitied concrete surroundings.

Sights & museums

❤ Gedenkstätte Berliner Mauer

Bernauer Strasse 111 (467 986 666, www.berliner-mauer-gedenkstaette.de). U8 Bernauer Strasse; S1, S2 Nordbahnhof. **Open** *Documentation centre 10am-6pm Tue-Sun.* **Admission** *free.* **Map** *p113 N4.*

Immediately upon reunification, the city bought this stretch of the Wall on Bernauer Strasse to keep as a memorial. For a sense of how brutally Berlin was severed in two, a visit to this impeccably restored area of the Wall is a must. It extends along 1.4km (0.8 miles) of Bernauer Strasse and includes the death strip, watch tower and border fortifications. On this particular street, neighbours woke up one morning to find themselves in a different country from those on the opposite side of the road, as soldiers brandishing bricks and mortar started to build what the East German government referred to as the 'Anti-Fascist Protection Wall'.

Don't miss the excellent **Documentation Centre** across the street from the Wall, which includes a very good aerial video following the route of the Wall in 1990: it's the best chance you have of really getting your head around it. From the centre's tower, you can look down over the Wall and the **Kapelle der Versöhnung** (Chapel of Reconciliation). Further down the road in the old **Nordbahnhof** station is an fascinating exhibition, 'Border Stations and Ghost Stations in Divided Berlin', which tells the story of how East Germany closed and then fiercely guarded stations through which West German trains travelled during the Cold War.

Volkspark Humbolthain

Main entrance Brunnenstrasse 101. S1, S2, S25, S41, S42, U8 Gesundbrunnen; S1, S2, S25, S8 Humboldthain. **Open** *Park 24hrs daily. Pool 10am-6pm daily in summer.* **Admission** *Pool €5.50; €3.50 reductions.* **Map** *p113 N2.*
On a warm summer's day, bring picnic blankets and swimsuits to enjoy the green pastures and open-air swimming pools of Humbolthain, a park built on the remains of rubble from World War II. For those interested in history, there are guided tours available from April to October of the partially demolished Flak Tower, and for those who simply want to perambulate, the hidden rose garden with its high hedges is ideal for a romantic stroll.

Restaurants & cafés

Café Pförtner €€

Uferstrasse 8-11 (5036 9854, www. pfoertner.co). U8 Pankstrasse. **Open** *9am-11pm Mon-Fri; 11am-11pm Sat.* **No cards.** **Map** *p113 L1* ⑩ *Modern Italian*
Make the trip across town for the photo opportunity this former bus repair station affords. It's a little out of the way, but you'll quickly be won over by the inventive modern Italian food featuring flavours such as beetroot, melon and pork belly. Portions are a bit small and service can be lax, but eating in the converted BVG bus is an experience not to be missed.

Shikgoo €€

Tegeler Strasse 25 (8501 2045). U6, U9 Leopoldplatz. **Open** *6pm-midnight Thur-Tue.* **No cards.** *Korean*
This tiny restaurant is run by a hospitable Korean couple, who request shoes off when entering. It's a traditional Korean-style eaterie with low tables and cushions on the floor. Try the hot stone soup, and be sure to order extra kimchi.

Bars & pubs

Basalt Bar

Utrechter Strasse 38 (www. facebook.com/basaltberlin). U6, U9 Leopoldplatz. **Open** *8pm-late Tue-Sat.* **No cards.**

In the know
Labyrinth Kindermuseum

Budding builders shouldn't miss the massive Labyrinth Kindermuseum (Osloer Strasse 12, 800 931 150, www.labyrinth-kindermuseum.de) in Wedding. It's an enormous DIY indoor maze made up of wooden walls filled with hands-on installations that help kids learn how things come together. They even teach children to use electrical tools safely.

Black walls with an emerald-green tiled bar and an array of leafy jungle plants make this botanical-themed cocktail bar one of Wedding's best-looking secrets. The house cocktail, the Mescalmule, arrives in a bronze mug and is a daring concoction of smoked tequila, chili, cucumber and passionfruit. It's delicious.

♥ Eschenbräu
Triftstrasse 67 (0162 493 1915 mobile, eschenbraeu.de). U6, U9 Leopoldplatz. **Open** *3pm-late daily.* **No cards**.
This brewery has an excellent microbrew prepared for almost every occasion and an enormous courtyard in which to sample them. There's also tasty *Flammkuchen* (German pizza) to share with some friends.

Moritz Bar
Adolfstrasse 17 (0173 680 7670 mobile, www.moritzbar.com). U6, S41, S42 Wedding. **Open** *7pm-late daily.* **No cards**.
Wedding's very own living-room bar, complete with upcycled wooden counter, Augustiner by the bottle and assorted vintage furniture. The south German brothers who run the place offer special events, such as a weekly vegan food night, gay student Mondays and communal viewings of cult German TV detective series *Tatort*.

♥ Vagabund Brauerei
Antwerpener Strasse 3 (5266 7668, www.vagabundbrauerei.com). U6 Seestrasse. **Open** *5pm-late Mon-Fri; 1pm-late Sat, Sun.* **No cards**.
Three old friends from Maryland have fulfilled their dream of starting a craft brewery thanks to a wildly successful crowdfunding initiative. They run a homely taproom at the microbrewery, with a rotating menu of beers

that includes their own citrusy American Pale Ale and unctuous Coffee Stout, as well as local guests from the likes of Heidenpeters and Eschenbräu.

Shops & services

♥ Leopoldplatz Flohmarkt
Leopoldplatz on Müllerstrasse (www.bbm-maerkte.de). U6, U9 Leopoldplatz. **Open** *Farmer's market 10am-5pm Tue, Fri; flea market 10am-4pm Sat, winter 3pm. Market*
On Saturdays, this square is transformed into one of Berlin's best but least known flea markets. Forget Mauerpark, if you want real rummage bargains, wake up early and get ready to haggle. For a cheap breakfast post bargain-hunting, head over to **Simit Evi** for a selection of Turkish sesame breads (*simit*), savoury yoghurt dipping sauce and an ample serving of freshly cooked eggs. Tuesday and Friday's market sells fresh produce.

Entertainment

silent green Kulturquartier
Plantagenstrasse 31 (1208 2210, www.silent-green.net). S41, S42, U6 Wedding. **Open** *performance times vary. Café/bar 11am-6pm Mon-Fri, 10am-6pm Sat, Sun.* **Map** *p113 K2* ❺ *Cultural venue*
In 2013, a private group transformed the historic Wedding Crematorium into an independent space for research and experimentation in the arts. The result is fantastic, and for a former crematorium, just spooky enough. A number of arts collectives are headquartered here, and the building's architecture plays a central role: the domed Cupola, once a place for mourning, now hosts concerts.

Friedrichshain & Lichtenberg

As Prenzlauer Berg and Mitte saw rents soar in the
1990s, Berlin's alternative squat community migrated
to Friedrichshain and politicised this formerly working-
class district. Much of the area is pretty bleak: one of the
hardest hit during World War II, it is dominated by big
communist-era housing blocks and slashed through by
railway tracks. The area bordering the Spree contains
the remains of industrial buildings, but, with the arrival
of luxury apartments and hotels, the banks of the river
here may soon be unrecognisable. Friedrichshain is also
home to East Berlin's first post-war civic building project
– a broad boulevard named originally Stalinallee and
then Karl-Marx-Allee.

Best dance clubs
://about blank *p131*, Berghain *p132*

Best street art & culture
Urban Spree Bookshop & Art
Gallery *p130*

Best landmark
East Side Gallery *p126*

Most immersive museum
Gedenkstätte Berlin-
Hohenschönhausen *p134*

Best brunch
Café Schönbrunn *p127*,
Silo Coffee *p128*

There's more to Friedrichshain today than a photoshoot at the East Side Gallery – though this is well worth a visit; there's a thriving alternative culture here, supporting flea markets and vegetarian restaurants. The district is also a nightlife hotspot, with a concentration of bars and clubs by Ostkreuz and along the Spree. Here too is the globally renowned club Berghain, a giant on the city's techno scene.

Further east, Lichtenberg has a couple of key former Stasi strongholds and the East Berlin zoo.

Friedrichshain

The best way to get a feeling for both Friedrichshain and the old GDR is to head east from Alexanderplatz down **Karl-Marx-Allee**. From Lichtenberger Strasse onwards, the street truly impresses in its Communist monumentalism, with rows of grand apartment blocks draped in stone and Meissen tiles stretching to the twin towers of Frankfurter Tor and beyond. To take a break from the socialist bombast, visit the **Computerspielemuseum** (Computer Games Museum; *p127*) or spend some time exploring the

huge **Volkspark Friedrichshain**, formed from the rubble of World War II bombing.

South of Karl-Marx-Allee there are increasingly touristy shops, bars and restaurants in the grid of streets around Boxhagener Platz and some of the city's best nightlife around Ostkreuz. Most visitors, however, make a beeline for the **East Side Gallery** (*see p126*), a stretch of the Berlin Wall along the Spree that was turned into a mural memorial in 1990. There are great views of the red-brick, double-decker **Oberbaumbrücke** from the riverside here.

→ Getting around

The two main transport hubs for Friedrichshain are Warschauer Strasse, on the U1 line, and Frankfurter Tor, served by the U5, which runs directly through the middle of the district. The Ostbahnhof and Ostkreuz stations can be reached by both S-Bahn and regional lines. For the *fussfaul* (foot-lazy), tram lines run along Boxhagener Strasse, Wülischstrasse and Warschauer Strasse.

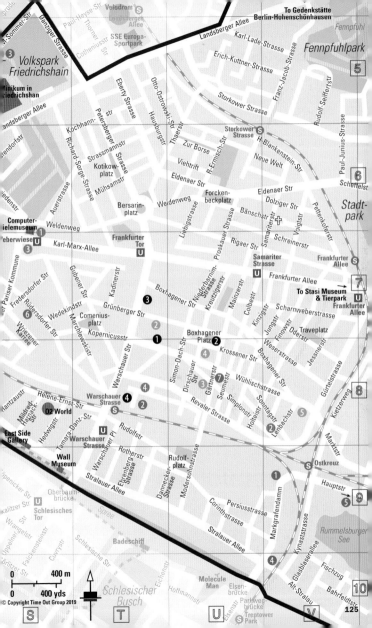

❤ East Side Gallery

Mühlenstrasse (www. eastsidegallery-berlin.de). U1, S5, S7, S75 Warschauer Strasse or S5, S7, S75 Ostbahnhof. **Open** *24hrs daily.* **Admission** *free.* **Map** *p125 S8.*

Running along the River Spree for 1.3km (0.8 mile) from Oberbaum Bridge to Ostbahnhof is one of Berlin's most photographed tourist sights. This is the largest remaining section of the Wall still standing, and it is decorated with 101 paintings by international artists from 1990. Dmitri Vrubel's striking portrait depicting Brezhnev and

Hönecker's kiss – a Soviet sign of great respect – is easily its most iconic image. The murals were steadily defaced in the ensuing years, and controversy still rages over the gallery's 2009 restoration, with certain artists objecting to copies being painted over their originals. In 2017, in an attempt to prevent further vandalism, a metre-high (three-foot) metal fence was erected around the perimeter of the Wall, an irony not lost on visitors.

Although the Wall is undeniably shabby and there's better street art to be seen elsewhere in the city, the East Side Gallery

Test The Best (Test The Rest) by Birgit Kinder

remains a lasting physical testimony to the story of the city's division and reunification.

However, visiting the East Side Gallery will not give you a sense of the reality of living with the Wall: the reinforced concrete, barbed wire and patrolling Soviet guards who were ordered to shoot on sight. For that, you could check out the convenient but pricey **Wall Museum** (Mühlenstrasse 78-80, 9451 2900, www.thewallmuseum.com, €12.50, €6.50 reductions), or, better still, visit Gedenkstätte Berliner Mauer (*see p120*) and Haus am Checkpoint Charlie (*see p138*).

Pneumohumanoiden by Jens-Helge Dahmen

Sights & museums

Computerspielemuseum

Karl-Marx-Allee 93A (6098 8577, www.computerspielemuseum.de). U5 Weberwiese. **Open** *10am-8pm daily.* **Admission** *€9; €6 reductions.* **Map** *p125 S6.*

This excellent museum traces the history of video games with interactive displays and well-curated installations from early arcade classics, such as Pong, to groundbreaking genre-definers, such as Sim City. It's a great way for families with older kids to while away a few hours. Adult gamers will love it too, if they don't mind waiting their turn behind the younger crowds.

Restaurants & cafés

♥ Café Schönbrunn €€

Volkspark Friedrichshain (4530 56525, www.schoenbrunn.net). Bus 200; Tram M4, M6, M8. **Open** *10am-late daily.* **Map** *p125 R5* ❶ *Café*

A favoured hangout for those who love to while away lazy Sundays in the park. A couple of years ago, this waterside place sold basic coffee and snacks to an elderly crowd, but now older parkgoers sip their first afternoon beer on the terrace while the in-crowd tucks into a post-clubbing breakfast. The unspectacular concrete front is unchanged, and the lounge furniture is pure 1970s.

Nil €

Grünberger Strasse 52 (2904 7713, www.nil-imbiss.de). U5 Frankfurter Tor. **Open** *11am-11.30pm daily.* **No cards.** **Map** *p125 T7* ❷ *Imbiss/Sudanese*

In a city full of vegetarians, Nil was an instant hit with its Sudanese spin on the falafel wrap: it's fried to order for extra crispness and served with plenty of fresh salad and the magic ingredient, a creamy peanut sauce. **Other locations** Oppelner Strasse 4, Kreuzberg (4881 6414).

Schneeweiss €€-€€€
*Simplonstrasse 16 (2904 9704, www.schneeweiss-berlin.de). U1, S5, S7, S75 Warschauer Strasse. **Open** 6pm-1am Mon-Fri; 10am-1am Sat, Sun. **Map** p125 U8* ③ *Southern German/Austrian*
With its statement 'snow-white' decor, Schneeweiss certainly lives up to its name. The menu offers 'Alpine' dishes – essentially a fusion of Italian, Austrian and south German cuisine. There are daily lunch and dinner menus, plus breakfast, snacks, shakes and schnitzels throughout the day. Although upmarket for the area, it's great quality for the price and deservedly popular, so do book.

♥ Silo Coffee €€
*Gabriel-Max Strasse 4 (0151 6451 8685 mobile, www.silogoods. com). U5 Frankfurter Tor. **Open** 8.30am-5pm Mon-Fri; 9.30am-7pm Sat; 10am-7pm Sun. **Map** p125 U8* ④ *Café*
It's a well-known fact that Berliners are lazy and reluctant to leave their home districts, favouring local hotspots over schlepping across town. However, Silo's classic but expertly prepared breakfast menu – including oven-baked pancakes, avocado toast, baked eggs, and of course, the house-roasted Fjord Coffee – pulls Berliners in from all over the city. Homesick Australians will also find comfort here. You may have to wait for a table, particularly at weekends.

Vöner €
*Boxhagener Strasse 56 (0176 9651 3869 mobile, www.voener.de) S4, S41, S42, S5, S7, S75, S8, S86 Ostkreuz. **Open** noon-10pm Mon-Thu; noon-11pm Fri-Sun. **Map** p125 V8* ⑤ *Vegan*

Silo Coffee

Vegans, vegetarians and all those exhausted by Germany's love for *Fleisch* will find respite at this hip café. Here you're free to indulge in classic hangover or munchie food normally off-limits to veggies, including *Currywurst*, döner kebabs and seitan nuggets – all without any risk of getting the dreaded meat sweats.

Bars & pubs
Briefmarken Weine
*Karl-Marx-Allee 99 (4202 5292, www.briefmarkenweine.de). U5 Weberwiese. **Open** 7pm-midnight Mon-Sat. **Map** p125 S7* ①
Situated on Karl-Marx-Allee, former East German stamp shop turned purveyor of Italian goods, Briefmarken retains much of its old charm. Briefmarken is a mini oasis of regional Italian wine, fresh mozzarella antipasti and quiet candlelit conversations, and easy to distinguish by its neon green sign.

Chapel Bar

*Sonntagsstrasse 30 (0157 3200 0032 mobile, www.chapel.berlin) S3, S41, S42, S5, S7, S75, S8, S85 Ostkreuz. **Open** 6pm-1am Tue, Wed; 6pm-2am Thu; 6pm-3.30am Fri, Sat.* **No cards**. *Map p125 V8*

With artfully distressed walls, amber glowing table lamps and an eclectic assortment of vintage furniture, Chapel is evocative of dark smoky jazz joints. What really sets this place apart from other Berlin bars is the high quality of the artisan cocktails. The bar staff are happy to design you a signature drink, to play around with something experimental (artichoke liquor anyone?), or to simply rustle up an old favourite. The gin basil smash is superb.

CSA

Karl-Marx-Allee 96 (2904 4741, www.csa-bar.de). U5 Weberweise. **Open** 7pm-late Mon-Sat; *by reservation only Sun.* **No cards**. *Map p125 S7* ❸

This ultra-modern bar, housed in the old Czech Airlines building, has the feel of a futuristic airport lounge as dreamed up in the 1970s. The angular furniture and white plastic fittings contrast magnificently with its shabby location and the vast concrete sweep of Karl-Marx-Allee. The atmosphere is relaxed; the design-conscious crowd come for the excellent drink selection.

Zum Schmutzigen Hobby

Revaler Strasse 99 (3646 8446). U1, S5, S7, S75 Warschauer Strasse. **Open** *from 6pm daily.* **No cards**. *Map p125 T8* ❹

In 2010, famed drag queen Nina Queer moved her popular gay bar from Prenzlauer Berg to this graffiti- and bottle-strewn party zone of reclaimed buildings next to the Spree. Nina has since left the bar, but it remains as good as ever. It's intensely fun, especially later in the night when loud US pop hits fill the air. The large outdoor patio hosts viewing parties for *Germany's Next Top Model*, Eurovision and other TV events of gay interest.

Shops & services

Big Brobot

Kopernikusstrasse 19 (7407 8388, www.bigbrobot.com). U5 Frankfurter Tor. **Open** 11am- 8pm Mon-Fri; 11am-6pm Sat. *Map p125 T8* ❶ *Gifts & souvenirs*

A paradise for graphics nerds, with hundreds of collectible toys, comics and books on tattoo art or vintage typography. Big Brobot also stocks high-end skate labels such as Stüssy and Kid Robot. The refreshingly unpretentious staff are happy to help.

Big Brobot

Urban Spree

Flohmarkt am Boxhagener Platz

Boxhagener Platz (Flea market 0152 1134 2683 mobile, Farmers' market 0178 476 2242 mobile). U5 Samariterstrasse. **Open** *9am-3.30pm Sat; 10am-6pm Sun.* **No cards.** *Map p125 U7* ❷ *Market*
The Boxi market used to be more of a makeshift affair, full of bric-a-brac and punk clothing but, much like the surrounding area, it's now got with the times, offering a thriving farmers' market on Saturdays, and handicrafts, art and vintage clothing on Sundays. Stock up on local organic vegetables while chomping on a *lahmacun* (Turkish flatbread) roll.

Shakespeare & Sons

Warschauer Strasse 74 (4000 3685, www.shakesbooks.de, www. finebagels.com) U5 Frankfurter Tor. **Open** *8am-8pm Mon-Sat; 10am-8pm Sun.* **Map** *p125 T7* ❸ *Books*
Those looking for a respite from the bustle of Simon-Dach-Kiez would do well to retreat to this English- and French-language bookshop. With coffee and bagels provided by in-house Jewish-American bakery Fine Bagels, Shakespeare & Sons has a well-curated selection of reading matter, knowledgeable staff and plenty of solitary spots for you to hunker down in peace.

♥ Urban Spree Bookshop & Gallery

Revaler Strasse 99 (7407 8597, www.urbanspree.com). U1, S5, S7, S75 Warschauer Strasse. **Open** *General noon-midnight Mon-Thur, Sun; noon-3am Fri, Sat. Shop & gallery noon-6.30pm Tue-Sun.* **No cards.** *Map p125 T8* ❹ *Books & art*
Run by the team behind the now-closed HBC, Urban Spree's

ground-floor space functions as a gallery devoted to street art, graffiti and photography. There's also an excellent bookshop specialising in these topics, with limited editions and books from small publishers such as Fabulatorio. Gigs and performances also take place here, and a visit to the on-site *Biergarten* is highly recommended.

Entertainment

♥ ://about blank
Markgrafendamm 24C (no phone, http://aboutparty.net). S5, S7, S8, S9, S41, S42, S75 Ostkreuz. **Open** *midnight-late Thur-Sat.* **Admission** *€5-€15. No cards.* **Map** *p125 V9* ❶ *Club*
Particularly famed for its open-air parties, this club near Ostkreuz station is a favourite with the city's more adventurous hedonists – not least for its monthly gay night Buttons (formerly Homopatik).

Astra Kulturhaus
Revaler Strasse 99 (2005 6767, www.astra-berlin.de). U1, S3, S5, S7, S9 Warschauer Strasse. **Open** *varies.* **Admission** *varies.* **Map** *p125 T8* ❷ *Live music*
Berlin's premier alternative venue, Astra is part of the large RAW Tempel complex on old industrial warehouse grounds that's somewhat reminiscent of Christiania in Copenhagen. Arrive early as it gets crowded, and pillars can mean tricky sightlines. The likes of Bill Callahan, Godspeed You! Black Emperor, Death Cab for Cutie and Damon Albarn have played here.

Filmtheater Am Friedrichshain
Bötzowstrasse 1-5 (4284 5188, www. yorck.de). Bus 200. **Tickets** *€7-€9; €5.50 under-12s. 3D films €9.50-€11.50.* **Map** *p125 R5* ❸ *Cinema*

This charming five-screen cinema is right on the park in Friedrichshain and has a lovely beer garden that's open during the summer.

Salon zur Wilden Renate
Alt-Stralau 70 (2504 1426, www. renate.cc). S5, S7, S8, S9, S41, S42, S75 Ostkreuz. **Open** *varies.* **Admission** *varies. No cards.* **Map** *p125 V10* ❹ *Club*
This knackered old house was perennially at risk of being torn down and turned into – of course – trendy apartments. Once-sporadic parties follow a regular weekend rhythm these days, usually going till the last man standing. Students and wasted ravers press up against ex-pats from Mitte in the reliably crowded rooms, which are still set up like the flats they once were – complete with the odd bed. On languid summer afternoons, the club hops across the river to an intimate open-air wonderland called Else.

Sisyphos
Hauptstrasse 15 (9836 6839, www.sisyphos-berlin.net). S3 Rummelsburg. **Open** *midnight Fri-10am Mon every other weekend.* **Admission** *€10. No cards.* **Map** *p125 W9* ❺ *Club*
You don't make the trek out to Sisyphos just for a snoop and a couple of beers. It's an 'in for a penny, in for a pound' sort of place, where the party begins on Friday and trundles on non-stop until Monday. Vast indoor and outdoor spaces at this former dog-biscuit factory help create a festival-like spirit that's pitch-perfect for sunny weekends. Music ranges from pumping techno inside to more housey tunes out by the 'lake' – more of a scummy pond, really. Crowd-wise, expect it all: fresh-faced student revellers and wizened

❤ Berghain

Am Wriezener Bahnhof (no phone, www.berghain.de). U1, S3, S5, S7, S9 Warschauer Strasse. **Open** *midnight-late Fri, Sat, Sun.* **Admission** *€10-€14. No cards.* **Map** *p125 S7* ❻ *Club*

Easily the city's most famous club – and some would say the best club in the world – Berghain is not just a techno club: it's a way of life for many of the tireless regulars who call it 'church'. Housed within an imposing former power station, it emerged in 2004 from the ashes of its legendary gay predecessor, Ostgut, which had fallen victim to the city's massive infrastructure projects. Even 'non-club' people will be intoxicated by the open atmosphere, liberal attitudes, eccentric characters, the carefully preserved industrial fabric of the building and, of course, the gargantuan sound system. It's open, complete with darkrooms, from Friday midnight until well into Monday morning.

The club's reputation for a difficult and random door policy is not entirely undeserved: doorman Sven (recognisable by his facial tattoos) looms large all night with a seemingly haphazard attitude to who gets in. At peak times on a Saturday night, only a third of the people in the queue will get past him – you'll know you're in if he nods; if he points to his left, hard luck. Don't argue the toss, even if you're feeling brave. We recommend that you be calm, sober and respectful in the queue; it goes without saying that drunken stag dos aren't welcome. Once inside, a zero-tolerance camera ban is enforced – expect to be immediately ejected if you're discovered flaunting the rules. Other than that, you can go wild, safe in the knowledge that nothing you get up to will ever return to haunt you on social media.

Panorama Bar, up a flight of stairs from Berghain, is a smaller dancefloor that plays old-school house and features oversized artworks by Wolfgang Tillmans. Be here when the shutters open just after sunrise for one of the most climactic moments of the weekend.

▶ *Where should you go if you can't get into Berghain (or don't want to risk getting turned away)? For techno, try Tresor (see p96); for electro, try Ritter Butzke (see p148); and for a grope in the dark, try the KitKatClub (see p96).*

ravers of a dreadlocked persuasion are among the regulars.

Süss War Gestern

Wühlischstrasse 43. S5, S7, S8, S9, S41, S42, S75 Ostkreuz. **Open** *varies.* **Admission** *varies. No cards.* **Map** *p125 U8* ❼ *Club*
With a name meaning 'sweet was yesterday', the 1970s-style décor comes as no surprise. What is a surprise is the free entrance and €2.50 beers. There are three areas for dancing, drinking and hanging out, with different rooms playing different genres of music, from conventional techno to novelty hip hop. Check the website before you go.

Lichtenberg

Lichtenberg is generally unappealing, but it does contain the **Tierpark Berlin-Friedrichsfelde** (Zoo) and both the **Stasi Museum** and the **Gedenkstätte Berlin-Hohenschönhausen** (*see p134*), a former Stasi prison turned chilling exhibit of state oppression.

Sights & museums

Stasimuseum (Forschungs- und Gedenkstätte Normannenstrasse)

Ruschestrasse 103 (553 6854, www. stasimuseum.de). U5, S8, S9, S41, S42, S85 Frankfurter Allee; U5 Magdalenenstrasse. **Open** *10am-6pm Mon-Fri; 11am-6pm Sat, Sun. Tours (in English) 3pm Mon, Sat, Sun.* **Admission** *€6; €4.50 reductions. No cards.*

In January 1990, a few weeks after the Wall was breached, crowds stormed the Stasi headquarters at Normannenstrasse to vent anger at their former tormentors and to prevent the destruction of secret documents, which Stasi agents had been working overtime with shredders to destroy. Thanks to their efforts, many of the six million or so files were saved; since reunification they have been administered by a special authority charged with reviewing them and making them available to prosecutors and everyday people curious to find out what the Stasi knew about them. Not surprisingly, the files contained embarrassing revelations, with many people being listed as unofficial informers, a status hard to dispute or verify.

Visitors can explore the former headquarters and see displays of bugging devices and spy cameras concealed in books, plant pots and car doors. You can even poke around the offices of secret police chief Erich Mielke – his old uniform still hangs in the wardrobe – and apply at the front desk to see your own Stasi records, should any exist. Since early 2015, a permanent exhibition has explored the Stasi's structure, methods and activities, giving an insight into the most insidious police surveillance state in all of history. Tours are also offered of the Stasi Archives next door.

Tierpark

Am Tierpark 125 (515 310, www. tierpark-berlin.de). U5 Tierpark. **Open** *Late Mar-mid Sept 9am-6pm daily. Mid Sept-late Mar 9am-4.30pm daily.* **Admission** *€14; €6-€7 reductions.*

East Berlin's zoo is still one of Europe's largest, with an impressive amount of roaming space for the herd animals, although others are still kept in rather small cages. Residents include bears, big cats, elephants and penguins. One of the continent's biggest snake farms is also here. In the north-west corner is the Baroque Schloss Friedrichsfelde.

Stasimuseum

❤ Gedenkstätte Berlin-Hohenschönhausen

Genslerstrasse 66 (9860 8230, www.stiftung-hsh.de). Tram M5, M6. **Open** *Exhibition 9am-6pm daily. Guided tours (in German) 10am-4pm hourly; (in English) 10.30am, 12.30pm, 2.30pm daily.* **Admission** *€6; €1-3 reductions. No cards.*

It's claimed that at some point in their lives, one in three citizens worked as unofficial informers for East Germany's Ministerium für Staatssicherheit, better known as the Stasi. There were around 90,000 full-time agents and 175,000 *Inoffizielle Mitarbeiter* (unofficial employees, aka informers) – that's around 2.5 per cent of those aged between 18 and 60. One thing's for sure: the secret police apparatus was the most pervasive in the history of state-sponsored repression; compare, for example, the Gestapo, which in its 1940s heyday only had about 30,000 members.

The Stasi's grip on everyday life in the GDR was exhaustive, with hidden cameras and microphones, a network of informers and infamous secret prisons where political prisoners were held, brutalised, and psychologically broken before being sent to labour camps. A visit to this sprawling former remand prison is gut-wrenchingly bleak. First the site of a canteen for the Nazi social welfare organisation, the building was turned into 'Special Encampment No.3' by the Soviets before being expanded by the Stasi. Excellent and

highly personal guided tours are led daily by ex-prisoners; their personal testimony adds chilling immediacy to the bureaucratically spare interrogation rooms, the concrete 'tiger cage' in which 30 minutes of walking per day was permitted and the cramped cells where prisoners were forced to sleep in a mandated position. The museum houses a permanent exhibition, which reveals the stories of former prisoners during their incarceration, and there are temporary exhibitions which change throughout the year, often curated from the memorial's own immense collection of 15,000 historical artefacts from the GDR.

▶ *A 15-minute walk from the museum will bring you to the Mies van der Rohe Haus (Oberseestrasse 60, 9700 0618, www.miesvanderrohehaus.de), designed in 1933 and used by the Stasi as a laundry. It now hosts art exhibitions.*

Kreuzberg & Treptow

Kreuzberg is divided quite firmly into halves, according to its old postcodes – Kreuzberg 36, the eastern part, is scruffy and hip, great for a night out; Kreuzberg 61, in the west, is quieter, prettier, duller after dark but lovely during the day. Further east, Treptow is a quiet residential area concealing leafy Treptower Park, a huge war memorial and an abandoned amusement park.

Best monument
Soviet Memorial *p150*

Best for foodies
Lode & Stijn *p145*,
Markthalle Neun *p147*,
Nobelhart & Schmutzig *p141*

Best open-air fun
Badeschiff *p149*,
Club der Visionaere *p149*

Best cocktails
Marques Bar *p146*,
Schwarze Traube *p146*

Best night out
Roses *p146*, SO36 *p149*

Best museums
Haus am Checkpoint Charlie *p138*,
Jüdisches Museum *p140*,
Museum der Dinge *p144*

West Kreuzberg

The north-western portion of Kreuzberg, bordering Mitte, is not the prettiest, but it's where you'll find most of the area's museums and tourist sights. You can get an expensive overview from the tethered balloon on the corner of Wilhelmstrasse & Zimmerstrasse: **Berlin Hi-Flyer** (226 678 811, www.air-service-berlin.de, €23; €10-€18 reductions).

To the south are some of the most picturesque streets in West Berlin, especially north and east of **Viktoriapark**. The park contains the actual Kreuzberg ('Cross Hill') after which the borough is named; there are commanding views from the monument at the summit.

Sights & museums

Berlinische Galerie
Alte Jakobstrasse 124-128 (7890 2600, www.berlinischegalerie.de).

U6 Kochstrasse. **Open** *10am-6pm Mon, Wed-Sun.* **Admission** *€8; €5 reductions; free under-18s.* **Map** *p137 O9.*
Founded in 1975, the Berlinische Galerie moved into this spacious renovated industrial building near the Jewish Museum in 2004. It specialises in art created in Berlin, dating from 1870 to the present, including painting, sculpture, photography and architecture. Its collections cover Dada Berlin, the Neue Sachlichkeit and the Eastern European avant-garde. Enjoy half-price admission every first Monday of the month.

▶ *Visitors pay the reduced price if they have bought a ticket to the Jüdisches Museum (see p140) within the previous 48 hours.*

Berlin Story Bunker
Schöneberger Strasse 23A (2655 5546, www.berlinstory.de). S1, S2, S25 Anhalter Bahnhof. **Open** *10am-7pm daily.* **Admission** *Hitler*

→ Getting around

The most enjoyable way to explore both Kreuzberg and Treptow is by bike, thanks to the numerous green parks and residential spaces – just watch out for the cobblestones on the side roads. Kreuzberg is well served by the U-Bahn, with the U1 running from east to west through the centre, and the U6, 7 and 8 covering the rest of the district. Note that, even if you use the U-Bahn, you're likely to do some walking, as distances between stations are significant. Treptow is served primarily by the S-Bahn to Treptower Park.

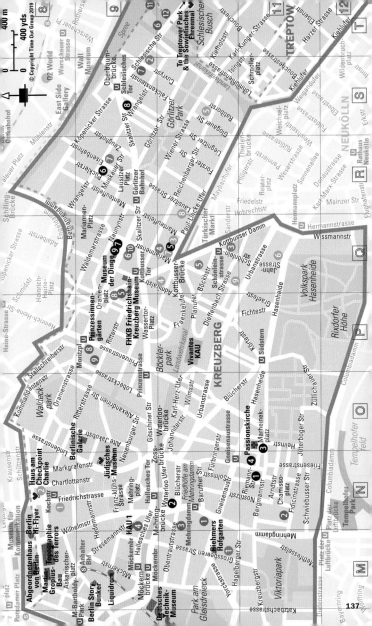

❤ Haus am Checkpoint Charlie

*Friedrichstrasse 43-45 (253 7250, www.mauermuseum.de). U6 Kochstrasse. **Open** 9am-10pm daily. **Admission** €14.50; €6.50-€9.50 reductions. **Map** p137 N8.*

A little tacky, but essential for anyone interested in the Cold War, this private museum opened not long after the GDR erected the Berlin Wall in 1961, making it the oldest documentation of the Wall in existence. The founder of the museum, Dr Rainer Hildebrandt, opened it as a non-violent protest against the Wall, with the purpose of recording the events that were taking place at this, the best-known crossing point. He believed that it was essential to be 'as close as possible to the injustice itself, where human greatness fully unfolds'. Haus am Checkpoint Charlie is not just a testament to the unfolding of history but played an active role in planning and assisting escapes.

The exhibition charts the history of the Wall and details the ingenious and hair-raising ways people escaped from the GDR – as well as exhibiting some of the actual contraptions that were used, such as a home-made hot-air balloon, a mini-submarine and getaway cars. Today, the museum also features permanent displays that look beyond Berlin and Germany towards other forms of non-violent protest.

For some *Ostalgie* (nostalgia for the GDR), head a few steps down from the Haus am Checkpoint Charlie to the **Trabi Museum** (Zimmerstrasse 14-15, 3020 1030, www.trabi-museum.com) dedicated to the cult Eastern bloc vehicle. And, to really max out on German kitsch, especially if you have bored and hungry kids in tow, finish off your visit with a trip to the nearby **Deutsches Currywurst Museum** (Schützenstrasse 70, 8871 8647, currywurstmuseum.com).

Deutsches Technikmuseum Berlin

exhibition €12; €9 reductions.
Berlin Museum €6; €4.50
*reductions. **Map** p137 M9.*
This is one of only two World War II
bunkers that is open to the public.
The five-storey structure served
as an air-raid shelter for the long-
destroyed Anhalter Bahnhof and
today provides a fitting setting
for two exhibitions. 'Hitler – How
could it happen?' charts the
Nazi's rise to power in Germany,
while the Berlin Museum offers a
chronological journey through the
city's history.

▶ *Another Nazi-era bunker*
houses the Sammlung Boros art
collection (see p79).

Deutsches Technikmuseum Berlin

Trebbiner Strasse 9 (902 540, www.
sdtb.de). U1, U7 Möckernbrücke.
***Open** 9am-5.30pm Tue-Fri;*
*10am-6pm Sat, Sun. **Admission***
*€8; €4 reductions. **Map** p137 M9.*
Opened in 1982 in the former goods
depot of the Anhalter Bahnhof, the
German Museum of Technology
is an eclectic, eccentric collection
of new and antique industrial
artefacts. The rail exhibits have

pride of place, with the station
sheds providing an ideal setting for
locomotives and rolling stock from
1835 to the present. Other displays
focus on the industrial revolution;
street, rail, water and air traffic;
computer technology; and printing
technology. Behind the main
complex is an open-air section with
two functioning windmills and
a smithy. Oddities, such as 1920s
vacuum cleaners, make this a fun
place for implement enthusiasts.
The nautical wing has vessels
and displays on inland waterways
and international shipping, while
another wing covers aviation and
space travel. Electronic information
points offer commentaries in
English on subjects from the
international slave trade to the
mechanics of a space station. The
Spectrum annex, at Möckernstrasse
26, houses over 200 interactive
devices and experiments.

Martin-Gropius-Bau

Niederkirchnerstrasse 7 (254 860,
www.gropiusbau.de). S1, S2, S25
Anhalter Bahnhof; U6 Kochstrasse
***Open** 10am-7pm Mon, Wed-Sun.*
***Admission** varies. **Map** p137 M8.*

❤ Jüdisches Museum

Lindenstrasse 9-14 (2599 3300, guided tours 2599 3305, www. jmberlin.de). U1, U6 Halle-sches Tor. **Open** *(last entry 1hr before closing) 10am-8pm daily.* **Admission** *€8; €3 reductions.* **Map** *p137 N9.*

The idea of a Jewish museum in Berlin was first mooted in 1971, the 300th birthday of the city's Jewish community. In 1975, an association was formed to acquire materials for display; in 1989, a competition was held to design an extension to the Baroque Kollegienhaus to house them. Daniel Libeskind emerged as the winner, the foundation stone was laid in 1992 and the permanent exhibition finally opened in 2001.

The ground plan of Libeskind's remarkable building is in part based on an exploded Star of David, in part on lines drawn between the site and former addresses of figures in Berlin's Jewish history, such as Mies van der Rohe, Arnold Schönberg and Walter Benjamin. The entrance is via a tunnel from the Kollegienhaus. The underground geometry is startlingly independent of the above-ground building. One passage leads to the exhibition halls, two others intersect en route to the Holocaust Tower and the ETA Hoffmann Garden, a grid of 49 columns, tilted to disorientate. Throughout, diagonals and parallels carve out surprising spaces, while windows slash through the structure and its zinc cladding like the knife-wounds of history. And then there are the

'voids' cutting through the layout, negative spaces that stand for the emptiness left by the destruction of German Jewish culture.

The permanent exhibition struggles in places with such powerful surroundings. What makes it engaging is its focus on the personal: it tells the stories of prominent Jews and what they contributed to their community, and to the cultural and economic life of Berlin and Germany. After centuries of prejudice and pogroms, the outlook for German Jews seemed to be brightening. Then came the Holocaust. The emotional impact of countless stories of the eminent and the ordinary, and the fate that almost all shared, is hard to convey adequately in print. The museum is undoubtedly a must-see, but expect long queues and big crowds.

▶ *Visitors pay the reduced price if they have bought a ticket to the Berlinische Galerie (see p136) within the previous 48 hours.*

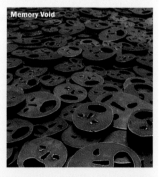

Memory Void

Topographie des Terrors

Cosying up to where the Wall once stood (a short, pitted stretch still runs nearby along the south side of Niederkirchnerstrasse), the Martin-Gropius-Bau is named after its architect, uncle of the more famous Walter. Built in 1881, it has been renovated and is now used for large-scale art exhibitions.

Topographie des Terrors

Niederkirchnerstrasse 8 (2545 0950, www.topographie.de). S1, S2, S25 Anhalter Bahnhof; U6 Kochstrasse. **Open** *Outdoor exhibition 10am-dusk daily. Indoor exhibition 10am-8pm daily.* **Admission** *free.* **Map** *p137 M8.*
Essentially a piece of waste ground, this was once the site of the Prinz Albrecht Palais, headquarters of the Gestapo, and the Hotel Prinz Albrecht, which housed offices of the Reich SS leadership. It was from here that the Holocaust was managed and the Germanisation of the east was dreamed up. There's an outdoor exhibition that gives a fairly comprehensive chronology of Hitler's rise to power, as well as an indoor documentation centre. A segment of the Berlin Wall runs along the site's northern boundary.

Restaurants & cafés

♥ Nobelhart & Schmutzig
€€€
Friedrichstrasse 218 (2594 0610, www.nobelhartundschmutzig. com). U6 Kochstrasse. **Open** *from 6.30pm Tue-Sat.* **Map** *p137 N8* ❶
Modern German
This restaurant's tagline is 'vocally local' – meaning they refuse to import food from beyond the capital and its immediate surroundings. Sadly, this means no chocolate. However, chef and sommelier Billy Wagner has ways of helping you temporarily forget: he uses neglected traditional methods to create a seasonally shifting menu of bold, contemporary flavours that evoke, impossibly, the authentic taste of Berlin. The outside is nondescript, visible only to those in the know, and you must ring a bell before you are ushered into the eatery – a long wooden table with just 28 seats. Booking essential.

Tim Raue €€€€
Rudi-Dutschke-Strasse 26 (2593 7930, www.tim-raue.de). U6 Kochstrasse. **Open** *noon-1pm, 7-9pm Wed-Sat.* **Map** *p137 N8* ❷
Fine dining

In contrast to many of Berlin's fine-dining establishments, this small restaurant, decorated with Chinese ceramics and dark wood furniture, prides itself on its informality. Not that this detracts from the exacting dishes. The tasting menu might include *amuse-bouches* of spicy cashews, prawn sashimi and marinated pork belly, moving on to main courses of wagyu beef, lobster, Australian winter truffle and tofu, all flaunting Japanese techniques and served with blobs, smears or foams of contrasting flavours and colours. Book ahead.

English Theatre Berlin

Bars & pubs

Galander Kreuzberg

Grossbeerenstrasse 54 (3850 9030, www.galander.berlin/galander-kreuzberg). U7 Gneisenaustrasse. **Open** *6pm-late daily.* **Map** *p137 M10* ①
This low-lit haven, complete with squishy leather armchairs and a piano at the back, offers a decadent array of spirits and home-made cordials to please the most demanding cocktail connoisseur. The friendly and attentive staff are brimming with encyclopaedic knowledge on mixology and won't hesitate to create something special or even regale you with a tune. The basil smash is divine.

Shops & services

Another Country

Riemannstrasse 7 (6940 1160, www.anothercountry.de). U7 Gneisenaustrasse. **Open** *2-8pm Mon; 11am-8pm Tue-Fri; noon-6pm Sat.* **Map** *p137 N11* ① *Books*
This second-hand bookshop was established by Sophia Raphaeline long before the area was laden with cafés, restaurants and shops, and offers a window into Kreuzberg of the past. It now has legendary status but retains a whiff of bohemia. The rooms have the feel of a private study, with piles of books laid out on tables and a fridge for beers; a projector is set up for film nights, and quizzes and dinners are also held.

Hallesches Haus

Tempelhofer Ufer 1 (no phone, hallescheshaus.com). U1, U6 Hallesches Tor. **Open** *10am-7pm Mon-Fri; 10am-6pm Sat, Sun.* **Map** *p137 N10* ② *Homewares*
Succulents, copper kettles, angora wool throws, over-sized lightbulbs, seaweed and samphire unguents – there is a dizzying array of artfully curated knick-knacks and treasures

to buy here, all tastefully arranged on wooden crates and industrial shelving. There's also a very good café, with a locally sourced, seasonal menu and plenty of places to sit and mull over those pretty things you never knew you needed.

Marheineke Markthalle

*Marheinekestrasse 15 (5056 6536, meine-markthalle.de). U7 Gneisenaustrasse. **Open** 8am-8pm Mon-Fri; 8am-6pm Sat. **Map** p137 N11* ❸ *Market*

A lovely covered market with French butchers, Italian charcuterie, flowers and organic produce, as well as plenty of prepared foods to take away. You'll find a Veganz supermarket upstairs, and a variety of snack bars with seating along the front wall.

Space Hall

*Zossener Strasse 33 & 35 (694 7664, www.space-hall.de). U7 Gneisenaustrasse. **Open** 11am-8pm Mon-Wed, Sat; 11am-10pm Thur, Fri. **Map** p137 N11* ❹ *Music*

A favourite of Berlin's resident DJs and producers, Space Hall has a huge selection of new and second-hand CDs and vinyl. Techno, house and electronica are the mainstay, but there's also hip hop, indie and rock.

Entertainment

BKA Theater

*Mehringdamm 34 (202 2007, www.bka-theater.de). U6, U7 Mehringdamm. **Box office** 5-9pm daily. **Tickets** €18-€24. **Map** p137 N10* ❶ *Theatre*

With a long tradition of taboo-breaking acts, BKA still has some of the weirdest and most progressive performers in town: intelligent drag stand-up, freaky chanteuses, power-lunged divas. There are private tables and arena seats overlooking the stage.

English Theatre Berlin

*Fidicinstrasse 40 (691 1211, www.etberlin.de). U6 Platz der Luftbrücke. **Tickets** €6-€18. **Map** p137 N11* ❷ *Theatre*

Directors Günther Grosser and Bernd Hoffmeister present a high-quality programme. Expect house productions, international guest shows and co-productions with performers from Berlin's lively international theatre scene, all in English. Theater Thikwa, one of Europe's most renowned companies working with disabled actors, is also based here.

Gretchen

*Obentrautstrasse 19-21 (2592 2702, www.gretchen-club.de). U1, U6 Hallesches Tor, or U6, U7 Mehringdamm. **Open** varies. **Admission** €8-€15. No cards. **Map** p137 N10* ❸ *Club*

Coming straight out of left field, Gretchen hosts an impressive array of nights that aren't afraid of forgoing Berlin's ubiquitous tech-house loops in favour of some trap, dubstep, drum 'n' bass or hip hop. The picturesque vaulted ceilings and intricate columns of this former Prussian stable create a wonderfully incongruous setting for the avant-garde sounds.

HAU

*HAU2, Hallesches Ufer 32, Kreuzberg (259 0040, tickets 2590 0427, www.hebbel-am-ufer.de). U1, U7 Möckernbrücke, or U1, U6 Hallesches Tor. **Box office** 3-7pm Mon-Sat. **Tickets** vary. **Map** p137 N9* ❹ *Theatre*

Since opening in 2003, HAU – the amalgamation of the century-old former Hebbel Theater (HAU1), Theater am Halleschen Ufer (HAU2) and Theater am Ufer (HAU3) – has gained an incredible reputation for hosting Berlin's most innovative and radical theatre programming, with work by the likes of Forced Entertainment, Nature Theater of

Oklahoma, Alain Platel, Jerome Bel and long-standing HAU regulars Gob Squad and Rimini Protokoll.

East Kreuzberg

In the 1970s and '80s, this part of Kreuzberg formed the eastern periphery of inner West Berlin. Enclosed by the Wall and the canal, its decaying tenements came to house Berlin's biggest and most militant squat community. No area of West Berlin has changed so much since reunification, as this once-isolated pocket found itself recast as desirable real estate. However, gentrification was slow to take off and Kreuzberg regained its appeal for young bohemia. Today it's full of cafés, bars and clubs, and dotted with independent cinemas; it's also the centre of Turkish Berlin and bustles with kebab shops and Anatolian travel agents.

Sights & museums

❤ Museum der Dinge
Oranienstrasse 25 (9210 6311, www.museumderdinge.de). U1, U8 Kottbusser Tor. Open noon-7pm Mon, Thur-Sun. Admission €6; €4 reductions. No cards. Map p137 Q9.
On the top floor of a typical Kreuzberg apartment block, the 'Museum of Things' contains every kind of small object you could imagine in modern design from the 19th century onwards – from hairbrushes and fondue sets to beach souvenirs and Nazi memorabilia. It's not a musty collection but a sleek and minimalist space organised by themes such as 'yellow and black' or 'functional vs kitsch', rather than by era or type, so that the 'things' appear in new contexts. It can get a little confused at times – hardly surprising, given the 20,000 objects – but it's a fascinating place. There's a great shop too.

Restaurants & cafés

Cocolo €
Paul-Lincke Ufer 39-40 (9833 9073, www.kuchi.de). U1, U8 Kottbusser Tor. Open noon-11pm Mon-Sat; 6-11pm Sun. No cards. Map p137 Q10 ③ Japanese
This ramen bar sparked Berlin's on-going obsession with bone broth and expanded from a tiny bar in Mitte to this spacious branch by the canal in Kreuzberg. All the classic ramen styles are served, but the cognoscenti always pick *tonkotsu*: the pork stock is kicked up to a piggy 11/10 by the addition of liquor derived from boiling bones, collagen and fat for hours. It's then topped with a soft-boiled egg, pickled ginger, crispy seaweed, slices of roast pork and braised sweet pork belly. **Other location** Gipsstrasse 3, Mitte (2838 6622).

Doyum Grillhaus €-€€
Admiralstrasse 36 (6165 6127). U1, U8 Kottbusser Tor. Open 7am-midnight daily. No cards. Map p137 Q10 ④ Turkish
One of the best *ockabasi* (Turkish grillhouses) in Kotti is somehow hidden in plain sight. Tourists flock to the overrated Hasir, but the Turkish locals come to this beautifully tiled dining room for a plate of *iskender* kebab smothered in yoghurt sauce, or succulent minced lamb *adana*. No alcohol allowed.

Five Elephant €€
Reichenberger Strasse 101 (9608 1527, www.fiveelephant.com). U1 Görlitzer Bahnhof. Open 8.30am-7pm Mon-Fri; 10am-7pm Sat, Sun. No cards. Map p137 S10 ⑤ Café
You can feel the love at this café and roastery run by a charming Austro-American couple: she bakes the cakes; he roasts the beans. There's a selection of traditional cakes and tarts, but

Markthalle Neun p147

the Philadelphia cheesecake is transcendental: a wafer-thin layer of spice is all that separates the custardy interior from the velvety top. No WiFi, so bring a book if you plan to stay a while.

Hamy Café-Foodstore €
Hasenheide 10 (6162 5959, www.hamycafe.com). U7, U8 Hermannplatz. **Open** *noon-midnight daily.* **No cards.** *Map p137 Q11* ⑥ *Vietnamese*

Don't panic if there's no room here: get others to budge up and share their table, or wait – service is so speedy it won't take long. There are three specials a day, all priced at €4.90: glass noodle salad with octopus, perhaps, or a golden chicken curry. Tofu can be substituted for meat or fish. Alcohol is served, but you may prefer to skip the beer in favour of fresh lime juice or lassi.

Horváth €€€
Paul-Lincke-Ufer 44A (6128 9992, www.restaurant-horvath.de). U1, U8 Kottbusser Tor. **Open** *6.30-10pm Wed-Sun. Map p137 Q10* ⑦ *Contemporary German*

Operating outside the usual Berlin luxury hotel system, Austrian chef Sebastian Frank gained a Michelin star in 2011 at this canalside restaurant. Enjoy a tasting menu of typical rustic German ingredients transformed through novel techniques: onion, pigeon and kohlrabi, or sturgeon, rib and celery, are charred, abstracted and perfectly plated. The Austrian wine list is excellent. Booking advised.

❤ Lode & Stijn €€€
Lausitzer Strasse 25 (6521 4507, www.lode-stijn.de). U1 Görlitzer Bahnhof. **Open** *6-10pm Tue-Sat. Map p137 R10* ⑧ *Contemporary*

A contemporary dining experience and part of a wave of chic bistro restaurants sweeping Berlin. Lode & Stijn offers a tri-weekly rotating seasonal set menu with a no-nonsense approach to cooking (the beef *Bitterballen* are to die for). A shorter version of the set menu is served at the bar. Booking is recommended.

St Bart's €€€
Graefestrasse 71 (4075 1175, www.stbartpub.com). U8 Schönleinstrasse. **Open** *Bar 4pm-midnight Mon-Thur, Sun; noon-midnight Fri, Sat. Kitchen 6-10pm Mon-Thur, Sun; noon-3pm, 6-10pm Fri, Sat. Map p137 Q10* ⑨ *Gastropub*

This surprising little gastropub serves up a sumptuous feast of simple yet powerful flavours. The menu features the likes of burnt Jerusalem artichokes, green asparagus, lentils and goats cheese and heavenly buttermilk fried chicken. Everything comes paired with home-made sauces, and the booze menu is unpretentiously priced.

Bars & pubs

Barbie Deinhoff's
Schlesische Strasse 16. U1 Schlesisches Tor. **Open** *from 7pm-late daily.* **No cards.** *Map p137 S9* ❷
Sure, this is a queer performance space, but most people come to its bright, casual rooms for the young, mixed crowd, the top-notch local DJs and the hilarious art adorning the walls. Two-for-one Tuesdays are popular, attracting a particularly skint Kreuzberg crowd.

Bei Schlawinchen
Schönleinstrasse 34 (no phone). U8 Schönleinstrasse. **Open** *24hrs daily.* **No cards.** *Map p137 Q10* ❸
This dive bar situated just off Kottbusser Damm is a unique example of a Berlin *Kneipe* (pub), with its bizarre decorations of dolls, old bicycles and instruments. High unemployment in the neighbourhood means that it's usually rammed all day, with rowdy characters propping up the bar or hammering away at the table football. Naturally, the beer is both cheap and plentiful. Rumour has it, they haven't closed since 1978...

Das Hotel Bar
Mariannenstrasse 26a (8411 8433, www.dashotel.org). U8 Kottbusser Tor. **Open** *4pm-late daily.* **No cards.** *Map p137 Q9* ❹
Das Hotel occupies some attractive old *altbau* buildings, with an ice-cream parlour, brasserie, bar and dive club – pretty much everything except for actual hotel rooms. The bar is all candles and old pianos, and a Spanish DJ gets the downstairs dancefloor going on weekends. There are some 'secret' rooms to rent – phone or email for details.

♥ Marques Bar
Graefestrasse 92 (6162 5906). U8 Schönleinstrasse. **Open** *7pm-late daily.* **No cards.** *Map p137 Q10* ❺
Below a rather average Spanish restaurant is this 1920s time-capsule of a cocktail bar, where the decor is suitably solid and mahogany. A host takes you to an available table and asks for your preferred 'flavour profile' (ie what kind of drink you usually like). Then the bar staff do their magic, working with hundreds of booze varieties (plus over 30 tonics), vintage glassware and fist-sized rocks of ice.

♥ Roses
Oranienstrasse 187 (615 6570). U1, U8 Kottbusser Tor. **Open** *10pm-6am daily.* **No cards.** *Map p137 Q9* ❻
Whatever state you're in (the more of a state, the better), you'll fit in just fine at this boisterous den of glitter. It draws customers of all sexual preferences, who mix and mingle and indulge in excessive drinking amid the plush, kitsch decor. No place for uptights, always full, very Kreuzbergish.

♥ Schwarze Traube
Wrangelstrasse 24 (2313 5569). U1 Görlitzer Bahnhof. **Open** *7pm-late daily.* **No cards.** *Map p137 R9* ❼
This bar on a quiet backstreet shot to fame when the slight but magnificently bearded owner, Atalay Aktas represented Germany at the 2013 World Class Bartender of the Year final. Aktas describes his ideal ambience as 'noble trash'. It's

all about the detail here – ask bar staff for a custom-made cocktail to suit your taste, or request a classic.

Würgeengel
Dresdener Strasse 122 (615 5560, www.wuergeengel.de). U1, U8 Kottbusser Tor. **Open** *7pm-late daily.* **No cards.** **Map** *p137 Q9* 🔟
It's a bit of a mouthful, but this sultry boozer is named after Luis Buñuel's absurdist movie masterpiece *The Exterminating Angel*, in which a group of bourgeois worthies find themselves inexplicably unable to leave a lavish dinner party. The smartly dressed waiting staff, glass-latticed ceiling and leather booths certainly evoke an old-world sensibility, but it's still accessibly priced.

Shops & services

Hard Wax
Paul-Lincke-Ufer 44A (6113 0111, www.hardwax.de). U1, U8 Kottbusser Tor. **Open** *noon-8pm Mon-Sat.* **Map** *p137 Q10* ⑤ *Music*
Up a staircase at the back of a Kreuzberg courtyard lies this vinyl mecca, famous for its flawless selection of dub, techno and reggae. It was opened by dub techno pioneers Basic Channel, and many of the city's biggest DJs (Marcel Dettmann, DJ Hell) started out by working here. Beware – it's infamous for its haughty service.

❤ Markthalle Neun
Eisenbahnstrasse 42-43 (610 734 73, www.markthalleneun.de). U1 Görlitzer Bahnhof. **Open** *General 8am-8pm daily. Market noon-6pm Fri; 10am-6pm Sat. Street food 5-10pm Thur.* **No cards.** **Map** *p137 R9* ⑥ *Market*
During the late 19th century, 14 municipal covered markets were opened to replace traditional outdoor markets and improve hygiene standards. Local residents

saved this one from closure in 2009, filling it with stalls serving heritage veg and locally sourced meats. It's also home to the excellent Heidenpeters microbrewery and the Sironi bakery from Milan. Aligned with the Slow Food movement, the market hosts regular themed events, including the hugely popular and influential **Street Food** showcase on Thursday evenings (www.facebook.com/StreetFoodThursday) and **Cheese Berlin**, where'll you find a multitude of artisanal European cheeses.

Modern Graphics
Oranienstrasse 22 (615 8810, www.modern-graphics.de). U1, U8 Kottbusser Tor. **Open** *11am-8pm Mon-Sat.* **Map** *p137 Q9* ⑦ *Books & magazines*
Shelves of European and alternative comics, plus graphic novels, anime, T-shirts and calendars.

Motto
Skalitzer Strasse 68 (4881 6407, www.mottodistribution.com). U1 Schlesisches Tor. **Open** *noon-8pm Mon-Sat.* **Map** *p137 S9* ⑧ *Books & magazines*
Tucked away in a disused frame factory in a courtyard off Schlesisches Tor, Motto is Swiss by origin and Swiss in its super design-consciousness. Fanzines, back issues, artists' books, posters, rare print-runs and cult classics are spread in a come-hither way across a long central table.

Voo Store
Oranienstrasse 24 (6110 1750, www.vooberlin.com). U1, U8 Kottbusser Tor. **Open** *10am-8pm Mon-Sat.* **Map** *p137 Q9* ⑨ *Fashion*
The Voo concept store brings sleek fashions to an area usually associated with punkier looks. Expect well-crafted outerwear from minimal Swedish favourite Acne,

classic New Balance sneakers, and a selection of accessories. At the in-store coffee bar, **Companion Coffee**, you can get a fine macchiato while perusing upmarket magazines such as *The Travel Almanac*.

Entertainment

Babylon Kreuzberg
Dresdener Strasse 126 (6160 9693, www.yorck.de). U1, U8 Kottbusser Tor. **Tickets** *€7-€9. No cards.* **Map** *p137 Q9* ⑤ *Cinema*
Another Berlin perennial, this twin-screen theatre runs a varied programme featuring indie crossover and UK films. Once a local Turkish cinema, its films are almost all English-language and it offers a homely respite from the multiplex experience.

Chalet
Vor dem Schlesischen Tor 3 (6953 6290, www.chalet-berlin.de). U1 Schlesisches Tor. **Open** *midnight-late Tue-Sun.* **Admission** *€10-€12. No cards.* **Map** *p137 T10* ⑥ *Club*
Chalet was opened by some of the late, great Bar 25 crew – and these guys know a thing or two about getting their groove on. Located in a grand, 150-year-old townhouse, it has multiple levels and rooms to explore, as well as a large luscious garden in which to shoot the breeze when the beats get too much. An altogether stylish and sultry club with a party pretty much every night; more local on weekdays, more touristy at weekends.

Lido
Cuvrystrasse 7 (6956 6840, tickets 6110 1313, www.lido-berlin.de). U1 Schlesisches Tor. **Open** *varies.* **Admission** *varies. No cards.* **Map** *p137 S9* ⑦ *Live music*
A true Kreuzberg institution, this indie concert venue was a cinema in the 1950s and retains its curved

bar and neon signage. Saturday's Karrera Klub has championed guitar-driven music for over a decade, with a live gig followed by DJs playing indie dance classics. Other live music acts range from the avant-garde (Laibach, Lydia Lunch) to more contemporary bands (Kurt Vile, These New Puritans). Friendly Fires, Taking Back Sunday, The Front Bottoms, We Are Scientists, Shitdisco and The Horrors have all graced the stage in the past.

Prince Charles
Prinzenstrasse 85F (no phone, www.princecharlesberlin.com). U8 Moritzplatz. **Open** *11pm-late Thur-Sat.* **Admission** *varies. No cards.* **Map** *p137* ⑧ *Club*
Walking down the concrete underpass to the entrance, it feels more like the approach to a car park than a trendy little club. It's situated in a former swimming pool, and the tiled walls and soft lighting create an intimate atmosphere. Artfully dishevelled young things bop along to the house-heavy soundtrack, pausing for a breather outside on the extremely lounge-worthy wooden decking.

▶ *Next door is the cheekily named Parker Bowles supper club (Prinzenstrasse 85D, 5527 9099, www.parker-bowles. com, closed Sun, €€€).*

Ritter Butzke
Ritterstrasse 26 (no phone, www. ritterbutzke.de). U8 Moritzplatz. **Open** *midnight-late Fri, Sat.* **Admission** *varies. No cards.* **Map** *p137 P9* ⑨ *Club*
This enormous old factory is a party hotspot thanks to its imaginative decor and reliable booking policy; events include 'Wasted Unicorns Summer Party' with AKA AKA and 'Playfulness' with Jake the Rapper. It held illegal

parties for years but has now gone legit and even allows its parties to be promoted in listings mags from time to time. It's the antithesis of Berghain, thanks to crowds of locals and amiable bouncers who are occasionally dressed as knights (*Ritter* means 'knight'), but brace yourself for a massive queue if you arrive between 1 and 3.30am.

♥ SO36

Oranienstrasse 190 (tickets 6110 1313, 6140 1306, www.so36.de). U1, U8 Kottbusser Tor. **Open** *8pm-late daily.* **Admission** *€3-€20. No cards.* **Map** *p137 Q9* ⑩ *Live music*
Still going strong since the punk heyday of the late 1970s, and with no sign of betraying its highly politicised origins, SO36 is suitably scummy inside, with decades of sweat, beer and blood ingrained into the woodwork. While plenty of touring punk and hardcore bands grace the black stage, the venue embraces all sorts of alternative lifestyles; the long-running queer Turkish night, Gayhane is especially popular.

Treptow

The canal and lack of U-Bahn keeps this large district just east of Kreuzberg relatively isolated, although Schlesische Strasse has become a nightlife hotspot in recent years. The grand tree-lined Puschkinallee neatly segues into expansive Treptower Park, location of the **Sowjetisches Ehrenmal** (Soviet Memorial; *see p150*). Roam the park to find the charming **Insel der Jugend** (www.inselberlin.de), a tiny landscaped islet that hosts summer events, and the abandoned **Spreepark** (www.berliner-spreepark.de), a massively popular amusement park in GDR days that ran into debt after the Wall fell. Now the rides are all overgrown and

the ferris wheel creaks eerily in the wind – it's wonderfully atmospheric. Guided tours are available from the main gate (book in advance through the website).

Entertainment

♥ Badeschiff

Arena Berlin, Eichenstrasse 4, (016 2545 1374, www.arena-berlin. de/badeschiff). U1 Schlesisches Tor, or S8, S9, S41, S42 Treptower Park. **Open** *May-Sept from 8am daily.* **Admission** *€5.50; €2-€3 reductions. No cards.* **Map** *p137 T9* ⑪ *Pool*
This former barge has been converted into a heated open-air swimming pool suspended in the Spree, with a beach area, deckchairs and a bar on the riverside. Swimming here is a unique experience. In winter, it becomes a covered sauna. The old warehouses that make up the Arena Berlin complex host events and club nights.

♥ Club der Visionaere

Am Flutgraben (6951 8942, www. clubdervisionaere.com). U1 Schlesisches Tor, or S8, S9, S41, S42 Treptower Park. **Open** *2pm-late Mon-Fri; noon-late Sat, Sun.* **Admission** *€5. No cards.* **Map** *p137 T10* ⑫ *Club*
One of the first and best, this summer-only canalside club is nestled under an enormous weeping willow. There's a small indoor dancefloor and a rickety open-air area of wooden decking with a large jetty stretching out across the water. You can drop in during the week for a beer, but the place comes to life at the weekend, filling up with an after-hour crowd, happy to chill, drink and dance the day away. Winter parties are now held in the nearby Hoppetosse boat.

❤ Soviet Memorial (Sowjetisches Ehrenmal am Treptower Park)

Treptower Park (www.treptower park.de). S8, S9, S41, S42 Treptower Park.

This Soviet war memorial (one of three in Berlin) and military cemetery is tucked away in beautiful Treptower Park. Architect Yakov Belopolsky's design to commemorate the loss of 80,000 Soviet soldiers was unveiled just four years after World War II ended, on 8 May 1949, and its epic scale and brawny symbolism made it a war memorial for all East Germany. During the GDR era, the monument was part of the obligatory itinerary for Westerners during trips to the East, and it also played its part in installing reverence for the Soviet Union among East Germans. Parts of the monument are created from the marble of Hitler's demolished New Chancellery.

On entering, you're greeted by statues of two kneeling soldiers, and the view unfolds across a geometrical expanse flanked by 16 stone sarcophagi, one for each of the 16 Soviet republics, which mark the burial site of the 5,000 Soviet soldiers who died in the final Battle of Berlin in spring 1945. At the end is a 12-m (40-ft) statue of a Soviet soldier holding a rescued German child and a massive lowered sabre, a broken swastika crushed beneath his boot. It is claimed that this depicts the deeds of Sergeant of Guards Nikolai Masalov, who risked a hail of German gunfire to save the life

of a three-year-old German girl. While the origins of the story are disputed, the symbolism cannot be lost on anyone: it's an arresting image, whether surrounded by foliage in summer, or bleak snow in winter. When you visit, don't be surprised to see flowers and miniature bottles of vodka inside the small memorial hall – even today visitors come to pay their respect to the fallen Soviets.

Neukölln

Neukölln is, arguably, Berlin's hippest district. With a vibrant ethnic mix dominated by the Turkish community, it's also home to plenty of bohemians and artists. While gritty bars and pubs are giving way to boutiques and high-end eateries, gentrification is patchy and has yet to creep far beyond the Ringbahn, the S-Bahn line that encircles Berlin's inner districts. At its northernmost tip, the area hugging the canal is known as Kreuzkölln and is fertile ground for charming cafés and restaurants. Following Weserstrasse south-east takes you past living-room bars and cocktail joints towards the picturesque 18th-century 'village' of Rixdorf. Cross Karl-Marx-Strasse westwards and you'll be in Schillerkiez, another café and dining hotspot that is gateway to the vast expanse of Tempelhofer Feld.

Best for kite-flying
Tempelhofer Feld *p158*

Best for R&R
Stadtbad Neukölln *p160*

Best budget eats
Azzam *p152*,
Türkischer Markt *p156*

Best desserts
Coda *p154*

Best vintage fashion
Aura *p156*, Sing Blackbird *p155*

Best late-night drinking
Geist im Glas *p155*,
Villa Neukölln *p159*

Kreuzkölln

The small strip bordering the canal just across from Kreuzberg was, until about 15 years ago, a quiet, mainly working-class area with a large Turkish population. But now, other languages are heard on the streets – English, French, Spanish, Swedish, Italian, Japanese – and it's full of charming cafés and restaurants. The canalside Maybachufer, home to the lively **Türkischer Markt** and **Nowkoelln Flowmarkt**, makes for a jolly stroll. From here, head south for espresso bars, and vintage fashion and wooden-toy shops. Quiet by day, Weserstrasse comes alive at night and is adjacent to the Levantine food paradise that is Sonnenallee.

Restaurants & cafés

Ankerklause €
Kottbusser Damm 104 (693 5649, www.anklerklause.de). U8 Schönleinstrasse. **Open** *4pm-late Mon; 10am-late Tue-Sun.* **No cards.** **Map** *p153 Q10* ❶ *Café*

Café by day and bar by night, the nautically themed Ankerklause has firmly resisted the temptation to gentrify itself, despite its enviable location, with balcony seating hanging over the canal. The coffee is average, and you might want to avoid drinking too much of the house wine, Chateau Migraine, but the breakfasts and cakes are hearty and delicious. Give market days a skip (Tuesdays and Fridays), when it's inevitably rammed.

❤ Azzam €
Sonnenallee 54 (3013 1541). U7, U8 Hermannplatz. **Open** *8am-midnight daily.* **No cards.** **Map** *p153 R11* ❷ *Lebanese*

People flock from all over the city to sample Azzam's houmous, made fresh throughout the day. The grilled minced lamb is perfectly seasoned, and the falafel a crunchy, sesame-speckled delight. You get a lot for your money too: each dish comes with raw veg, bitter olives, garlicky mayo or tahini sauce, and a basket of stacked pitta bread, which doubles as cutlery.

→ Getting around
Neukölln is well served by public transport, including the U7, U8 and various S-Bahn lines. Bus services include the notorious M41, a ride on which will immerse you in a perfect microcosm of the district's diverse communities.

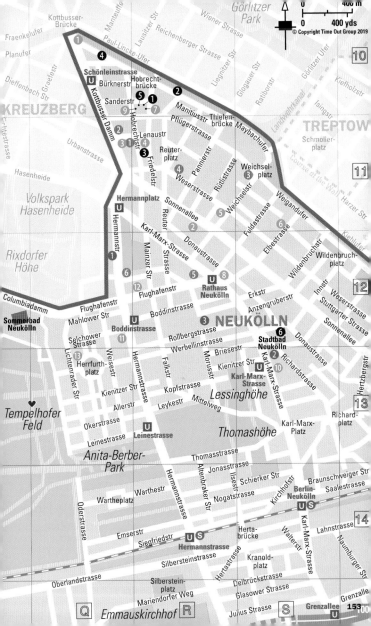

Ankerklause p152

Café Brick €
Lenaustrasse 1 (223 52595,
www.brick-coffee.com).
U7, U8 Hermannplatz; U8
Schönleinstrasse. **Open** *9am-10pm*
Mon-Thur; 9am-midnight Fri;
10am-midnight Sat; 10am-10pm
Sun. **Map** *p153 Q11* ❸ *Café*
A welcome addition to this end
of Kottbusser Damm, Café Brick
makes the best coffee around.
Small but beautiful, this cosy
neighbourhood spot offers delicious
and fairly priced cakes, bagels and
sandwiches. With free WiFi, a laid-
back vibe and a cheeky little cocktail
list, you may find yourself spending
a lot longer here than intended.

❤ Coda €€
Friedelstrasse 47 (9149 6396,
www.coda-berlin.com).
U7, U8 Hermannplatz; U8
Schönleinstrasse. **Open** *7pm-late*
Tue, Thur-Sat. **Map** *p153 R11* ❹
Desserts
Offering a menu composed entirely
of desserts and drinks, concept
restaurant Coda is due a Michelin
star any day now. Masterminded by
chef René Frank, with an emphasis

on the surprising and experimental,
plates are artfully composed using
the freshest ingredients. You'll
find no unctuous, stodgy puddings
here. Come by for the full blow-out
six-course tasting menu, which
pairs desserts with drinks (from
€98). Or head to the bar for a single
exquisite pud and a superlative
cocktail.

Dr To's €€
Weichselstrasse 54 (0152 16667022,
www.dr-tos.de). U7 Rathaus
Neukölln. **Open** *6pm-midnight*
Mon-Sat. **No cards.** **Map** *p153*
R11 ❺ *Asian*
Menus that describe their food
as 'Asian' are often a bad sign in
Berlin, but at Dr To's you'll find
thoughtful and creative tasting
plates, such as Japanese roast beef
with fresh mint and pomegranate,
and calamari salad with green
beans, seaweed and miso. Portions
are small so don't under order.

Eins44 €€€
Elbestrasse 28/29 (6298 1212,
www.eins44.com). U7 Rathaus
Neukölln. **Open** *12.30-2.30pm,*

*7pm-midnight (last orders
10.30pm) Tue-Fri; 7pm-midnight
(last orders 10.30pm) Sat.* **Map** *p153
S11* ⑥ *Fine dining*

Situated in a former schnapps
factory, Eins44 pairs industrial
design with fine dining. Proving
there's a place for high-end eating
in down-and-dirty Neukölln, the
restaurant serves both lunch and
dinner. Lunches tend towards the
classic, while in the evenings you
can select three (€46) or up to six
courses (€73) from flexible menus
featuring highly seasonal dishes,
such as venison with shiitake
mushrooms, radish and ginger, and
prawns served with yellow beetroot
and vermouth. Wine pairings are
recommended.

Fräulein Frost €

*Friedelstrasse 39 (9559 5521). U8
Schönleinstrasse.* **Open** *2-8pm
daily.* **No cards**. **Map** *p153 R10* ⑦
Ice-cream

The opening of the city's numerous
ice-cream parlours is Berliners'
favourite herald of spring, and
Fräulein Frost is one of the best.
Sledges provide outside seating
(and fun) for kids. Refresh yourself
with their signature GuZiMi
(cucumber, lemon, mint) or go
all out with a velvety pistachio,
a buttermilk orange, or Elvis's
favourite, the divine Graceland.

Imren Grill €

*Karl-Marx-Strasse 75 (no phone,
www.imren-grill.de). U7 Rathaus
Neukölln.* **Open** *9am-3am daily.*
No cards. **Map** *p153 R12* ⑧ *Imbiss*

Part of a small chain, Imren Grill
provides some of the best Turkish
snacks in town. Lunch specials
include baked fish with stew and
rice – but first things first: order
the classic *Döner im Brot* (kebab in
toasted bread), with its stuffing of
lamb grilled in neck fat, fresh salad,
sesame sauce and chilli flakes.

❤ Sing Blackbird €

*Sanderstrasse 11 (5484 5051, www.
facebook.com/singblackbird). U8
Schönleinstrasse.* **Open** *1-7pm
daily.* **No cards**. **Map** *p153 R10* ⑨
Café

An instant hit on opening, this
charming vegetarian café doubles
up as an excellent vintage clothes
shop, where you can bring in your
clothes for trade or credit. The
café does cakes and is also home
to the cold-pressed Daily Dose
juice company.

Bars & pubs

Galatea

*Lenaustrasse 5 (6583 4970, www.
facebook.com/GalateaWineBerlin).
U7, U8 Hermannplatz.* **Open**
*7.30pm-1am Wed, Thur;
7.30pm-2am Fri, Sat.* **Map** *p153
Q11* ①

A Spanish wine bar, Galatea
offers *pinchos* alongside a wine
list featuring a rounded selection
of Iberian wines. Friendly and
popular with local music lovers,
Galatea hosts live concerts a
few nights a week. Expect an
enthusiastic crowd and anything
from swing to folk and jazz.

❤ Geist im Glas

*Lenaustrasse 27 (0176 5533
0450 mobile, www.facebook.
com/geistimglas). U7, U8
Hermannplatz.* **Open** *7pm-late
Mon-Fri; 10am-late Sat, Sun.* **No
cards**. **Map** *p153 Q11* ②

The space here is built up with
wooden platforms, and there's
great attention to detail in the
decor, including Victorian curios
laid into the bar and an esoteric
toilet. The speciality is infused
alcohols, shots of which are poured
out of a giant bottle at the bar or
mixed into house cocktails, such
as the Geist Russian, a rich blend
of vodka infused with vanilla,
cinnamon, Kahlúa and cream. The

weekend brunch features *huevos rancheros*, chicken with waffles and fabulous bloody marys, but you'll need to get there early.

Nathanja & Heinrich

*Weichselstrasse 44 (no phone, www.nathanja-heinrich.de). U7 Rathaus Neukölln. **Open** 3pm-late Mon-Fri; 1pm-late Sat-Sun. **No cards**. **Map** p153 S11* ❸

Serving up a devastatingly good gin basil smash, Nathanja & Heinrich put equal effort into their beer selection. This beautiful bar – full of wood, mirrors and fresh flowers – hosts plenty of freelancers tapping at their MacBooks over coffee during the day. In the evenings, it's crowded with hipsters sipping mixed drinks late into the night.

SilverFuture

*Weserstrasse 206 (7563 4987, www.silverfuture.net). U7, U8 Hermannplatz. **Open** 5pm-2am Mon-Thur, Sun; 5pm-3am Fri, Sat. **Map** p153 R11* ❹

Neukölln is the new frontier of cool in Berlin, and this is its longstanding queer destination. 'You are now leaving the heteronormative zone' announces a playful sign above the bar – and it's not kidding. Fun for groups of any sexual or gender definition, this neighbourhood bar is welcoming, witty and charmingly rough around the edges.

Shops & services

❤ Aura

*Sanderstrasse 13 (178 148 4444 mobile, www.auraberin.com). Transport. **Open** 1-8pm Mon-Fri; noon-7pm Sat. **Map** p153 R10* ❶ *Vintage fashion*

Set next to two other vintage shops (Vintage Galore and Sing Blackbird; *see opposite and p155*), Aura has a back room bursting at the seams with a vast collection of vintage Japanese kimonos in jewel-like colours. The front room is devoted to vintage ladies' wear and accessories, including sunglasses. A good place for unusual finds and not over-priced.

Nowkoelln Flowmarkt

*Maybachufer between Friedelstrasse and Pannierstrasse (no phone, www.nowkoelln.de). U8 Schönleinstrasse. **Open** Apr-Nov 10am-6pm every 2nd Sun. Closed Dec-Mar. **No cards**. **Map** p153 R10* ❷ *Flea market*

This massively popular canalside flea market has grown considerably in recent years. Plenty of local trendsters hawk vintage apparel, and there's a strong food section with smoked fish sandwiches, *Käsespätzle* and hot apple pie on offer. Note that the market doesn't operate over winter.

Oye Kreuzkölln

*Friedelstrasse 49 (8937 2815, www.oye-records.com). U7, U8 Hermannplatz. **Open** 1-8pm Mon-Fri; 2-8pm Sat. **Map** p153 R11* ❸ *Music*

The southern branch of Oye Records, this small shop packs in a quality pick of house, techno and bass vinyl. Big-name DJs often do in-store events.

❤ Türkischer Markt

*Maybachufer between Kottbusser Damm and Hobrechtstrasse (no phone, www.tuerkenmarkt. de). U8 Schönleinstrasse. **Open** 11am-6.30pm Tue, Fri, Sat. **No cards**. **Map** p153 Q10* ❹ *Market*

On Tuesdays and Fridays, the Maybachufer buzzes with traders selling fruit, veg, organic and artisanal produce and street food. On Saturdays, the groceries give way to crafts, jewellery, a German-only wine stand, plants and haberdashery. The market continues to be very much a local

Türkischer Markt

This beautifully decorated single-screen cinema is hidden in plain sight by a row of concrete apartment buildings just up the hill from Hermannplatz. It opened in the 1920s under the name Rixdorfer Lichtspiele and charms down to the smallest details. The original Sarotti kiosk is a highlight, and the typically simple programme feels refreshing rather than limited.

Schillerkiez & Rixdorf

As rents shot up in Kreuzkölln, and following the closure of Tempelhof Airport in 2008, the now-peaceful **Schillerkiez** quickly became recognised as one of Berlin's most desirable neighbourhoods. With leafy Herrfurthplatz at its heart, Schillerkiez stretches from Hermannstrasse in the east to the awesome Tempelhofer Feld (*see p158*) in the west. Much quieter than raucous Weserstrasse, it's an area where Spanish restaurateurs, Swedish fashion designers and English bar-owners throw in their lot with the Turkish kebab shops and betting parlours.

East of the busy shopping street of Karl-Marx-Strasse is the historic and charming village of **Rixdorf**, centred around Richardplatz. Buildings dating from the original early 18th-century Bohemian settlement include a blacksmith and farmhouse, as well as the older 15th-century Bethlehemskirche. There's even a horse-and-carriage business still in operation, and the square regularly holds traditional events including a Christmas craft market.

For a break from sightseeing and window-shopping, take a dip at the marvellous **Stadtbad Neukölln**.

affair, and it's a great, if somewhat hectic, introduction to the neighbourhood. Once you've run the gamut of the market, you can relax with a beverage of choice and check out the buskers performing at the far end.

Vintage Galore
Sanderstrasse 12 (6396 3338, www.vintagegalore.de). U8 Schönleinstrasse. **Open** *2-8pm Wed-Fri; noon-6pm Sat.* **Map** *p153 R10* **5** *Homewares*
Vintage Galore is one of the best places to find authentic mid-century Danish furniture: it stocks everything from floor lamps to snack plates in the distinctive rounded teak style.

Entertainment
Neues Off
Hermannstrasse 20 (6270 9550, www.yorck.de). U7, U8 Hermannplatz. **Tickets** *€7-€9.* **Map** *p153 Q12* **1** *Cinema*

💙 Tempelhofer Feld

Main entrance at Herfurthstrasse and Oderstrasse (www.gruen-berlin.de/tempelhofer-feld). U8 Boddinstrasse. **Open** *dawn-dusk daily.* **Admission** *free.* **Tours** *€12; reductions from €6.* **Map** *p153 O12.*

Famous for its Nazi and Cold War history, Tempelhof Airport ceased operation in 2008. Now you can stroll down the runways where World War II Stuka dive-bombers took off and where, during the Berlin Airlift of 1948 when the Soviets blockaded West Berlin, the Western Powers landed supplies for the city's 2.5 million residents in one of the greatest feats in aviation history. Today, the 368-hectare open space of runways and grasslands is much enjoyed by – among others – walkers, kite-surfers, cyclists, runners, skaters and goshawks. There are designated sections for dogs to run free, basketball courts, a baseball field, beer gardens and even small allotments where Berliners can grow their own veg. Few experiences can compare with zooming down the central runway on two wheels, filling your lungs with the famously inspiring 'Berliner Luft'. However, the future of the *Feld* is far from secure. Controversially, Berliners voted against building on this vast space in a 2014 city-wide referendum, despite promises of affordable housing and a new library. In 2015, the airport buildings became temporary shelter for up to 3,000 refugees seeking sanctuary in Germany; the numbers have since dwindled to a few hundred. By 2018 it was unclear whether the huge hangars would return to hosting concerts and trade fairs, such as fashion extravaganza Bread & Butter, or be re-purposed to house a proposed creative district, visitor centre, rooftop gallery and a museum about the Berlin Airlift. One thing is certain, however: Berliners won't be giving up this grand open-air playground without a fight.

▶ *For details of all the park's entrances and opening hours, see the website. A comprehensive tour of the airfield can be booked at touren@berlinkompakt.net.*

Restaurants & cafés

Café Rix €-€€
*Karl-Marx-Strasse 141 (686 9020, www.caferix.de). U7 Karl-Marx-Strasse. **Open** 9am-midnight Mon-Thur; 9am-1am Fri, Sat; 10am-midnight Sun. **No cards**. Map p153 S13* ⑩ *Café*
Hidden behind the noisy shopping street of Karl-Marx-Strasse is this oasis – a grand café housed in a former 19th-century ballroom. There's a lovely courtyard where you can enjoy a coffee and cake or the breakfast menu, which is served until 5pm.

Isla €
*Hermannstrasse 37 (no phone, www.facebook.com/ Islacoffeeberlin). U8 Boddinstrasse. **Open** 7.30am-6pm Mon-Fri; 9am-6pm Sat, Sun. Map p153 Q12* ⑪ *Café*
A delicious brunch, lunch and coffee outfit, Isla has a zero-waste policy, a cool, minimalist interior and friendly waiting staff. Try the pea, houmous, spinach and cheese sandwiches. Weekdays are popular with the freelancer crowd, but the weekend laptop ban leaves space for brunching. In 2018, the staff were also hosting pop-up dining events.

Lavanderia Vecchia €€
*Flughafenstrasse 46 (6272 2152, www.lavanderiavecchia.de). U8 Boddinstrasse. **Open** noon-3pm, 7.30pm-midnight Tue-Fri; 7.30pm-midnight Sat. Map p153 R12* ⑫ *Italian*
This cute Italian joint has white linen strung along the ceiling, as a nod to the building's original role as a laundry house. Tricky to locate, it's in a courtyard set back from the street. There's just one set menu for dinner (booking essential), costing €65 a head including wine. Changing weekly, it features lots of classic antipasti (*vitello tonnato*, squid salad, sardines), followed by a pasta starter and homely mains, accompanied by a choice of wines from the Sabina region of Italy. Lunch is a more affordable affair.

La Pecora Nera €€
*Herrfurthplatz 6 (6883 2676, www.pecoraberlin.de). U8 Boddinstrasse. **Open** 6pm-late Tue-Sun. **No cards**. Map p153 Q13* ⑬ *Italian*
Schillerkiez really upped its restaurant game with the arrival of La Pecora Nera, a charming Venetian place with an authentic menu and excellent choice of wines. The speciality is *bigoli*, a buckwheat pasta peculiar to the Veneto region. There are fish specials on Fridays.

Bars & pubs

Klunkerkranich
*Karl-Marx-Strasse 66 (no phone, www.klunkerkranich. de). U7 Rathaus Neukölln. **Open** 4pm-2am; Wed-Fri; noon-2am Sat, Sun. **No cards**. Map p153 R12* ⑤
This rooftop bar with a view over the city is not easy to find but worth the effort. It's set on top of the Neukölln Arcaden shopping centre; to get there take a lift to the fifth-floor parking lot and walk up. Extremely popular in summer, Klunkerkranich hosts regular events; check the website to see what's on. When DJs are playing, expect a cover charge of €5.

❤ Villa Neukölln
*Hermannstrasse 233 (6272 8948, www.villaneukoelln. de). U8 Boddinstrasse. **Open** 4.30pm-2.30am Mon, Tue; 4.30pm-4am Wed, Thur; 2.30pm-4am Fri-Sun. **No cards**. Map p153 Q12* ⑥
A much-loved institution, Villa Neukölln is the definition of shabby-chic. With two front rooms, one a haven for smokers,

and plenty of street-side seating in good weather, the real draw is the old ballroom out back. Part the velvet curtains to find yourself in a different era. Hosting swing nights, concerts and dancing lessons, the Villa scores high on character and low on attitude. Pop in for a drink or check the website to see what's on.

Shops & services

♥ Stadtbad Neukölln
Ganghoferstrasse 3 (682 4980, www.berlinerbaeder.de/baeder/ stadtbad-neukoelln). U7 Rathaus Neukölln. **Open** *sauna 10am-10.30pm Mon-Sun; pool varies Mon-Sun.* **Admission** *sauna from €16, reductions €13. Pool from €3.50, reductions €2. No cards.* **Map** *p153 S12* **6**
Built for Berlin's workers and first opened in 1914, Stadtbad Neukölln is a jewel. Architect Reinhold Kiehl drew inspiration from the ancient thermal baths of classical Rome, and the two large pools and assortment of saunas, steam rooms and plunge pools feature statues of Greek gods, pillars, mosaics, fountains, cupolas and a café-bar. Splashing about in such palatial surroundings is an unforgettable experience. While the changing rooms are basic, the sauna complex, is excellent, and though they're not quite fit for serious lane swimming, Stadtbad Neukölln's two pools are perfect for families and recreational swimmers. Check the hours on the website before showing up, though, since Berlin's pools are infamous for last-minute schedule changes.

Entertainment

Sameheads
Richardstrasse 10 (7012 1060, www. sameheads.com). U7 Karl-Marx-Strasse. **Open** *6pm-late Tue-Sat.*

Admission free-€3. No cards. **Map** *p153 S13* **2** *Club*
A friendly international hipster enclave that steadfastly refuses to be pigeonholed. What began as an offbeat fashion boutique quickly evolved into a bar and late-night party space. Vintage threads are still on sale in the day, while all manner of antics kick off as the sun goes down. You might stumble upon any or all of the following: comedy open mics, art shows, pub quizzes, film screenings and sweaty raves. It's all masterminded by three British brothers – Nathan, Leo and Harry – aka the Sameheads.

SchwuZ
Rollbergstrasse 26 (5770 2270, www.schwuz.de). U7 Rathaus Neukölln; U8 Boddinstrasse. **Open** *varies.* **Admission** *varies. No cards.* **Map** *p166 R12* **3** *LGBT club*
One of Berlin's longest-running dance institutions, SchwuZ moved into the old Kindl brewery in 2013. A variety of mainstream and more underground events takes place throughout the week attracting a mixed and ready-to-mingle crowd who take full advantage of the warehouse-like space and multiple dancefloors.

In the know
Hufeisensiedlung

Fans of modern architecture should head far south into Britz to check out the Hufeisensiedlung (Lowise-Reuter-Ring, U7 Parchimer Allee), one of six modernist housing estates in the city to be listed as a UNESCO World Heritage Site. Built in the late 1920s by Bruno Taut and Martin Wagner, the large horseshoe-shaped complex contains 1,200 flats overlooking a large green space. Many of the flats retain their original Bauhaus fittings and distinctive brightly coloured doors.

Charlottenburg & Schöneberg

The old heart of West Berlin runs all the way from the Tiergarten to Spandau, from Tegel Airport in the north to wealthy, residential Wilmersdorf in the south. Often derided as staid and stagnant in comparison to its edgier eastern neighbours, Charlottenburg is undeniably bourgeois – the fur coat/small dog quotient is high – but it's far from boring. As well as charming hotels and lovely squares, it boasts the magnificent Schloss Charlottenburg and the Kurfürstendamm shopping street as well as some odd seedy little corners. East of Wilmersdorf is Schöneberg, also well-heeled and residential. Berlin's long-established gay scene is focused on its northern reaches. It's also where you'll find department store KaDeWe, Berlin's answer to Harrods.

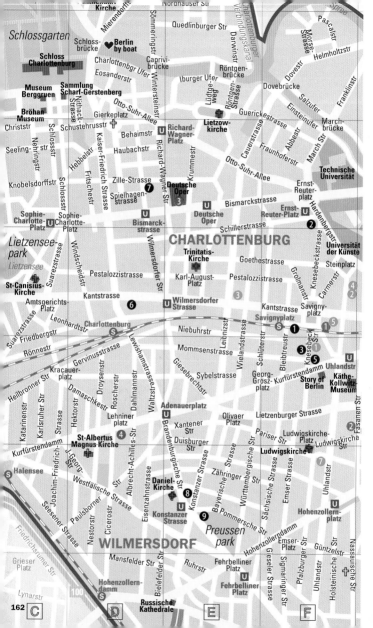

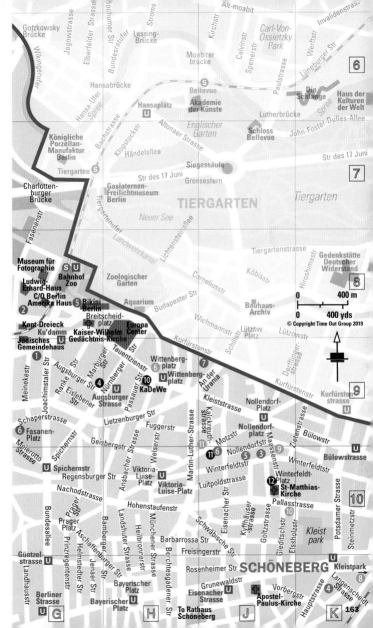

Best museums
Museum Berggruen *p171*,
Story of Berlin *p165*

Best tastes of Thailand
Thai Park *p173*

Best department stores
KaDeWe *p41*, Manufactum *p167*

Best historic drinking dens
Diener Tattersall *p167*, Neues
Ufer *p175*

Best old-time shops
Erich Hamann Bittere
Schokoladen *p173*, Harry
Lehmann *p172*

Best brunch
1900 Café Bistro *p166*, Benedict
p172, Café Aroma *p174*

Best landmarks
Kaiser-Wilhelm-Gedächtnis-
Kirche *p165*, Schloss
Charlottenburg *p171*

Bahnhof Zoo & the Ku'damm

During the Cold War, **Bahnhof Zoologischer Garten** (Zoo Station) was the main entry point to the West. It was a spooky anomaly: located in the middle of West Berlin but policed by the East Berlin authorities, who controlled the intercity rail system. It was also a seedy hangout for junkies and winos, and served as the central backdrop to the infamous cult film *Christiane F*. Since then, attempts have been made to spruce up the area, including the redevelopment of the **Bikini Berlin** complex, which backs onto the zoo. The area's most notable landmark is the **Kaiser-Wilhelm-Gedächtnis-Kirche**; south-west from the church stretches the **Kurfürstendamm** (Ku'damm), the main shopping street in West Berlin. For more shops, chic restaurants and cafés, explore Kantstrasse, Savignyplatz and Bleibtreustrasse.

Sights & museums

C/O Berlin Amerika Haus
Hardenbergstrasse 22-24 (284 441 662, www.co-berlin.org). U2, U9, S5, S7, S75 Zoologischer Garten. **Open** *Exhibition and bookshop 11am-8pm daily. Café 10am-8pm daily.* **Admission** *€10; €6 reductions.* **Map** *p162 G8.*
Built by the US in the 1950s to promote transatlantic cultural exchange, Amerika Haus housed embassy offices until the new Pariser Platz site was completed in 2006. Since 2014, following extensive renovations, it has been an exhibition space for the much-loved photography gallery C/O Berlin, which exhibits museum-quality photography and visual media from around the world.

➜ **Getting around**
Charlottenburg is well-served by U-Bahn, S-Bahn and bus lines. The 15-minute journey by S-Bahn from Mitte to Charlottenburg is a treat, offering views over Museum Island, the River Spree, Tiergarten and the zoo; join the S5, S7 or S75 and jump off at Zoologischer Garten or Savignyplatz. Nollendorfplatz is the main U-Bahn station serving north Schöneberg; for Kleistpark and around, use the U7.

❤ Kaiser-Wilhelm-Gedächtnis-Kirche

Breitscheidplatz (218 5023, www.gedaechtniskirche.com). U2, U9, S5, S7, S75 Zoologischer Garten. **Open** *9am-7pm daily. Guided tours 10.15am-3.15pm hourly Mon, Fri, Sat; 12.15-3.15pm hourly Tue-Thur, Sun.* **Admission** *free.* **Map** *p162 G8.*

The Kaiser Wilhelm Memorial Church is one of Berlin's best-known sights and one of its most dramatic at night. The neo-romanesque structure was built in 1891-95 by Franz Schwechten in honour of – you guessed it – Kaiser Wilhelm I. Much of the building was destroyed during an Allied air raid in 1943. These days, the church serves as a stark reminder of the damage done by the war, although some might argue it improved what was originally a profoundly ugly building. Inside the rump of the church is a glittering art nouveau-style ceiling mosaic depicting members of the House of Hohenzollern on pilgrimage towards the cross. There's also a cross made from nails from Coventry's war-destroyed cathedral, and photos of the church before and after the war. The wrap-around blue stained glass in the chapel is simply stunning. Guided tours in English can be booked.

Käthe-Kollwitz-Museum

Fasanenstrasse 24 (882 5210, www.kaethe-kollwitz.de). U1, U9 Kurfürstendamm. **Open** *11am-6pm daily.* **Admission** *€7; €4 reductions; free under-18s. No cards.* **Map** *p162 F9.*

Käthe Kollwitz's powerful, deeply empathetic work embraces the full spectrum of life, from the joy of motherhood to the pain of death (with a particular fascination for the latter). A committed socialist and pacifist, she is held in great esteem by Berliners. The collection includes her famous lithograph *Brot!*, as well as charcoal sketches, woodcuts and sculptures, all displayed to impressive effect in this grand villa off the Ku'damm. For refreshments, the Café im Literaturhaus next door is a lovely spot.

Museum für Fotografie

Jebensstrasse 2 (266 424242, www.smb.museum/mf). U2, U9, S5, S7, S75 Zoologischer Garten. **Open** *11am-7pm Tue, Wed, Fri-Sun; 11am-8pm Thur.* **Admission** *€10; €5 reductions.* **Map** *p162 G8.*

Shortly before his death in 2004, Berlin-born Helmut Newton – who served his apprenticeship elsewhere in Charlottenburg at the studio of Yva – donated over 1,000 of his nude and fashion photographs to the city and provided funds towards the creation of a new gallery. This museum, doubling as a home for the Helmut Newton Foundation (www.helmutnewton.com), was the result. Housed in a former casino behind Bahnhof Zoo, it's now the largest photographic gallery in the city. The ground and first floors are dedicated to Newton's work. Six colossal nudes, modelled on 1930s Nazi propaganda photos, glare down at you on entering the building and set the tone for the big, garish, confrontational pieces that dominate the exhibits. The top floor has changing shows on the history of photography, drawn from the collection of the Berlin State Museums.

❤ Story of Berlin

Kurfürstendamm 207-208 (8872 0100, www.story-of-berlin.de). U1 Uhlandstrasse. **Open** *10am-8pm daily; last entry 6pm.* **Admission** *€12; €5-€9 reductions.* **Map** *p162 F9.*

If you're interested in the city's turbulent history, the Story of Berlin is a novel way of approaching it. The huge space is filled with well-designed rooms and multimedia exhibits created by a wide range of authors, designers and film and stage specialists, telling Berlin's story from its founding in 1237 to the present day. The 20 themed displays are labelled in both German and English and are fairly child-friendly. Underneath all this is a massive nuclear shelter. Built by the Allies during the 1970s, the low-ceilinged, oppressive bunker is still fully functional and can hold up to 3,500 people. Guided tours of the bunker are included in the price of the ticket.

Story of Berlin p165

Restaurants & cafés

You don't have to stay at the **25hours Hotel** (see p188) in order to relish the fine views and the excellent Middle Eastern nosh at its top-floor restaurant, **Neni**.

❤ 1900 Café Bistro €
Knesebeckstrasse 76 (8871 5871). S5, S7, S75 Savignyplatz. **Open** *8am-7pm Mon-Fri; 9am-7pm Sun.* **No cards.** **Map** *p162 F9* ❶ *Café*
Booking is recommended for weekend brunch at this kitschy café, where plates overflow with cold cuts, cheese and fruit. Traditional tray-baked crumble cakes and a salad menu are also available.

Arirang €
Uhlandstrasse 194 (4502 1248). U2, U9, S5, S7, S75 Zoologischer Garten. **Open** *noon-11pm daily.* **No cards.** **Map** *p162 F8* ❷ *Korean*
This fabulous restaurant used to be a closely guarded secret in a shabby Wedding location, but in 2014 it moved to Charlottenburg. There's nothing special about the surroundings or the service, but the food is authentic. As is the norm in Korea, dishes are served with a selection of kimchi, pickled salads and rice, so take care not to over-order. The fiery kimchi and noodle stew, and the spring onion and seafood pancakes are perfect for sharing.

Aroma €-€€
Kantstrasse 35 (3759 1628). S5, S7, S75 Savignyplatz. **Open** *noon-2.30am daily.* **No cards.** **Map** *p162 E8* ❸ *Chinese*
If you're hankering for a dim sum fix, head to Aroma in Berlin's mini Chinatown on Kantstrasse. You can enjoy assorted dumplings in the traditional, genteel tea-time style of *yum cha* or as part of a full dinner with more substantial plates. Go with classics such as *har gao* (steamed shrimp dumplings), fried turnip cakes or *cheong fun*, pillowy steamed rice noodle rolls stuffed with prawn or beef.

Glass €€€-€€€€
Uhlandstrasse 195 (5471 0861, www.glassberlin.de). U2, U9, S5, S7, S75 Zoologischer Garten. **Open** *6-11pm Tue-Sat.* **Map** *p162 F8* ❹ *Fine dining*
Inside a brutalist apartment building, chef Gal Ben-Moshe spins straw into culinary gold. The Arab-

influenced set menu of six to eight courses features starters impaled on smoking cinnamon sticks; soups adorned with savoury sorbets; and finely tuned, playful desserts. Wine pairings are available.

Schwarzes Café €-€€

Kantstrasse 148 (313 8038, www. schwarzescafe-berlin.de). S5, S7, S75 Savignyplatz. **Open** *24 hours Wed-Mon; from 10am Tue.* **No cards.** **Map** *p162 F8* ❺ *Café*
A Charlottenburg institution, Schwarzes Café is open round the clock, closing only between 3am and 10am on Tuesday mornings. The menu features hearty middle-European fare, including *Schnitzel* and *Knödel*. If you come to eat, you won't leave hungry. Noisy and sociable, this is an unpretentious spot with a big student following.

Witty's €

Wittenbergplatz 5 (6391 1666, www.wittys-berlin.de). U1, U2, U3 Wittenbergplatz. **Open** *10am-midnight Mon-Sat; 11am-midnight Sun.* **No cards.** **Map** *p162 H9* ❻ *Imbiss*
Yearning for an authentic sausage fix but concerned about the industrially processed content of your average Imbiss offering? Look no further. Witty's features a fully organic menu of Berlin staples, including *Currywurst* and fries. Gluten-free options available.

Bars & pubs

♥ Diener Tattersall

Grolmanstrasse 47 (881 5329, www.diener-berlin.de). S5, S7, S75 Savignyplatz. **Open** *6pm-late daily.* **No cards.** **Map** *p162 F8* ❶
Ex-boxer Franz Diener took this place over in 1954 and, with his artist friends, turned it into one of the central hubs of West Berlin cultural life. The chattering classes flocked here from concert halls and theatres to gossip and to spot off-duty actors drinking the night away. In a city fascinated with *Ostalgie* and the rapid rhythms of gentrification, raise a toast (or four) to this previous age of West Berlin bohemians.

Shops & services

For fashion and designer homewares, check out the permanent retailers and pop-ups in **Bikini Berlin**; highlights include the Artek Concept Store and Samsø & Samsø.

Bücherbogen

Stadtbahnbogen 593, Savignyplatz (3186 9511). S5, S7, S75 Savignyplatz. **Open** *10am-8pm Mon-Fri; 10am-6pm Sat.* **No cards.** **Map** *p162 F8* ❶ *Books*
An art-lover's dream, this massive bookshop takes up three whole railway arches, with rows of books on art, design and architecture, plus exhibition catalogues and lots of rare or out-of-print volumes.

♥ Manufactum

Hardenbergstrasse 4-5 (2403 3844, www.manufactum.de). U1, U2 Ernst-Reuter-Platz. **Open** *10am-8pm Mon-Fri; 10am-6pm Sat.* **Map** *p162 F7* ❷ *Department store*
Founded in 1988 by a high-profile Green Party politician as a counterpoint to cheap mass production, Manufactum quickly developed a cult following for its ironic catalogue blurbs and impeccable selection of products. It continues in the same vein today, with an emphasis on German-made goods that demonstrate high production values, classic design and sustainability. Prices reflect the quality. Don't miss the on-site bakery and café, **Brot & Butter**, which serves vast sourdough loaves, almond croissants and small lunch specials.

❤ Berlin by boat

While Berlin's claims to be the 'Prussian Venice' may meet with deserved scepticism, the German capital is still an engagingly watery place. The River Spree meanders through Berlin on its journey from the Czech Republic to the Elbe, creating a maze of interlocking rivers, lakes and canals that are an integral part of the German capital.

A range of city-centre tours is offered by **Stern und Kreis** (www. sternundkreis.de), **Reederei Winkler** (www.reederei winkler. de) and **Reederei Riedel** (www. reederei-riedel.de). Circular tours of the Spree and the Landwehrkanal usually last three to four hours and take in the city's top sights, including the Reichstag and Museum Island; they also pass under Berlin's numerous bridges, including the picturesque Oberbaumbrücke. Passengers can hop on and off at landing stages en route, and basic food and drink is served on board. For a complete tour, expect to pay around €19 per adult. Shorter trips and evening sailings are also available. There are convenient landing stages at the Schlossbrücke in Charlottenburg, at the Haus der Kulturen der Welt in Tiergarten, at Märkisches Ufer, at Jannowitzbrücke and in the Nikolaiviertel. Note that many services operate only from mid-March to late November.

A short train journey (20-30 minutes) to Wannsee (*see p183*) offers more boating opportunities. Stern & Kreis's Seven Lakes Trip (7-Seen-Rundfahrt) slides gently past the handsome mansions surrounding the Kleiner Wannsee. Or you can take a round trip to Potsdam and Sanssouci. For further details, consult the operator's website. However, savvy visitors on a budget may prefer to take advantage of the hourly year-round **BVG ferry** from Wannsee to Kladow, which is part of the local transport network; a standard A-B zone ticket (€2.80) is valid for both the S-Bahn journey to Wannsee and the ferry. It's a beautiful ride, and there's even a decent pub by the pier in a quasi-rural setting on the other side. Other BVG passenger ferries, including a rowing boat service, operate on and around the Müggelsee (*see p182*).

Marga Schoeller Bücherstube

Knesebeckstrasse 33 (881 1112, www.margaschoeller.de). S5, S7, S75 Savignyplatz. **Open** *9.30am-7pm Mon-Wed; 9.30am-8pm Thur, Fri; 9.30am-6pm Sat.* **Map** *p162 F9* ❸
Books

This bookshop (established 1930) won renown when owner Marga shook a fist at the Nazi regime by removing all Nazi-related texts from her shelves. In the '70s, it relocated down the road from its original Ku'damm spot. English books are displayed in an inviting alcove. It goes further than most to provide new non-fiction titles, from philosophical and political texts to theatre studies.

Michas Bahnhof

Nürnberger Strasse 24A (218 6611, www.michas-bahnhof.de). U3 Augsburger Strasse. **Open** *10am-6.30pm Mon-Fri; 10am-3.30pm Sat.* **Map** *p162 G9* ❹
Gifts & souvenirs

Unsurprisingly in such an engineering-mad country, Berlin has some fantastic model-train shops, and Michas Bahnhof is one of the best. The small space is rammed with engines, old and new, from around the world – and everything that goes with them.

Steiff Galerie

Kurfürstendamm 38 (8862 5006, www.steiff.de). U1 Uhlandstrasse. **Open** *10am-8pm Mon-Sat.* **Map** *p162 F9* ❺ *Gifts & souvenirs*

Inventor of the teddy bear (so named in the US after a hunting story involving 'Teddy' Roosevelt), Steiff has been in business since the late 19th century. The company's whole range of artisan animals (not just bears) are here. Prices are aimed at adult hobbyists rather than kids.

Entertainment

Astor Film Lounge

Kurfürstendamm 255 (883 8551, www.astor-filmlounge.de). U1, U9 Kurfürstendamm. **Tickets** *€12-€18.* **Map** *p162 G9* ❶ *Cinema*

The first 'premium cinema' in Germany offers a luxury cinematographic experience, complete with a welcome cocktail, doorman and valet parking. The building dates from 1948, when a café was converted into a small cinema called the KiKi (Kino im Kindl). It was later redesigned and renamed the Filmpalast and become one of West Berlin's classiest *Kinos*. After thorough renovations and another name change, it's still a grand example of 1950s movie-going luxury, with an illuminated glass ceiling, comfortable seats and a gong to announce the show.

Delphi Filmpalast am Zoo

Kantstrasse 12A (312 1026, www.delphi-filmpalast.de). U2, U9, S5, S7, S75 Zoologischer Garten. **Tickets** *€7-€10.* **Map** *p162 G8* ❷ *Cinema*

The Delphi was originally a 1920s dance palace. Bombed out during the war, it was rebuilt as the Delphi Filmpalast and became a major Cinemascope and 70mm venue, where films such as *Ben Hur* and *My Fair Lady* would run for up to a year. It's the last cinema in the city still to have balcony seating. Now part of the excellent Yorck cinema group, it shows mainly new German arthouse films. Just next door, at Kantstrasse 10, is another fabulous Yorck cinema, **Delphi LUX** (322 931040), which serves as a designated audience cinema for the European Film Awards.

Deutsche Oper

Bismarckstrasse 35 (343 8401, tickets 3438 4343, www. deutscheoperberlin.de). U2 Deutsche Oper. **Box office** *11am-7pm Mon-Sat; 10am-2pm Sun; or online.* **Tickets** *vary.* **Map** *p162 E7* ❸ *Opera*

With roots dating from 1912, the Deutsche Oper built its present 1,900-seat hall in 1961, just in time to carry the operatic torch for West Berlin during the Wall years. Since reunification it has lost out in profile to the grander Staatsoper. Following the death of former long-time intendant Götz Friedrich in 2000, a revolving door of German opera luminaries has struggled to provide the house with a distinct artistic profile, but it retains a solid reputation for productions of the classics, including by the Staatsballett Berlin. Dietmar Schwarz has been in charge since 2012. Discounted tickets are available half an hour before performances.

Schaubühne

Kurfürstendamm 153 (890 023, www.schaubuehne.de). U7 Adenauerplatz, or S3, S5, S7, S9 Charlottenburg. **Box office** *11am-6.30pm Mon-Sat; 3-6.30pm Sun.* **Tickets** *€7-€43; €9 reductions.* **Map** *p162 D9* ❹ *Theatre*

Of the Big Five, the Schaubühne is most popular with English audiences and has a long history of Anglophile collaboration. It was the theatre that established Brits Mark Ravenhill and Sarah Kane as Germany's favourite playwrights. Under artistic director Thomas Ostermeier, the house style treads a happy medium between German radicalism and British realism, which, coupled with the frequent surtitling of performances in English, makes it an ideal starting point for anyone looking for an introduction to German theatre.

Zoo Palast

Hardenbergstrasse 29A (01805 222 966 premium phone, www. zoopalast-berlin.de). U2, U9, S5, S7, S75 Zoologischer Garten. **Tickets** *€11-€12.50; 3D films €13-€17.50.* **Map** *p162 G8* ❺ *Cinema*

In the Cold War, West Berlin premières were always held in this striking 1950s building, which in a different reincarnation during the Nazi era was the venue for Albert Speer's most spectacular light shows. Much like the surrounding Zoo area, it fell into disrepair after 1990 but reopened in late 2013 with seven new screens showing traditional multiplex blockbuster fare.

Schloss Charlottenburg & around

The palace that gives Charlottenburg its name lies a few kilometres north-west of Bahnhof Zoo. In contrast to the commercialism and crush of the latter, this part of the city is wealthy and serene. Intended as Berlin's answer to Versailles, **Schloss Charlottenburg** was built in the 17th century as a summer palace for Queen Sophie-Charlotte. Nearby are some impressive museums of 20th-century art.

Sights & museums

Bröhan-Museum

Schlossstrasse 1A (3269 0600, www. broehan-museum.de). U2 Sophie-Charlotte-Platz; U7 Richard-Wagner-Platz. **Open** *10am-6pm Tue-Sun.* **Admission** *€8; €5 reductions; free under-18s. Special exhibitions varies.* **Map** *p162 C6.*

This quiet museum contains three floors of international art nouveau and art deco pieces that businessman Karl Bröhan began collecting in the 1960s and donated to the city of Berlin on his 60th birthday. The paintings, sculptures, furniture, porcelain, glass and silver date from 1890 to 1939 and are thoughtfully laid out, although the labelling is in German only. Among the pieces of fine art, Hans Baluschek's paintings of social life in the 1920s and '30s, and Willy Jaeckel's portraits of women are the highlights. The furniture is superb too.

❤ Museum Berggruen

Westlicher Stülerbau, Schlossstrasse 1 (266 424 242, www. smb.museum/mb). U2 Sophie-Charlotte-Platz; U7 Richard-Wagner-Platz. **Open** *10am-6pm Tue-Fri; 11am-6pm Sat, Sun.* **Admission** *€10; €5 reductions.* **Map** *p162 C6.*
Heinz Berggruen was one of Picasso's dealers in Paris and went on to become a major modernist collector. In 2000, he sold his entire collection to Berlin for a knockdown $100 million; it is now displayed across three easily manageable circular floors. Inevitably, the astonishingly prolific and diverse output of Pablo Picasso dominates. Some of the many highlights include the 1942 *Reclining Nude* and his late-period *The Woman of Algiers* (1955). Works by Braque, Giacometti, Cézanne and Matisse also feature, while most of the second floor is given over to the wonderful paintings of Paul Klee.

Sammlung Scharf-Gerstenberg

Schlossstrasse 70 (266 424242, www.smb.museum/ en/museums-institutions/ sammlung-scharf-gerstenberg). U2 Sophie-Charlotte-Platz. **Open** *10am-6pm Tue-Fri; 11am-6pm Sat, Sun.* **Admission** *€10; €5 reductions.* **Map** *p162 C6.*
Housed in the eastern Stüler building and in the Marstall

(stables wing) opposite Schloss Charlottenburg, this gallery exhibits works by the Surrealists and their forerunners. Featured artists range from Piranesi, Goya and Redon to Dalí, Magritte and Ernst. The original collection was amassed by Otto Gerstenberg around 1910 and added to by his grandsons, Walter and Dieter Scharf.

❤ Schloss Charlottenburg

Spandauer Damm 10-22 (0331 969 4200, www.spsg.de). U2 Sophie-Charlotte-Platz; U7 Richard-Wagner-Platz. **Open** *Apr-Oct 10am-5.30pm Tue-Sun. Nov-Mar 10am-4.30pm Tue-Sun. Belvedere & Mausoleum closed Nov-Mar.* **Admission** *Combined ticket €17; €13 reductions. Gardens free.* **Map** *p162 C6.*
Friedrich III (later King Friedrich I) built this sprawling palace and gardens in 1695-99 as a summer home for his queen, Sophie-Charlotte. Severely damaged in World War II, it has been restored and is now the largest surviving Hohenzollern palace.

The easiest option is to buy the combination ticket, which allows entrance to all parts of the palace – with the exception of the state and private apartments of King Friedrich I and Queen Sophie-Charlotte in the Altes Schloss (Old Palace), which are only accessible on a guided tour (€8, €5 reductions).

The one must-see is the Neue Flügel (New Wing). The upper floor contains the state apartments of Frederick the Great and the winter chambers of his successor, King Friedrich Wilhelm II. The contrast between the two sections is fascinating: Frederick's rooms are all excessive rococo exuberance, while Friedrich Wilhelm's far more modestly proportioned rooms reflect the more restrained classicism of his time.

The Neue Pavillon (New Pavilion) was built by Karl Friedrich Schinkel in 1824 for Friedrich Wilhelm III – the king liked it so much that he chose to live here in preference to the main palace. Inside is an excellent exhibition on the architect's legacy.

The huge, impeccably kept gardens are a major draw. Laid out in 1697 in formal French style, they were reshaped in a more relaxed English style in the 19th century. Here you'll find the Belvedere (built in 1788 as a teahouse, now containing a collection of Berlin porcelain) and the sombre Mausoleum (containing the tombs of Friedrich Wilhelm III, his wife Queen Luise, Kaiser Wilhelm I and his wife).

Shops & services

♥ Harry Lehmann

Kantstrasse 106 (324 3582, www. parfum-individual.de). S5, S7, S75 Charlottenburg; U7 Wilmersdorfer Strasse. **Open** *9am-6.30pm Mon-Fri; 9am-2pm Sat.* **No cards.** **Map** *p162 D8* ❻ *Perfume*
In business since 1926, Harry Lehmann's is a jewel of a store where perfumes are sold by weight. Famously, Marlene Dietrich was a fan of the lavender scent. You can choose your own favourite from the rows of glass flacons, or the staff will concoct you a mix to take away in a beautiful retro bottle.

Rogacki

Wilmersdorfer Strasse 145-146 (343 8250, www.rogacki.de). U7 Bismarckstrasse. **Open** *9am-6pm Mon-Wed; 9am-7pm Thur; 8am-7pm Fri; 8am-4pm Sat.* **Map** *p162 D7* ❼ *Food & drink*
A trip to Rogacki, a German-Polish delicatessen-cum-food market, is like stepping back in time. The draw here is the fish: specialities include *Bratherings* (fried and

brined herring), *Rollmops* (pickled herrings rolled around gherkin) and *Senfgurken* (white gherkins from Spreewald). Alongside the excellent quality produce, you'll find gourmet islands inside where you can pull up a stool and order a *Fischbrötchen* or oysters and wine for much less than you'll pay at the KaDeWe. Excellent for people-watching!

Wilmersdorf

The middle-class residential area of Wilmersdorf is a great place to get a feel for how the other half of Berlin lives, away from the street art and piercings of the east. The area was farmland until the mid 19th century, when a property boom created the *Millionenbauern* (peasant millionaires). It became an affluent neighbourhood and was home to a large Jewish population during the Weimar years.

Visit at the weekend to explore the flea market on Fehrbelliner Platz and the enormous informal Thai food market in the **Preussen Park**.

▶ *From Fehrbelliner Platz, it's a five-minute bus journey (bus 115) to the Brücke-Museum (see p180).*

Restaurants & cafés

♥ Benedict €€

Uhlandstrasse 49 (9940 40997, www.benedict-breakfast.de). U3, U9 Spichernstrasse. **Open** *Restaurant 24hrs daily. Bakery 7.30am-6.30pm daily.* **Map** *p162 F10* ❼ *Breakfast*
Brunch is the quintessential Berlin meal, but in recent years locals have been hankering after something more than the eggs, cold cuts and cheese that make up the typical offering. Since it opened in 2017, Benedict has been overwhelming Berliners with its

Thai Park

menu, which fuses the flavours of Tel Aviv and New York, and serves them with European flair. Eggs Benedict may be the titular dish, but the menu runs from *shakshuka* (baked eggs in tomato sauce), to a Russian breakfast, to the most mouth-watering pancakes in town.

Bars & pubs

Rum Trader
Fasanenstrasse 40 (881 1428). U3, U9 Spichernstrasse. Open varies. No cards. Map p162 F9 ②
Subtitled the 'Institute for Advanced Drinking', this tiny bar is a Berlin classic, thanks to its eccentric owner, Gregor Scholl, who is ever present, smartly dressed in bow tie and waistcoat. There is no menu: Scholl will ask which spirit you like and whether you want something '*süss oder sauer*' (sweet or sour). Don't waste his time (or talent) by asking for a mojito. Hugely atmospheric and

with room for only 15 guests, Rum Trader is best avoided if you're on a budget.

Shops & services

♥ Erich Hamann Bittere Schokoladen
Brandenburgische Strasse 17 (873 2085, www.hamann-schokolade. de). U7 Konstanzer Strasse. Open 9am-6pm Mon-Fri; 9am-1pm Sat. Map p162 E10 ⑧ *Food & drink*
This beautiful Bauhaus building houses Berlin's oldest functioning chocolate factory. Everything is still done with an eye to period detail: chocolate thins are boxed by hand in beautifully old-fashioned packaging, while the signature chocolate 'bark' is still made in the original purpose-built machine.

♥ Thai Park
Preussenpark. U7 Konstanzer Strasse. Open varies. Admission free. Map p162 E10 ⑨ *Food market*
Thai Park began when Thai Berliners started an impromptu foodie get-together in this sedate little park. When other visitors to the park started asking if the food was for sale, the Thai locals saw a business opportunity and set up shop from their picnic blankets, knocking up authentic pad thai or green papaya salad with nothing more than portable gas burners and Tupperwares full of ingredients. The city authorities turned a blind eye, and, soon, what had been a few noodle and saté stands had burgeoned into the largest Thai street-food market outside Asia. Still an informal set-up with no official hours, Thai Park is busiest on Sundays, though stalls sometimes open on weekdays as well in good weather. With a carnival atmosphere – helped by the caipirinhas and massages on offer alongside all the food – this is a great place to bring a blanket and

savour delicious soups, dumplings and deep-fried treats alfresco. Children romp, clubgoers wearing shades feed their hangovers, while the Thais catch up on the week's gossip. In 2018, there was talk of the city authorities shutting down the whole operation but, to date, the entrepreneurs of Thai Park continue to cook, indifferent to the controversy, in true Berlin style.

Entertainment

Bar jeder Vernunft

Spiegelzelt, Schaperstrasse 24 (883 1582, www.bar-jeder-vernunft.de). U3, U9 Spichernstrasse. **Box office** *noon-6.30pm Mon-Fri; 3-5.30pm Sat, Sun. Performances from 7pm daily.* **Tickets** *€12.50-€29.50.* **Map** *p162 G9* ⑥ *Cabaret*

Some of Berlin's most celebrated entertainers perform in this snazzy circus tent of many mirrors, which takes in shows, comedy, cabaret, literature and theatre. Dinner is an extra €29. It's not the cheapest night out, but it'll be worth it if the place revives its much-lauded production of *Cabaret*.

Schöneberg

Geographically and atmospherically, Schöneberg lies between Charlottenburg and Kreuzberg but has a charm all of its own. Developed in the 19th century, it's devoid of conventional sights, but has beautiful squares, such as Viktoria-Luisa Platz, grand buildings and one of Europe's oldest, wildest and wealthiest gay communities, centred around Nollendorf Platz. At its north-west corner on Tauentzienstrasse is **KaDeWe** (Kaufhauf des Westens; *see p41*), Berlin's iconic department store.

Restaurants & cafés

❤ Café Aroma €€

Hochkirchstrasse 8 (782 5821, www.cafe-aroma.de). U7, S1, S2 Yorckstrasse. **Open** *5pm-midnight Mon-Sat; 11am-midnight Sun.* **Map** *p162 L11* ⑧ *Italian*

In a brunch-mad city, this lovely Italian trattoria is a Berlin foodie favourite for its multi-course marathon of cold cuts, poached salmon, fried risotto balls and roast vegetables. One of the first restaurants to sign up to Germany's Slow Food association in the early 1990s, it takes pains to source sustainable and authentic produce.

Café Berio

Maassenstrasse 7 (216 1946, www.cafeberio.de). U1, U2, U3, U4 Nollendorfplatz. **Open** *6am-3am daily.* **No cards.** **Map** *p162 J10* ⑨ *Café*

One of the best daytime cafés in Berlin, this Parisian-style café is full of attractive, trendy young men (including the waiters), with a good people-watching terrace in summer. Decent food is served all day, should you get hunger pangs at an ungodly hour. It's a gay café historically, but no one will be turned away.

Ixthys €

Pallasstrasse 21, on Winterfeldtplatz (8147 4769). U1, U2, U3, U4 Nollendorfplatz. **Open** *noon-10pm Mon-Sat.* **Map** *p162 J10* ⑩ *Korean*

Reams of handwritten scripture adorn the wall at this Christian Korean café, and the menu has bizarre flow diagrams explaining man's relationship with original sin. Brisk service brings *bulgogi*-marinated meats, or spicy broths, but the star of the show is the *bibimbap*, a classic dish of rice, layered with sautéed vegetables, chilli paste and sliced beef, crowned with a glistening fried egg and served in a scalding stone bowl so it will continue sizzling on the table.

Sissi €€-€€€

Motzstrasse 34 (2101 8101, www. sissi-berlin.de). U1, U2, U3, U4 Nollendorfplatz. **Open** *from 5pm daily.* **Map** *p162 J10* ⑪ *Austrian*
Sissi is just darling! Some of the best *Schnitzel* in town and other hearty Austro-German dishes are complemented by excellent wines and attentive service. It's much bigger than it looks, thanks to a sizeable upstairs dining area, and the bright pink walls and an abundance of candlelight ensure the atmosphere is warm and inviting.

Bars & pubs

Green Door

Winterfeldtstrasse 50 (215 2515, www.greendoor.de). U1, U2, U3, U4 Nollendorfplatz. **Open** *6pm-3am Mon-Thur, Sun; 6pm-4am Fri, Sat.* **No cards.** **Map** *p162 J10* ③
Behind an actual green door (ring the bell for entry) lies this popular cocktail bar, which attracts a solid crowd of upmarket regulars as well as booze tourists on the Berlin quality cocktail trail. Inside it's quietly classy with a touch of kitsch. The impressive drinks menu runs the gamut of spirit-based mixology and includes the house Green

In the know
Ich bin ein Berliner

Contrary to widely held belief, President Kennedy did not call himself a doughnut in front of half a million Berliners outside Rathaus Schöneberg in 1963. A *Berliner* is only a doughnut in the north and west of Germany; in Berlin, doughnuts are known as *Pfannkuchen*. What's more, his addition of the indefinite *ein* was grammatically correct, implying solidarity with the city's embattled citizens.

Door cocktail, a refreshing mix of champagne, lemon, sugar and mint.

❤ Neues Ufer

Hauptstrasse 157 (7895 7900, www. neuesufer.de). U7 Kleistpark. **Open** *2pm-2am daily.* **No cards.** **Map** *p162 K11* ④
Established in the early 1970s, this is one of the city's oldest gay cafés. Formerly known as Anderes Ufer ('The Other Side'), it was an old haunt of David Bowie, who used to live just two doors away.

Stagger Lee

Nollendorfstrasse 27 (2903 6158, www.staggerlee.de). U1, U2, U3, U4 Nollendorfplatz. **Open** *7pm-late daily.* **Map** *p162 J10* ⑤
This vaudeville bar takes its name from a 1920s folk song about the true-life exploits of a violent pimp from St Louis, Missouri. Low-hanging saloon lamps, Victorian wallpaper and an enormous mechanical till add to its faux-Americana charm. The cocktails are outstanding. If you're choosing between here and the Green Door, pick Stagger Lee if you're all about the rye – but they are both excellent.

Tom's Bar

Motzstrasse 19 (213 4570, www. tomsbar.de). U1, U2, U3, U4 Nollendorfplatz. **Open** *10pm-6am daily.* **No cards.** **Map** *p162 J9* ⑥
Once described by *Der Spiegel* as the climax of the night, Tom's is something of a cruising institution for the gay community. The front bar is fairly chatty but the closer you get to the steps down to the darkroom, the more intense things become. It's very popular with men of all ages and styles, especially on 2-for-1 Mondays.

Shops & services
KaDeWe (*see p41*) is still the queen of consumerism in this part of the city.

Prinz Eisenherz

Motzstrasse 23 (313 9936, www. prinz-eisenherz.com). U1, U2, U3, U4 Nollendorfplatz. **Open** *10am-8pm Mon-Sat.* **Map** *p162 J10* ⓫ *Books*

One of the finest queer bookshops in Europe, with many titles unavailable in Britain included among its large English-language stock. There's a good art and photography section, plus magazines, postcards and news of book readings and other events. There's a solid section of feminist lit, too.

Winterfeldtplatz Market

Winterfeldtplatz (0175 437 4303 mobile). U1, U2, U3, U4 Nollendorfplatz. **Open** *8am-1pm Wed; 8am-4pm Sat.* **Map** *p162 J10* ⓬ *Food & drink*

In the leafy square surrounding St-Matthias-Kirche, this thriving farmers' market buzzes with life twice a week. There are more than 250 stalls; some stock traditional market tat, but most offer high-end gastronomic produce. The emphasis is on the local and seasonal, such as wild herbs and edible flowers, foraged mushrooms and local salami. Plenty of vendors serve cooked food; look out for Bauer Lindner, which sells *Bratwurst* made from their own pigs raised organically in Brandenburg.

Entertainment

Kleine Nachtrevue

Kurfürstenstrasse 116 (218 8950, www.kleine-nachtrevue.de). U1, U2, U3 Wittenbergplatz. **Box office** *from 8pm Wed-Sat. Performances 9pm Wed-Sat; 11.45pm Fri, Sat.* **Tickets** *€20-€35. No cards.* **Map** *p162 J9* ❼ *Cabaret*

Used as a location for many films, this is as close as it gets to real nostalgic German cabaret – intimate, dark, decadent, but very friendly. Shows consist of short song or dance numbers sprinkled with playful nudity and whimsical costumes. Special weekend performances vary from erotic opera to a four-course meal served to songs sung by the male 'reincarnation' of Marlene Dietrich.

In the know
Marlene Dietrich

Berlin is rightfully proud of Marlene Dietrich, the city's most iconic actress. Born in 1901 on Schöneberg's Rote Insel, she first found fame in silent films and on stage. Her breakthrough film was *Der Blaue Engel* (*The Blue Angel*, 1930), filmed at the Babelsberg studios (see *p184*), whose success enabled her to move to Hollywood. In the 1930s, Dietrich spurned Nazi offers to return to Germany and instead became a key figure in the effort to raise Allied war bonds. Her film career subsided, but she continued to perform on stage as a cabaret artist for several decades, until ill health forced her to retire. She died in Paris in 1992. Her will stated that she was to be buried in Schöneberg, but only after the Wall fell. Her grave can be found in the Städtischer Friedhof III cemetery on Stubenrauchstrasse.

Marlene Dietrich

West of the Centre

As it consists of two cities – once divided and now fused back together – it's not surprising that Berlin sprawls for miles in every direction. Although most of the fun stuff is in the gentrified East, and the key sites are in the centre, the outlying western boroughs are well worth exploring. Sleepy, a touch staid but with plenty of culture and history, the western districts feel a world away from the *Plattenbauten* (high-rises) and industrial sites in the East. Visiting the leafy streets and villas of Grunewald and Wannsee is like stepping back in time. The most popular excursion is to Potsdam, located just beyond the confines of the city in the state of Brandenburg. Potsdam is to Berlin what Versailles is to Paris.

Best viewpoints
Funkturm *p178*,
Teufelsberg Berlin *p180*

Best historic buildings
Olympiastadion *p178*, Park
Sanssouci *p184*, Zitadelle *p179*

Best art museums
Bildergalerie *p184*,
Brücke-Museum *p180*,
Museum Barberini *p184*

Westend

A couple of kilometres south-west of Schloss Charlottenburg, within the vast Messe- und Ausstellungsgelände (Trade Fair & Exhibition Area), the **Funkturm** (Radio Tower) offers panoramic views. To the north-west, the imposing columns and conjoined rings of the **Olympiastadion** loom large; it's one of the few pieces of Fascist-era architecture still standing in Berlin. Nearby is the **Corbusierhaus**, a huge multicoloured apartment block, designed by Le Corbusier for the International Building exhibition of 1957, and the **Georg-Kolbe-Museum** with its charming garden café.

Sights & museums

❤ Funkturm

Messedamm (3038 1905, www. funkturm-messeberlin.de). U2 Theodor-Heuss-Platz or Kaiserdamm. **Open** *Platform 2-10pm Tue-Fri; 11am-10pm Sat, Sun. Restaurant 6-11pm Tue-Fri; 11.30am-11pm Sat, Sun.* **Admission** *€5; €3 reductions. No cards.*
The 147-m (482-ft) Radio Tower was built in 1926 and looks a bit like a smaller version of the Eiffel Tower. There's a zippy lift up to the observation deck, but challenge-seekers can attempt the 610 steps; vertigo sufferers can seek solace in the restaurant, only 55m (180ft)

from the ground. The tower closes in summer for repairs, so ring ahead.

Georg-Kolbe-Museum

Sensburger Allee 25 (304 2144, www.georg-kolbe-museum.de). S3, S9 Heerstrasse or bus X34, M49, X49. **Open** *10am-6pm daily.* **Admission** *€7; €5 reductions; free under-18s. No cards.*
Georg Kolbe's former studio has been transformed into a showcase for his work. The Berlin sculptor, regarded as Germany's best in the 1920s, focused on naturalistic human figures. There are examples of his earlier graceful pieces, as well as his later more sombre and bombastic works, created in accordance with Nazi aesthetic ideals. His famous *Figure for Fountain* is in the sculpture garden, where there's also a great café for coffee and cake.

❤ Olympiastadion

Olympischer Platz 3 (2500 2322, www.olympiastadion-berlin.de). U2 Olympia-Stadion or S3, S9 Olympiastadion. **Open** *varies.* **Admission** *€8; €5.50 reductions. Guided tours €11; €9.50 reductions. No cards.*
Built on the site of Berlin's original 1916 Olympic stadium, the current structure was designed by Werner March and opened in 1936 for the infamous 'Nazi Olympics' (you can see where the swastikas were removed from the old bell). The 74,000-seat stadium underwent a

major and long-overdue refitting for the 2006 World Cup, including better seats and a roof over the whole lot. Home of Hertha BSC, it also hosts the German Cup Final, plus other sporting events and concerts. You can book a guided tour at the visitor centre by the Osttor (eastern gate). After the war, the former *Reichssportfeld* became the headquarters of the British military occupation forces.

Spandau & around

Founded in the 13th century, Berlin's western neighbour and eternal rival Spandau is a little Baroque town that makes for a low-key escape from the city. The old town centre is mostly pedestrianised, with 18th-century townhouses interspersed with modern stores; visit in December to see the famous Christmas market in full swing. To the north, at the confluence of the Spree and Havel rivers, is the dominating presence of the **Zitadelle** (Citadel). Some distance south of Spandau is

the **Luftwaffenmuseum der Bundeswehr Berlin-Gatow**.

Sights & museums

Luftwaffenmuseum der Bundeswehr Berlin-Gatow

Kladower Damm 182, Gatow (3687 2601, www.luftwaffenmuseum.de). U7 Rathaus Spandau, then bus 135, then 15-min walk. **Open** *10am-6pm Tue-Sun.* **Admission** *free.*
For propeller heads only, this museum is on the far western fringes of the city at what was formerly the RAF base in divided Berlin; it's a long journey by public transport followed by a 15-minute walk from the bus stop (or you can get a cab from the U-Bahn station). Then there's a lot more walking to take in more than 100 aircraft scattered around the airfield, plus exhibits in two hangars and the former control tower. The emphasis is on the history of military aviation in Germany since 1945, although there's also a World War I triplane, a restored Handley Page Hastings (as used during the Berlin Airlift) and a whole lot of missiles.

❤ Zitadelle

Am Juliusturm 64 (354 9440, tours 334 6270, www.zitadelle-spandau. net). U7 Zitadelle. **Open** *10am-5pm daily.* **Admission** *€4.50; €2.50 reductions. No cards.*
The bulk of the Zitadelle was constructed between 1560 and 1594 in the style of an Italian fort to dominate the confluence of the Spree and Havel rivers. Since then it has been used as everything from a garrison to a prison to a poison-gas laboratory. The oldest structure here (and the oldest secular building in Berlin) is the Juliusturm, probably dating back to an Ascanian fortress from about 1160. The present tower was home until 1919 to 120-million gold Marks, a small part of the five

Funkturm

billion paid as French reparations to Germany in 1874 after the Franco-Prussian War. There are two museums within the Zitadelle: one tells the story of the building with models and maps; the other covers local history.

Grunewald & around

South-west of the city centre is the Grunewald, the largest of Berlin's many forests. Due to its easy accessibility by S-Bahn, its lanes and pathways fill with walkers, runners, cyclists and horse riders at weekends. Within the forest are a cluster of lakes, a wonderful eco park, **Naturschutzzentrum Ökowerk** (www.oekowerk.de) and the legendary **Teufelsberg Berlin**, with its eerie abandoned spy structure on the top. There are also a handful of worthwhile museums on the forest's eastern edge. To the south-west, the Grosser Wannsee is a wide inlet of the River Havel, with the largest inland beach in Europe on its eastern shore (see p182 Berlin's bathing lakes).

Sights & museums
Alliierten Museum
Clayallee 135, at Huttenweg (818 1990, www.alliiertenmuseum. de). U3 Oskar-Helene-Heim then 10 mins walk, or bus 115. **Open** *10am-6pm Tue-Sun.* **Admission** *free.*
The Allies arrived as conquerors, kept West Berlin alive during the 1948 Airlift and finally went home in 1994. In what used to be a US Forces cinema, the Allied Museum is mostly about the period of the Blockade and Airlift, documented with photos, tanks, jeeps, planes, weapons and uniforms. Outside is the former guardhouse from Checkpoint Charlie and an RAF Hastings TG 503 plane. Guided

tours in English can be booked in advance.

❤ Teufelsberg Berlin
*Teufelsseechaussee 10 (www. teufelsberg-berlin.de). **Open** Tours noon-8pm Wed-Sun. **Admission** €5-€15. No cards.*
During the Cold War, the Allies built this listening station on the top of one of Berlin's highest hills to eavesdrop on what the East Germans were up to on the other side of the Wall. The site was abandoned when the Iron Curtain fell, and soon became a favourite spot for urban explorers and ravers looking for a trippy place to throw an open-air party. The days of illegally exploring the site are now over, but the situation is still a bit disorganised. You can buy a ticket to explore the Teufelsberg online or at the site, but if you choose the latter, bring cash or you'll be turned away. Guided tours taking you through the decrepit structure are offered in German and English and cost extra, as does bringing in a camera (but not a smartphone). Beyond Teufelsberg's varied history, it's the stunning view over the city, the wild graffiti and the unnerving acoustics of the giant radar dome that are the real draws. Keep an eye on children; there's no health and safety here.

❤ Brücke-Museum
Bussardsteig 9 (831 2029, www. bruecke-museum.de). U3 Oskar-Helene-Heim then bus 115. **Open** *11am-5pm Mon, Wed-Sun.* **Admission** *€6; €4 reductions. No cards.*
This small but satisfying museum – reputedly a favourite of David Bowie – is dedicated to the work of *Die Brücke* (The Bridge), a group of expressionist painters that was founded in Dresden in 1905 before moving to Berlin. A large collection of oils, watercolours, drawings and sculptures by the main members

Teufelsberg Berlin

of the group – Schmidt-Rottluff, Heckel, Kirchner, Mueller and Pechstein – is rotated in temporary exhibitions.

Domäne Dahlem
Königin-Luise-Strasse 49 (666 3000, www.domaene-dahlem.de). U3 Dahlem-Dorf. **Open** *Museum 10am-5pm Wed-Sun.* **Admission** *Museum €5; €3 reductions. No cards.*
On this organic working farm, children can see how life was lived in the 17th century. Craftspeople preserve and teach their skills. It's best to visit during one of the several annual festivals, when kids can ride ponies, tractors and hay wagons. There's also a farm shop and, in good weather, a garden café.

Gedenkstätte Haus der Wannsee-Konferenz
Am Grossen Wannsee 56-58 (805 0010, www.ghwk.de). S1, S7 Wannsee then bus 114. **Open** *10am-6pm daily.* **Admission** *free.*
On 20 January 1942, a group of leading Nazis, chaired by Heydrich, gathered here to draw up plans for the Final Solution. Today, this infamous villa has been converted into the Wannsee Conference Memorial House, a place of remembrance, with a photo exhibit on the conference and its genocidal consequences. Call in advance if you want to join an English-language tour, though the information is in both English and German.

Museum Europäischer Kulturen
Arnimallee 25 (266 426802, www.smb.museum/en/ museums-institutions/museum-europaeischer-kulturen/home.html). U3 Dahlem-Dorf. **Open** *10am-5pm Tue-Fri; 11am-6pm Sat, Sun.* **Admission** *€8; €4 reductions.*
The museum covers everyday European culture from the 18th century to the present. One highlight is a mechanical model of the Nativity, displayed during Advent. Exhibitions will continue here until at least July 2019; thereafter the museum may relocate to the Kulturforum; check the website for updates.

Potsdam

Potsdam is the capital of the state of Brandenburg. Located just outside Berlin's city limits to the south-west, it's the capital's most beautiful neighbour, known for its 18th-century Baroque architecture. For centuries, Potsdam was the summer residence of the Hohenzollerns, and, despite the damage wrought during World War II and by East Germany's socialist planners, much remains of the

💙 Berlin's bathing lakes

Brandenburg, the state that encircles Berlin, is known as the land of 3,000 lakes, and a visit to one is the perfect antidote to any of the Berlin vices – beer, cigarettes, sausage – to which you may have succumbed. Starkly beautiful in winter and inviting in summer, a good number of the lakes are reachable by public transport, and, if you bring a bike, you stand a good chance of finding your own private lakeside sunbathing patch. Whether for sailing, swimming or strolling, each lake has its own distinct character, and every Berliner has his or her favourite. Striking out in any direction from Berlin, you'll be spoilt for choice.

The municipal bathing beaches – *Strandbäder* – are run by the city. You pay an entrance fee for access to showers, toilets, changing rooms and the services of a lifeguard. Usually, one end of the beach is favoured by nudists. Freikörperkultur (FKK), German for nudism, has a long history in these parts. Berliners are untroubled by the sight of a naked body, and at most lakes no one will care if you suit up or not.

▶ *For details of all the city's* Strandbäder *and other swimming pools, see www.berlinerbaeder.de.*

Müggelsee
S3 Friedrichshagen.
Officially Berlin's largest lake, Müggelsee in the east is over 4km (2.5 miles) long and 2.5km (1.5 miles) wide, so hiking round the lake is a great way to stretch your legs. If you're planning to do the whole circuit, you'll have

to take the tiny ferry between Müggelwerder and Müggelhort, which runs once an hour in summer; the crossing takes 10 minutes. Once over, follow the lake round and after 30 minutes you'll come to a lovely beer garden. There are plenty of sandy little spots to take a dip, but if you're looking for facilities, then head for **Strandbad Müggelsee** (www.strandbad-mueggelsee. de) – although the large colony of ducks here can make swimming a challenge!

Schlachtensee
S1 Schlachtensee.
A circuit of the Schlachtensee is 5.5km (3.5 miles), which is the perfect distance to work up an appetite that you can happily sate at the **Fischerhütte** (Fischerhüttenstrasse 136, 8049 8310, www. fischerhuette-berlin. de). In summer, there are rowing boats and paddle boards for hire (www.steh-paddler.com), and the particularly clean waters are ideal for a dip. The lake is just across the road from the station, but you may have to walk a few minutes along its perimeter to find a secluded spot.

Strandbad Plötzensee
Nordufer 26, Wedding (8964 4787, www.strandbad-ploetzensee.de). S41, S42 Beusselstrasse, or U9, S41, S42 Westhafen then 20-min walk. **Open** *May-Sept 9am-7pm daily (longer hours in good weather).* **Admission** *€5 (€3 reductions).*
Only 30 minutes from Alexanderplatz, Plötzensee is the perfect spot to relax with

a swim after a strenuous day's exploring. The Strandbad has 740m of sand, and there are plenty of refreshments on offer, so you can have a dip, crack open a beer – and still be back in the centre in time for dinner.

Strandbad Wannsee
Wannseebadweg 25, Nikolassee (2219 0011, www.berlinerbaeder. de/baeder/strandbad-wannsee). S1, S7 Nikolassee then 10-min walk, or Berlin Wannsee then shuttle bus. **Open** *Apr-mid Sept; see the website for daily opening times. No swimming in Apr.* **Admission** *€5.50, €3.50 reductions.*
Lie on the sandy beach at Strandbad Wannsee to watch the sailing boats dart up and down the River Havel and you'll be partaking in an experience enjoyed by Berliners for nearly a century. The waters of the Wannsee (an inlet of the river) are extensive and, in summer, warm enough for comfortable swimming; there's a strong current, though, so don't stray beyond the floating markers. Between May and September, there are boats, pedalos and two-person wicker sunchairs, called *Strandkörbe*, for hire, plus a playground and slides. Service buildings house showers, toilets, shops, cafés and kiosks. Children love it here.

Teufelsee
S7 Grunewald, then 15-min walk.
This small lake in the Grunewald is surround by a pleasant green meadow, ideal for stretching out on. On the lake itself, floating rafts draw swimmers who compete for space with the ducks. Prudes beware: naked swimming and sunbathing are common here.

Schlachtensee

legacy of these Prussian kings. The best-known landmark is **Sanssouci**, one of three royal parks flanking the town. For full details of Potsdam's many historic buildings, contact the **tourist office** (Brandenburger Strasse 3, 0331 2755 8899, www.potsdamtourismus.de). A **Potsdam Card** (48 hours from €23), provides free public transport and discounted entry to most attractions.

Sights & museums

❤ Museum Barberini

Humboldtstrasse 5-6 (0331 2360 14499, www.museum-barberini. com). Open Mon, Wed-Sun 10am-7pm. Admission €10-€14. In Potsdam's old town is this state-of-the-art museum, rebuilt on the site of the 18th-century Barberini Palace. It opened in 2017 to house a permanent collection of art produced in the GDR and to host temporary exhibitions from around the world. There's a café with a lovely view of the Alter Markt, with the domed Nikolaikirche on the north side, the Altes Rathaus to the right and the rebuilt Stadtschloss to the left.

❤ Park Sanssouci

Potsdam (0331 969 4200, www. spsg.de). Open Park 24hrs daily. Palace access is time-limited and must be booked online in advance. Admission Park free. Sanssouci+ ticket for all Potsdam palaces €19; €14 reductions. The sprawling Park Sanssouci is Potsdam's biggest tourist magnet. A legacy of Prussian King Friedrich II (Frederick the Great), 'Sans souci' means 'without worry' and reflects the king's desire for a sanctuary where he could pursue his cultural interests. He initially had the vineyard terraces and formal garden built, before

adding the rococo palace, **Schloss Sanssouci** (closed Mon, €8-€12). The palace is flanked to the west by the ornate **Neue Kammern** (New Chambers, closed Nov-Mar and closed Mon, €5-€6) and to the east by the **Bildergalerie** (Picture Gallery, closed Nov-Apr and closed Mon, €5-€6). Spreading out from these buildings are acres of grandly elegant gardens, which conceal several other features, including the Orangery; the toy fortress, built for Wilhelm II's sons; the Chinese Tea House; the pagoda-style Drachenhaus café and Schloss Charlottenhof, with its copper-plate engraving room. After victory in the Seven Years' War, Friedrich II built the huge **Neues Palais** (closed Tue, €6-€8) to the west of Sanssouci, which was used by Kaiser Wilhelm II as his favoured residence. It's free to wander through the park, and its size means you can always find your own grassy corner for a picnic.

In the know
Filmstudio Babelsberg

In the 1920s, the world's largest film studio outside Hollywood was located in Babelsberg, near Potsdam. It was here that Fritz Lang's *Metropolis*, Josef von Sternberg's *The Blue Angel* and other masterpieces were produced. During the Nazi period, it churned out thrillers, light entertainment and propaganda pieces. Today **Filmpark Babelsberg** (Grossbeerenstrasse 200, 0331 721 2750, www.filmpark.de, closed Nov-Mar, €15-€22) has modern facilities for all phases of film and TV production, plus studio tours, stunt displays and a theme park. The history of film-making at the studios is explored in more depth at the **Filmmuseum Potsdam** (Breite Strasse 1A, 0331 271 8112, www.filmmuseum-potsdam.de, closed Mon), housed in the former royal stables.

Berlin Essentials

Hackesche Höfe p85

Accommodation

Berlin is the third most popular European tourist destination after London and Paris but, for now, remains one of the least expensive European cities in which to stay. The average price for a room here is €105 per night, compared to the European-wide average of €131. By booking far enough in advance, it's possible to find high-quality affordable accommodation in the most desirable parts of town. And, after a day of graffiti-gazing and educational trips around museums with worrying names (looking at you, Topographie des Terrors), indulging a little with your lodgings may be just the ticket.

There are now so many places to choose from that hoteliers go the extra mile to stand out from the crowd: **Dude** near Heinrich-Heine Strasse has an all-day deli and a high-end steak restaurant; **Nhow** by the river in Friedrichshain attracts music-lovers with two recording studios and Gibson guitars available on room service, and the **Radisson Blu Hotel Berlin** has its own giant aquarium. On the luxury front, the **Adlon Kempinski** and the newer **Das Stue** steal the show, with extremely convenient central locations, but **Soho House** has secured itself an international hipster clientele by applying its studied vintage-chic aesthetic to an old Jewish department store with a swimming pool on the roof.

At the other end of the price spectrum, the city has an abundance of boutique hostels and budget hotels, offering arty DIY interiors at affordable prices: check out the **Circus Hostel** in Rosenthalerplatz and **Lekkerurlaub** in Graefekiez. Or, sleep in a vintage caravan parked in an old vacuum cleaner factory at the **Hüttenpalast** in Neukölln. Alternatively, choose from the hundreds of rooms and apartments available from **Airbnb** (www.airbnb.com) or the budget-friendly **WG-Gesucht** (www.wg-gesucht.de).

Prices and information

Hotels are graded according to an official star rating system – but we haven't followed it in this guide, as the ratings merely reflect room size and amenities, such as lifts or bars, rather than other important factors such as decor, staff or atmosphere. Instead, we've listed our accommodation selections in four price categories (see below In the know).

Many of the larger hotels refuse to publish any rates at all, depending instead on direct booking over the internet (often at a discount), which enables them to vary their prices daily. In addition to the hotels' own websites, check out discount specialists such as www.expedia.com, www.hotels.com and booking.com. It's wise to reserve in advance whenever possible, especially for weekend stays in Mitte, and always check the cancellation policy before you book.

Note that tourists pay an additional room tax of five per cent per night up to 21 successive days; business travellers are exempt but have to prove they're in Berlin for work.

Luxury

Although Berlin's hotels are comparatively cheap, the standards of luxury accommodation in the capital rival any other major European city. The flashy **Ritz-Carlton** (Potsdamer Platz 3, 337 777, www.ritzcarlton.com), elegant **Grand Hyatt** (Marlene-Dietrich-Platz 2, 2553 1234, www.berlin.grand.hyatt.com) and the **Waldorf Astoria**

(Hardenbergstrasse 28, Charlottenburg, 814 0000, www.waldorfastoriaberlin.com) all offer the facilities and service expected of these premium chains.

Adlon Kempinski Berlin

Unter den Linden 77, Mitte (226 10, www.hotel-adlon.de). U6 Französische Strasse, or S1, S2, S25 Brandenburger Tor. Map p70 M7.

Not quite the Adlon of yore, which burned down after World War II, this new, more generic luxury version was rebuilt by the Kempinski Group in 1997 on the original site next to the Brandenburg Gate. Apart from a few original features, you're really paying for the prime location and the superlative service: bellboys who pass you a chilled bottle of water when you return from a jog in nearby Tiergarten; as well as dining at Thai concept restaurant Sra Bua by Tim Raue or the extremely formal Lorenz Adlon Esszimmer, which has two Michelin stars. If you want to rent out one of the three bulletproof presidential suites (from where Michael Jackson once dangled his child), it will set you back around €15,000, but you do at least get a 24-hour private butler and limousine for your money.

Hotel de Rome

Behrenstrasse 37, Mitte (460 6090, www.roccofortehotels.com). U6 Französische Strasse. Map p70 N7.

This 19th-century mansion was originally built to house the headquarters of Dresdner Bank, but was transformed into a sumptuous hotel by Rocco Forte in 2006. Despite the intimidating grandeur, the young staff are approachable and friendly. All 146 rooms push the limits of taste, with plenty of polished wood, marble and velvet. The former basement vault houses a pool, spa and fully equipped gym. The lobby restaurant, La Banca, specialises in upscale Mediterranean cuisine with alfresco dining in the summer; cocktails and lighter fare are available at the Rooftop Terrace or the Opera Court, where high tea is served every afternoon.

Mandala

Potsdamer Strasse 3, Tiergarten (590 05 1221, www.themandala.de). U2, S1, S2, S25 Potsdamer Platz. **Map** p98 L8.
This privately owned addition to the Design Hotels portfolio is, given the address, an oasis of calm, luxury and taste. The 144 rooms and suites, most of which face onto an inner courtyard, are perfectly designed for space and light, decorated in warm white and beige, with comfortable minimalist furnishings and TVs. A sheltered path through the Japanese garden on the fifth floor leads to Facil, an ultra-modern restaurant with two Michelin stars. The Qiu lounge offers lighter fare, and the rooftop spa, windowed from end to end, offers spectacular city views. Reduced rates are available for longer stays.

Patrick Hellmann Schlosshotel

Brahmsstrasse 10, Grunewald, West of the Centre (895 8430, www.schlosshotelberlin.com). S7 Grunewald.
Designed down to the dust ruffles by Karl Lagerfeld, this restored 1914 villa on the edge of Grunewald is a luxury escape of which mere mortals can only dream. There are 12 suites and 54 rooms, with elegant marble bathrooms, a limousine and butler service, and well-trained staff to scurry after you. R&R is well-covered too, with a swimming pool, a golf course, tennis courts and two restaurants (with summer dining on the lawn, of course). This is a beautiful place in a beautiful setting, but so exclusive that it might as well be on another planet. It's worth checking the internet for deals, nonetheless.

Sofitel Berlin Gendarmenmarkt

Charlottenstrasse 50-52, Mitte (203 750, www.sofitel.com). U2, U6 Stadtmitte. **Map** p70 N7.
'Design for the senses' is the motto here. This is a truly lovely hotel, and rooms are often difficult to come by, but it's well worth the fight. So much attention has been paid to the details: from the moment you enter the lobby, with its soothing colour scheme and wonderful lighting, the atmosphere is intimate and elegant. This carries into the rooms, each beautifully styled, with perhaps the best bathrooms in the city. Even the conference rooms are spectacular, and the hotel's 'wellness' area includes plunge pools, a gym and a meditation room. In summer, you can wind down on the sun deck, which perches high above the surrounding rooftops overlooking the splendid domed cathedrals of Gendarmenmarkt.

Das Stue

Drakestrasse 1, Tiergarten (311 7220, www.das-stue.com). S3, S5, S7, S9 Tiergarten. **Map** p98 H8.
The hippest member of Berlin's luxury hotel family, Das Stue is located in the 1930s Royal Danish Embassy, restored to its former splendour by Spanish designer Patricia Urquiola. There's a long list of reasons to stay at this Design Hotel, including a pearl-white spa, rooms overlooking the Tiergarten, the original three-storey library, and the Michelin-starred Cinco restaurant (*see p108*), with a menu provided by superstar Catalan chef Paco Pérez. The central location means it's a short walk to most of Berlin's major sights. Some rooms overlook Berlin Zoo, with binoculars provided for close-up views of your four-legged neighbours.

Expensive

Reliable chain choices in this price bracket include **Bristol Berlin** (Kurfürstendamm 27, Charlottenburg, 884 340, www.bristolberlin.com); **Radisson Blu Hotel Berlin** (Karl-Liebknecht-Strasse 3, Mitte, 238 280, www.radissonblu.com/hotel-berlin) and **Sofitel Berlin Kurfürstendamm** (Augsburger Strasse 41, Charlottenburg, 800 9990, www.sofitel.com).

25hours Hotel Bikini Berlin

Budapester Strasse 40, Charlottenburg (120 2210, www.25hours-hotels.com). U2, U9, S3, S5, S7, S9 Zoologischer Garten. **Map** p162 G8.
You'll find a 149-room branch of Design Hotels' funky 25hours brand located

inside the Bikini Berlin 'concept' shopping mall (*see p167*) that adjoins the Tiergarten. The design is a blend of exposed brick and industrial lighting, softened by plenty of greenery and brightly coloured furnishings. There's great attention to detail, including window-side hammocks, free Mini rental and a fab Middle Eastern restaurant, Neni.

Art Nouveau Berlin

Leibnizstrasse 59, Charlottenburg (327 7440, www.hotelartnouveau.de). U7 Adenauerplatz, or S3, S5, S7, S9 Savignyplatz. **Map** *p162 E9.*
This is one of the most charming small hotels in Berlin. The rooms are decorated with flair, in a mix of Conran-modern and antique furniture, each with an enormous black and white photo hung by the bed. The en suite bathrooms are cleverly integrated into the rooms without disrupting the elegant townhouse architecture. Even the TVs are stylish. The breakfast room has a fridge full of goodies, should you feel peckish in the wee hours, and the staff are sweet.

Dormero Hotel Berlin Ku'damm

Eislebener Strasse 14, Wilmersdorf (214 050, www.dormero.de). U1, U9 Kurfürstendamm, or U3 Augsburger Strasse. **Map** *p162 G9.*
Tucked down a quiet street behind KaDeWe, this hotel offers modern luxury without the stuffiness. Staff are friendly, and the 72 rooms, all done out in a contemporary-elegant style, are warm and relaxing. There's a beautiful Japanese garden in the middle, surrounded by individually decorated salons available for meetings and special occasions. The Quadriga restaurant serves steaks and bistro fare.

Ellington

Nürnberger Strasse 50-55, Charlottenburg (683 150, www. ellington-hotel.com). U1, U2, U3 Wittenbergplatz, or U3 Augsburger Strasse. **Map** *p162 H9.*
This is one of the classiest, most sophisticated joints in Berlin. Hidden within the shell of a landmark art deco dance hall, it combines cool contemporary elegance with warmth and ease. The rooms, mostly white with polished wood accents, are brilliantly simple, with modern free-standing fixtures and half-walls, instilling absolute calm behind the original double windows. The staff are helpful and remarkably cheerful given the daft flat caps they're made to wear. An ambitious menu is served in the Duke restaurant, and there are Sunday jazz brunches in the central courtyard. All this and KaDeWe round the corner... the Duke himself would have been proud.

Garden Boutique Hotel

Invalidenstrasse 122, Mitte (2844 5577, www.honigmond.de). U6 Oranienburger Tor. **Map** *p70 M4.*
Along with its nearby sister Honigmond Boutique Hotel, this 20-room guesthouse is enchanting, and it doesn't cost an arm and a leg. Choose between large bedrooms facing the street, smaller ones overlooking the fish pond and Tuscan-style garden, or spacious apartments on the upper floor. As with all great places, the secret is in the finer detail. The rooms are impeccably styled with polished pine floors, paintings in massive gilt frames, antiques and iron bedsteads. There's also a charming sitting room overlooking the garden. Highly recommended. **Other location** Honigmond Boutique Hotel, Tieckstrasse 11 (284 4550).

Soho House

Torstrasse 1, Mitte (405 0440, www. sohohouseberlin.com). U2 Rosa-Luxemburg-Platz. **Map** *p70 P5.*
The average Berliner has a healthy scepticism for anything 'private' or 'exclusive', so eyebrows were raised when Soho House opened its branch in the German capital in 2010. But even the toughest critic would have to admit that the imposing Bauhaus building and its history deserved a new lease of life; it originally housed a Jewish-owned department store before it was taken over, first by the Nazis, then by

the Communist regime. These days, Soho House occupies eight floors; in addition to 65 guest rooms, there are 20 apartments and four lofts, plus the excellent Cowshed spa, a library and a cinema. Two floors are given over to The Store Berlin, Soho House's carefully curated shopping experience (see p39), where you'll find Cecconi's restaurant, serving northern Italian cuisine, and The Store Kitchen, which offers lighter fare throughout the day. In the rooms, beautiful old wooden floors and 1920s furniture mix with raw concrete walls. There's a touch of Britishness too, with a kettle and biscuits in each room, all of which combines to create a sense of *Gemütlichkeit* (cosy homeliness). A swim in the rooftop pool overlooking east Berlin rounds off the experience.

Moderate

Other good options include the **Circus Hotel** (see p192) and the **Monbijou Hotel** (www.monbijouhotel.com), both in Mitte's Scheunenviertel.

Almodovar Hotel

Boxhagener Strasse 83, Friedrichshain (692 097 080, www.almodovarhotel. com). U5 Samariterstrasse. **Map** *p125 V8.*
This boutique hotel is 'Berlin' through and through: fully vegetarian, with organic products in the rooms and even a complimentary yoga mat. Rooms are bright and spacious, and the penthouse suite even boasts its own sauna – but there's also a spa with ayurvedic treatments that's available to all guests. The lovely rosewood furniture was sustainably made specifically for the hotel.

Art'otel Berlin Mitte

Wallstrasse 70-73, Mitte (240 620, www. artotels.de). U2 Märkisches Museum. **Map** *p70 P7.*

A real gem on the Spree. This delightful hotel is a creative fusion of old and new, combining restored rococo reception rooms with ultra-modern bedrooms designed by Nalbach & Nalbach. As well as highlighting the artwork of George Baselitz – originals hang in the corridors and all 109 rooms – the hotel's decor has been meticulously thought out to the smallest detail, from the Philippe Starck bathrooms to the Breuer chairs in the conference rooms. Staff are pleasant, and the views from the top suites across Mitte are stunning.

Bleibtreu by Golden Tulip

Bleibtreustrasse 31, Charlottenburg (884 740, www.bleibtreu.com). U1 Uhlandstrasse, or S3, S5, S7, S9 Savignyplatz. **Map** *p162 F9.*
The Bleibtreu is a friendly, smart and cosy establishment popular with the media and fashion crowds. Although on the smaller side, the rooms are very modern and decorated with environmentally sound materials. Private massages are offered, as well as reflexology, making it a wonderful choice for the health-conscious, but good service and plenty of pampering mean it should appeal to anyone.

Dude

Köpenicker Strasse 92, Mitte (411 988 177, www.thedudeberlin.com). U8 Heinrich-Heine-Strasse. **Map** *p70 P7.*
Housed in an elegant 19th-century townhouse, this 27-room boutique hotel was created by an advertising executive to provide a humorous antidote to identikit hotels. There are a number of house rules – including no photography and no large groups – to help foster an atmosphere of anything-goes discretion. The rooms are quite stark, with brass beds offset by block-coloured walls, and there are Molton Brown goodies in the bathroom. Breakfast is served in the all-day deli, and the high-end steak restaurant, The Brooklyn, specialises in rare whiskies and Napa Valley wines.

Hotel Pension Funk

Fasanenstrasse 69, Charlottenburg (882 7193, www.hotel-pensionfunk.de). U1 Uhlandstrasse. **Map** *p162 G9.*

In the area around the Gedächtniskirche, not a lot is left of the charm and glamour that made the Ku'damm the most legendary street of pre-war Berlin. That makes this wonderful pension, which is hidden away on a quiet side street, a real find. The house, built in 1895, used to be home to the Danish silent movie star Asta Nielsen and has been lovingly restored, with elegant dark wood furniture and art deco detailing. The owner has done his best to make the bathrooms match modern standards without destroying the overall feel – one is hidden inside a replica wardrobe – but some fall slightly short of the quality you would expect from a newer hotel. However, the very reasonable prices and spotless surroundings make up for this. And the breakfast, served in the cosy dining room, is as good as anywhere more expensive.

Michelberger

Warschauer Strasse 39-40, Friedrichshain (2977 8590, www. michelbergerhotel.com). U1, S3, S5, S7, S9 Warschauer Strasse. **Map** *p125 T8.*

With its purposefully unfinished look and effortlessly creative vibe, Michelberger might seem like Berlin in a nutshell to some. While the cheaper rooms are characterised by a stylish simplicity reminiscent of a school gym, the pricier rooms have an air of tongue-in-cheek decadence – decked out in gold from floor to ceiling or in the style of a mountain resort – complete with sunken bathtubs and movie projectors. Michelberger might not be as spick and span as other hotels, but it's much more fun. The downside of the convenient location (right across from Warschauer Strasse U-Bahn station) is that some rooms are quite noisy; the quieter ones face the courtyard.

Nhow

Stralauer Allee 3, Friedrichshain (290 2990, www.nhow-hotels.com). U1, S3, S5, S7, S9 Warschauer Strasse. **Map** *p125 T9.*

If you're allergic to pink, you'd be well advised to check in elsewhere. New York designer Karim Rashid opened his eye-popping music and lifestyle hotel in a huge modern building right by the River Spree. Even the elevators are illuminated by different coloured lights, and some are decorated with photos of Rashid and his wife. As you'd expect from a music hotel with its own music manager, all rooms are equipped with iPod docking stations, and if you're in the mood for a spontaneous jam, you can order a Gibson guitar or an electric piano up to your room. More dedicated musicians can make use of the rehearsal rooms and two recording studios, or perform at one of the rooftop gigs and parties. As you can imagine, open mic night here is superb. The river view is beautiful, and the breakfast buffet leaves no wish unfulfilled. There's a pleasant sauna too.

Budget
The Circus Hostel

Weinbergsweg 1A, Mitte (2000 3939, www.circus-berlin.de). U8 Rosenthaler Platz. **Map** *p70 O4.*

Almost the standard by which other hostels should be measured, the Circus is a rarity – simple but stylish, warm and comfortable. And the upper-floor apartments have balconies and lovely views. The laid-back staff can help get discount tickets to almost anything, or give directions to the best bars and clubs, of which there are plenty nearby. The place is deservedly popular and is always full, so be sure to book ahead. The breakfast buffets are bountiful, with an excellent choice of organic granolas, and useful things such as laptops are available to rent, as well as bikes, Segways and even electric motorbikes. There's a quiet bar downstairs which often hosts evening events, such as poetry readings, and offers home

Just across the Platz, the owners also run the moderately priced **Circus Hotel** (Rosenthaler Strasse 1), whose 63 double rooms, each with private bath, surround a central terraced winter garden and café run by breakfast food maestros Commonground. There are also serviced apartments nearby at Choriner Strasse 84.

Eastern Comfort

Mühlenstrasse 73, Friedrichshain (6676 3806, www.eastern-comfort.com). U1, S3, S5, S7, S9 Warschauer Strasse. **Map** *p125 S9.*
Berlin's 'hostel boat' is moored on the Spree by the East Side Hotel, across the river from Kreuzberg. The rooms – or, rather, cabins – are clean and fairly spacious (considering it's a boat), and all have their own shower and toilet. The four-person room can feel a little cramped, but if you need to get up and stretch there are two common rooms, a lounge and three terraces offering lovely river views. The owners have now done up a second boat, the **Western Comfort**, which is moored across the river on the Kreuzberg bank.

Heart of Gold Hostel Berlin

Johannisstrasse 11, Mitte (2900 3300, www.heartofgold-hostel.de). S1, S2, S25 Oranienburger Strasse. **Map** *p70 N5.*
The prime location aside (it's only 50m from Oranienburger Strasse), this member of the Backpacker Germany Network (www.backpacker-network. de) is loosely themed on Douglas Adams' *The Hitchhiker's Guide to the Galaxy*. Rooms are bright and cheerful, with parquet floors. Lockers are free; individual bathrooms and showers, and a keycard system guarantee security. The laundry is cheap, as are the shots in the bar; and with rentable 'Sens-O-matic' sunglasses and Squornshellous Zeta mattresses to help you recover, what more could a backpacker (or hitchhiker) need? Towels, of course, which are available for free at reception.

Hüttenpalast

Hobrechtstrasse 66, Neukölln (3730 5806, www.huettenpalast.de). U7, U8 Hermannplatz. **Map** *p153 R11.*
The Hüttenpalast (literally 'Cabin Palace') is a large hall that was once the factory floor of an old vacuum cleaner company. Since 2011, it's been home to eight vintage caravans and three little cabins, each sleeping two people. It's set out like a mini indoor campsite, with separate male and female shower rooms and a tree in the middle. Each morning, guests emerge from their boltholes to discover the tree has borne fruit – well, little bags containing croissants. There's fresh coffee on hand and the streetfront café does an à la carte menu for those with particularly grumbling stomachs. Each caravan is different – Kleine Schwester (Little Sister) is decked out with white wood panelling and matching linen; the Herzensbrecher (Heartbreaker) has a domed metal ceiling; the Schwalbennest (Swallow's Nest) is big enough to squeeze in a table. If you're at all claustrophobic, the cabins, also unique in design and decoration, are slightly larger – and there are also regular loft-style hotel rooms of varying sizes.

Lekkerurlaub

Graefestrasse 89, Kreuzberg (177 257 7568, www.lekkerurlaub.de). U8 Schonleinstrasse. **No cards**. **Map** *p137 Q10.*
This charming bijou B&B is in one of the prettiest and buzziest bits of Kreuzberg, and it feels a little like staying at a chic but welcoming friend's place. Katrin, the host, goes out of her way to make you feel at home. Set on the ground floor of a typical Berlin tenement, the rooms are small but clean. Each room is unique and tastefully decorated, although two of the beds can only be reached by ladder, so avoid these if you're scared of heights. A generous breakfast is served up every morning, and the lovely café serves meals from 9am to 6pm; there are also dozens of bars and restaurants within a two-minute radius.

Getting Around

ARRIVING & LEAVING

By air

The new **Berlin Brandenburg Willy Brandt Airport (BER)** should have opened back in 2012, but current estimates suggest 2020 as the likely date. Until then, Berlin remains served by two airports, **Tegel** and **Schönefeld**, which are likely to cease operation when BER finally opens.

Flughafen Schönefeld (SXF)

Airport information 6091 1150, www. berlin-airport.de. **Open** *24hrs daily.*
The former airport of East Berlin is 18km (11 miles) south-east of the city centre. It's small, and much of the traffic is to eastern Europe and the Middle East. Budget airlines from the UK and Ireland also use it – EasyJet flies in from Bristol, Gatwick, Glasgow, Liverpool, Luton and Manchester; Ryanair from Dublin, East Midlands, Edinburgh and Stansted.

Train is the best means of reaching the city centre. S-Bahn Flughafen Schönefeld is a 5-min walk from the terminal (a free S-Bahn shuttle bus runs every 10mins, 6am-10pm, from outside the terminal; at other times, bus 171 also runs to the station). From here, the **Airport Express regional train (RB7 / RB14)** runs to Mitte (25mins to Alexanderplatz), Berlin Hauptbahnhof (30mins) and Zoo (35mins) every half hour from 5am to 11.30pm. You can also take S-Bahn line **S9**, which runs into the centre every 20mins (40mins to Alexanderplatz, 50mins to Zoo), stopping at all stations along the way. The **S45** line from Schönefeld connects with the Ringbahn every 20mins.

Bus X7, every 10 or 20mins, 4.30am-8pm, runs non-stop from the airport to Rudow U-Bahn (U7), from where you can connect with the underground. This is a good option if you're staying in Kreuzberg, Neukölln or Schöneberg. Bus 171 takes the same route.

Tickets from the airport to the city cost €3.40, and can be used on any combination of bus, U-Bahn, S-Bahn and tram.

A **taxi** to Zoo or Mitte is quite expensive (€30-€35) and takes around 45mins.

Flughafen Tegel (TXL)

Airport information 6091 1150, www. berlin-airport.de. **Open** *Terminal E 24hrs daily. All other terminals 4am-midnight daily.*
More upmarket scheduled flights from the likes of BA and Lufthansa, as well as new routes on discount airlines, use the compact Tegel airport, just 8km (5 miles) north-west of Mitte.

Buses 109 and **X9** (the express version) run via Luisenplatz and the Kurfürstendamm to Zoologischer Garten (also known as Zoo Station, Bahnhof Zoo or just Zoo) in western Berlin. Buses run every 5-15mins, and the journey takes 30-40mins. Tickets cost €2.80 (and can also be used on U-Bahn and S-Bahn services). At Zoo you can connect to anywhere in the city.

From the airport, you can also take bus 109 to Jacob-Kaiser-Platz U-Bahn (U7), or bus 128 to Kurt-Schumacher-Platz U-Bahn (U6), and proceed on the underground from there. One ticket (€2.80) can be used for the journey.

The **JetExpressBus TXL** is the direct link to Berlin Hauptbahnhof and Mitte. It runs from Tegel to Alexanderplatz, with useful stops at Beusselstrasse S-Bahn, Berlin Hauptbahnhof and Unter den Linden S-Bahn. The service runs every 10 or 20mins, 4.30am-12.30am (5.30am-12.30am at weekends) and takes 30-40mins; a ticket is €2.80.

A **taxi** to anywhere central will cost around €20-€25 and take 20-30mins.

By rail
Berlin Hauptbahnhof
0180 699 6633, www.bahn.de. **Map** *p98 L5.*

Berlin's central station is the main point of arrival for all long-distance trains, with the exceptions of night trains from Moscow and Kiev, which usually start and end at Berlin Lichtenberg.

Hauptbahnhof is located north of the government quarter, and is linked to the rest of the city by S-Bahn (S3, S5, S7, S9), and by the U55 underground line that runs to the Bundestag, though parts of this line are often shut for construction work. Eventually, the line will connect to the U5 at Alexanderplatz, via Museumsinsel and Unter den Linden.

By bus
Zentraler Omnibus Bahnhof (ZOB)
Masurenallee 4-6, Charlottenburg (3010 0175, www.zob.berlin). **Open** *24 hrs daily.* **Map** *fold-out map B8.*

Buses arrive in western Berlin at the Central Bus Station, opposite the Funkturm and the ICC. From here, U-Bahn line U2 runs into the city centre. The area around the ZOB is quite barren of cafés, shops or even green spaces to pass the time, so don't arrive for your bus hours in advance.

PUBLIC TRANSPORT

Berlin is served by a comprehensive and interlinked network of buses, trains, trams and ferries. It's efficient and punctual, but not especially cheap.

The completion of the inner-city-encircling Ringbahn in 2002 reconnected the former East and West Berlin transport systems, though it can still sometimes be complicated travelling between eastern and western destinations. But services are usually regular and frequent, timetables can be trusted, and one ticket can be used for 2hrs on all legs of a journey and all forms of transport.

The Berlin transport authority, the BVG, operates bus, U-Bahn (underground) and tram networks, and a few ferry services on the outlying lakes. The S-Bahn (overground railway) is run by its own authority, but services are integrated within the same three-zone tariff system.

Information

The **BVG** website (www.bvg.de) has a wealth of information (in English) on city transport, and there's usually someone who speaks English at the 24-hour **BVG Call Center** (194 49). The **S-Bahn** has its own website at www.s-bahn-berlin.de.

The Liniennetz, a map of U-Bahn, S-Bahn, bus and tram routes for Berlin and Potsdam, is available free from info centres and ticket offices. It includes a city-centre map. A map of the U- and S-Bahn can also be picked up free at ticket offices or from the grey-uniformed *Zugabfertiger* – passenger-assistance personnel.

Fares & tickets

The bus, tram, U-Bahn, S-Bahn and ferry services operate on an integrated three-zone system. Zone A covers central Berlin, zone B extends out to the edge of the suburbs and zone C stretches into Brandenburg.

The basic single ticket is the €2.80 *Normaltarif* (zones A and B). Unless going to Potsdam or Flughafen Schönefeld, few visitors are likely to travel beyond zone B, making this in effect a flat-fare system.

Apart from the longer-term *Zeitkarten*, tickets for Berlin's public transport system can be bought from the yellow or orange machines at U- or S-Bahn stations, and by some bus stops. These take coins and sometimes notes, give change and have a limited explanation of the ticket system in English. You can often pay by card, but don't count on it (if you do, don't forget to collect your card – infuriatingly, the machines keep the card until all the tickets are printed, making it very easy to forget)! An app, **FahrInfo Plus**, is also available for iOS and Android, which allows you to purchase and carry tickets on your smartphone; details on www. bvg.de/en/travel-information/mobile.

Once you've purchased your ticket, validate it in the small red or yellow box next to the machine, which stamps it with the time and date. (Tickets bought on trams or buses are usually already validated.) There are no ticket turnstiles at stations, but if an inspector catches you without a valid ticket, you will be fined €60. Ticket inspections are frequent and are conducted while vehicles are moving by pairs of plain-clothes personnel.

Single ticket (Normaltarif)

Single tickets cost €2.80 (€1.70 6-14s) for travel within zones A and B, €3.10 (€2.20) for zones B and C, and €3.40 (€2.50) for all three zones. A ticket allows use of the BVG network for 2hrs with as many changes between bus, tram, U-Bahn and S-Bahn as necessary, travelling in one direction. A four-ticket option (4-Fahrten-Karte) is available for €9.

Short-distance ticket (Kurzstreckentarif)

The *Kurzstreckentarif* (ask for a *Kurzstrecke*) costs €1.70 (€1.30 reductions) and is valid for three U- or S-Bahn stops, or six stops on the tram or bus. No transfers allowed.

Day ticket (Tageskarte)

A *Tageskarte* for zones A and B costs €7 (€4.70 reductions), or €7.70 (€5.30) for all three zones. A day ticket lasts until 3am the morning after validating.

Longer-term tickets (Zeitkarten)

If you're in Berlin for a week, it makes sense to buy a *Sieben-Tage-Karte* ('seven-day ticket') at €30 for zones A and B, or €37.50 for all three zones (no reductions). A stay of a month or more makes it worth buying a *Monatskarte* ('month ticket'), which costs €81 for zones A and B, and €100.50 for all three zones.

▶ *For details of tourist discount cards for public transport, sights and attractions, see p24.*

U-Bahn

The U-Bahn network consists of ten lines and 170-plus stations. The first trains run shortly after 4am; the last between midnight and 1am, except on Fri and Sat when most trains run all night at 15-min intervals. The direction of travel is indicated by the name of the last stop on the line.

S-Bahn

Especially useful in eastern Berlin, the S-Bahn covers long distances faster than the U-Bahn and is a more efficient means of getting to outlying areas. The Ringbahn, which circles central Berlin, was the final piece of the S-Bahn system to be renovated, though there are still disruptions here and there.

Buses

Berlin has a dense network of 150 bus routes, of which 54 run in the early hours. The day lines run from 4.30am to about 1am the next morning. Enter at the front of the bus and exit in the middle or at the back. The driver sells only individual tickets, but all tickets from machines on the U- or S-Bahn are valid. Most bus stops have clear timetables and route maps.

Trams

There are 21 tram lines (five of which run all night), mainly in the east, though some have been extended a few kilometres into the western half of the city, mostly in Wedding. Hackescher Markt is the site of the main tram terminus. Tickets are available from machines on the trams, at the termini and in U-Bahn stations.

Other rail services

Berlin is also served by the **Regionalbahn** ('regional railway'), which once connected East Berlin with

Potsdam via the suburbs and small towns left outside the Wall. Run by **Deutsche Bahn** (www.bahn.de), it still circumnavigates the city. The website has timetable and ticket information in English.

Travelling at night

Berlin has a comprehensive *Nachtliniennetz* ('night-line network') that covers all parts of town, with more than 50 bus and tram routes running every 30mins between 12.30am and 4.30am.

Maps and timetables are available from BVG kiosks at stations, and large maps of the night services are found next to the normal BVG map on station platforms. Ticket prices are the same as during the day. Buses and trams that run at night have an 'N' in front of the number.

On all buses travelling through zones B and C after 8pm, the driver will let you off at any point along the route via the front door.

Truncated versions of U-Bahn lines U1, U2, U3, U5, U6, U7, U8 and U9 run all night on Fridays and Saturdays, with trains every 15mins. The S-Bahn also runs at 30-min intervals.

TAXIS

Berlin taxis are pricey, efficient and numerous. The starting fee is €3.90 and thereafter the fare is €2 per km for the first 7km, and €1.50 per km thereafter. The rate remains the same at night. For short journeys, ask for a *Kurzstrecke* – up to 2km for €5, but only available when you've hailed a cab and not from taxi ranks. There is a €1.50 surcharge for payment by credit card; cabs are not obliged to accept credit card payments, so it's wise to have cash on hand.

Taxi stands are numerous, especially in central areas near stations and at major intersections. You can phone for a cab 24hrs daily on 261 026. Most firms can transport people with disabilities but require advance notice. **Funk Taxi Berlin** (261 026) operates vans that

can carry up to seven people (ask for a *grossraum Taxi*; same rates as for regular taxis) and has two vehicles for people with disabilities.

DRIVING

Despite some congestion, driving in Berlin presents few problems. Visitors from the UK and US should bear in mind that, in the absence of signs or other traffic signals, drivers must yield to traffic from the right, except at crossings marked by a diamond-shaped yellow 'priority' sign. Trams always have right of way. An *Einbahnstrasse* is a one-way street.

Breakdown services
ADAC *Bundesallee 29-30, Wilmersdorf (0180 222 2222)*. **No cards**. 24hr assistance for about €65/hr.

Parking
Parking is usually metered in Berlin side streets (residents get an *Anwohnerplakette* pass), but spaces are hard to find. Buy a parking ticket from a nearby machine; if you don't have one, or park illegally, you risk getting your car clamped or towed.

There are long-term car parks at Schönefeld and Tegel airports, and there are many Parkgaragen and Parkhäuser (multi-storey and underground car parks) around the city, open 24hrs, that charge around €2/hr.

Vehicle hire
Car hire is not expensive and all major companies are represented in Berlin, with car hire desks at all the city's airports. Car- and moped-sharing services such as **DriveNow** (www.drive-now.com), **Ubeeqo** (www.ubeeqo.com), **car2go** (www.car2go.com) and **COUP** (www.joincoup.com) are popular.

CYCLING

See p23 Berlin by bike.

Resources A-Z

ACCIDENT & EMERGENCY

Emergency numbers
Ambulance *(Rettungsdienst) 112*
Emergency doctor *(Notarzt) 112*
Fire brigade *(Feuerwehr) 112*
Police *(Polizei) 110*

A&E departments
All hospitals have a 24-hr emergency ward; these are the most central:
Charité Universitätsmedizin *Charitéplatz, Schumannstrasse 20-21, Mitte (45050, www.charite.de). U6 Oranienburger Tor.* **Map** *p70 M6.*
St Hedwig Krankenhaus *Grosse Hamburgerstrasse 5, Mitte (23110, www.alexianer-berlin-hedwigkliniken.de). S5, S7, S75 Hackescher Markt, or S1, S2 Oranienburger Strasse.* **Map** *p70 O5.*
Vivantes Klinikum Am Urban *Dieffenbachstrasse 1, Kreuzberg (13010, www.vivantes.de/kau). U7 Südstern, or bus M41.* **Map** *p137 P10.*

AGE RESTRICTIONS

Age of sexual consent 16
Drinking alcohol 16 (beer/wine), 18 (hard liquor)
Driving 18
Smoking 18

CLIMATE

Berlin has a continental climate, which means that it's hot in summer and cold in winter. In Jan and Feb, the city often ices over. Spring begins in late Mar/early Apr. May and June are the most clement months.

CUSTOMS

EU nationals over 17 years of age can import limitless goods for personal use, if bought with tax paid on them at source. For non-EU citizens and for duty-free goods, the following limits apply:

• 200 cigarettes or 50 cigars or 250 grams of tobacco
• 1 litre of spirits (over 22 % by volume) or 2 litres of fortified wine (under 22% by volume)
• 4 litres of non-sparkling wine
• 16 litres of beer
• Other goods to the value of €300 for non-commercial use, up to €430 for air/sea travellers.

Travellers should note that the import of meat, meat products, fruit, plants, flowers and protected animals is restricted and/or forbidden.

Travel Advice

For up-to-date information on travel to a specific country – including the latest on safety and security, health issues, local laws and customs – contact your home country government's department of foreign affairs. Most have websites with useful advice for would-be travellers.

Australia
www.smartraveller.gov.au

Canada
www.voyage.gc.ca

New Zealand
www.safetravel.govt.nz

Republic of Ireland
www.dfa.ie

UK
www.fco.gov.uk/travel

USA
www.state.gov/travel

DISABLED ACCESS

Many but not all U-Bahn and S-Bahn stations have ramps and/or elevators for wheelchair access; the map of the transport network (*see back flap*) uses a wheelchair symbol to indicate accessible ones. Passengers in wheelchairs are required to wait at the front end of the platform to signal to the driver that they need to board; a folding ramp will be supplied. All bus lines and most tram lines are also wheelchair-accessible.

Public buildings and most of the city's hotels have disabled access. However, if you require more specific information about access, contact one of the following organisations:

Beschäftigungswerk des BBV
Weydemeyerstrasse 2A, Mitte (5001 9100, www.bbv-tours-berlin.de). U5 Schillingstrasse. **Open** *8am-3.30pm Mon-Fri.* **Map** *p70 Q6.* The Berlin Centre for the Disabled provides legal and social advice, together with a transport service and travel information.

Touristik Union International *0511 5678 600, www.tui.com.*

The TUI provides information on accommodation and travel in Germany for the disabled.

DRUGS

Berlin is relatively liberal in its attitude towards drugs. In recent years, possession of hash or grass has been effectively decriminalized; anyone caught with an amount under 10g is liable to have the stuff confiscated but can otherwise expect no further retribution. Joint smoking is tolerated in some of Berlin's more youthful bars and cafés – a quick sniff will tell whether you're in one. Anyone caught with small quanitities of hard drugs will net a fine but is unlikely to be incarcerated.

Drogen Notdienst *Genthiner Strasse 48, Tiergarten (2332 40200, www. drogennotdienst.de). U1, U2, U3, U4 Nollendorfplatz.* **Open** *8.30am-9pm Mon-Fri; 2-9pm Sat, Sun.* **Map** *p98 K9.* Emergency drug service.

ELECTRICITY

Electricity in Germany runs on 230V, the same as British appliances. You will require an adaptor (G to F) to change the

Local Weather

Average monthly temperatures and rainfall in Berlin

	High (°C/°F)	Low (°C/°F)	Rainfall (mm/in)
January	2 / 36	-3 / 27	43 / 0.17
February	3 / 37	-2 / 28	38 / 0.15
March	8 / 46	0 / 32	38 / 0.15
April	13 / 55	4 / 39	43 / 0.17
May	18 / 64	8 / 46	56 / 0.22
June	22 / 72	11 / 52	71 / 0.28
July	23 / 73	13 / 55	53 / 0.21
August	23 / 73	12 / 54	66 / 0.26
September	18 / 64	9 / 48	46 / 0.18
October	13 / 55	6 / 43	36 / 0.14
November	7 / 45	2 / 36	51 / 0.20
December	3 / 37	-1 / 30	56 / 0.22

shape of the plug. US appliances (120V) require a voltage converter.

EMBASSIES & CONSULATES

Australian Embassy *Wallstrasse 76-79, Mitte (880 0880, www.germany. embassy.gov.au). U2 Märkisches Museum.* **Open** *8.30am-5pm Mon-Fri.* **Map** *p70 P7.*

British Embassy *Wilhelmstrasse 70, Mitte (204 570, www.gov.uk/ government/world/germany). S1, S2, S25 Brandenburger Tor.* **Open** *9.30am-noon Mon, Tue, Thur, Fri.* **Map** *p70 M7.*

Embassy of Canada *Leipziger Platz 17, Mitte (203 120, www. canadainternational.gc.ca/germany- allemagne). U2, S1, S2, S25 Potsdamer Platz.* **Open** *9am- noon Mon-Fri.* **Map** *p98 M8.*

Embassy of Ireland *Jägerstrasse 51, Mitte (220 720, www.embassyofireland. de). U2, U6 Stadtmitte.* **Open** *9.30am-12.30pm Mon-Fri, by appointment only.* **Map** *p70 N7.*

New Zealand Embassy *Friedrichstrasse 60 (206 210, www. mfat.govt.nz). U2, U6 Stadtmitte.* **Open** *9.30am-1pm, 2-4pm Mon-Fri.* **Map** *p70 N7*

US Embassy *Clayallee 170, Zehlendorf (83050, visa enquiries 032 221 093 243, https://de.usembassy.gov). U3 Oskar- Helene-Heim.* **Open** *US citizen services phoneline 2-3pm Mon-Thur. Visa enquiries phoneline 8am-8pm Mon-Fri. Adult passport walk-in service 12.30- 3pm Mon, Fri.* The main US embassy building is on Pariser Platz, next to the Brandenburg Gate, but consular services still operate out of the original embassy in Zehlendorf.

For all other embassies, see http:// embassy.goabroad.com.

HEALTH

EU citizens who hold a **European Health Insurance Card** (EHIC) are entitled to free emergency medical care. Should you fall ill in Berlin, you can take your EHIC to any doctor (*see opposite*) or hospital emergency department (*see p197*) to get treatment. The EHIC doesn't cover all medical costs (dental treatment, for example), so private travel/medical insurance is recommended. In the UK, the EHIC is available by phoning 0300 330 1350 or online at www.ehic.org.uk. **It is unclear whether UK citizens will still be eligible for an EHIC after Brexit in March 2019.** Citizens from non-EU countries should always take out private medical insurance before travelling.

ID

By law you are required to carry some form of ID at all times, which, for UK and US citizens, means a passport. If police catch you without one, they may accompany you to wherever you've left it.

LANGUAGE

English is widely spoken in Berlin; in parts of Kreuzberg, Neukölln, Prenzlauer Berg and Mitte, you will also hear French, Spanish, Turkish and Arabic on the streets. But, venture into less 'hip' districts and having a grasp of German becomes more essential.

LEFT LUGGAGE

Airports
There is a left-luggage office at Tegel (4101 2315; open 5am-10.30pm daily) and lockers at Schönefeld (in the Multi Parking Garage P4).

Rail & bus stations
There are left-luggage lockers at Bahnhof Zoo, Friedrichstrasse, Alexanderplatz, Potsdamer Platz, Ostbahnhof, Hauptbahnhof and Zentraler Omnibus Bahnhof (ZOB).

LGBT

Help & information
Lesbenberatung *Kulmer Strasse 20A, Schöneberg (215 2000, www.*

*lesbenberatung-berlin.de). U7, S2, S25
Yorckstrasse. **Open** 2-5pm Mon, Wed,
Fri; 10am-4pm Tue; 3-6.30pm Thur.*
Map *p162 K10.* Counselling in all
areas of queer/lesbian life, as well as
self-help groups, courses, cultural
events and an 'info-café'.

Mann-O-Meter *Bülowstrasse 106,
Schöneberg (216 8008, www.mann-o-
meter.de). U2, U3, U4 Nollendorfplatz.
Open 5-10pm Mon-Fri; 4-8pm Sat.* **Map**
p162 J9. English spoken.

Schwulenberatung *Niebuhrstrasse
59-60, Charlottenburg (2336 9070,
www.schwulenberatungberlin.de). U7
Wilmersdorfer Strasse. **Open** 9am-8pm
Mon-Fri.* **Map** *p162 E8.* Information
and counselling about HIV and AIDS,
crisis intervention and advice on all
aspects of gay life.

MONEY

One euro (€) is made up of 100 cents.
There are 7 banknotes and 8 coins. The
notes are: €5 (grey-green), €10 (red), €20
(blue), €50 (orange), €100 (green), €200
(yellow-brown), €500 (purple).The coins
(€2, €1, 50 cents, 20 cents, 10 cents, 5
cents, 2 cents, 1 cent) vary in colour, size
and thickness.

Compared to the rest of Germany,
Berlin (and the East at large) is pretty
affordable. It's still possible to eat a
good lunch for €5, making Berlin miles
cheaper than other Western European
capitals, though prices are slowly
creeping up. It's by no means difficult
to have a major blow-out weekend in
Berlin, but with a little effort, it's equally
possible to stay here on a budget.
Supermarkets are especially cheap.

ATMs

ATMs are found throughout the centre
of Berlin and are the most convenient
way of obtaining cash. Most major credit
cards are accepted, as well as debit cards
that are part of the Cirrus, Plus, Star or
Maestro systems. You will normally be
charged a fee for withdrawing cash.

Banks & bureaux de change

Foreign currency and travellers'
cheques can be exchanged in most
banks. *Wechselstuben* (bureaux de
change) are open outside normal
banking hours and give better rates
than banks, where changing money
often involves long queues. The
Wechselstuben of the Reisebank offer
good exchange rates, and can be found
at the bigger train stations.

Credit & debit cards

In general, German banking and retail
systems are less enthusiastic about
credit than their UK or US equivalents,
though this is gradually changing.
Many Berliners prefer to use cash for
most transactions, although larger
hotels, shops and restaurants usually
accept major credit and debit cards.
Contactless payment is virtually
unheard of in Berlin for the moment
but looks likely to become 'a thing' at
younger joints in coming years.

If you want to draw cash on your
credit card, some banks will give an
advance against Visa and MasterCard
cards. However, you may not be able
to withdraw less than the equivalent
of US$100. A better option is using an
ATM.

If you've lost a credit/debit card, or
had one stolen, phone your bank and/or
the relevant 24-hr emergency number:
American Express *069 9797 2000.*
Diners Club *069 900 150 135.*
Mastercard *0800 819 1040.*
Visa *0800 811 8440.*

Tax

Non-EU citizens can claim back German
value-added tax (*Mehrwertsteuer or
MwSt*) on goods purchased in the
country, although it's only worth the
hassle on sizeable purchases. Ask the
shop for a Tax-Free Shopping Cheque for
the amount of the refund and present
this, with the receipt, at the airport's
refund office before checking in.

OPENING HOURS

Most **banks** are open 9am-noon and 1-3pm or 2-6pm Mon-Fri.

Shops can stay open 6am-10pm, except on Sun and hols, though few take full advantage of the fact. Big stores tend to open at 9am and close between 8pm and 10pm. Most smaller shops will close around 6pm. An increasing number of all-purpose neighbourhood 'late shops' (*Späti*) stay open until around midnight. Many Turkish shops are open on Sat afternoons and 1-5pm Sun. Many bakers open to sell cakes 2-4pm Sun.

The opening times of **bars** vary, but many are open during the day, and most stay open until at least 1am, if not through until morning.

Most **post offices** are open 8am-6pm Mon-Fri and 8am-1pm Sat.

PHARMACIES

Prescription and non-prescription drugs (including aspirin) are sold only at pharmacies (*Apotheken*). You can recognise these by a red 'A' outside the front door. A list of the nearest pharmacies open on Sundays and in the evening should be displayed in the window of every pharmacy. A list of emergency pharmacies (*Notdienst-Apotheken*) is available online at www.akberlin.de/notdienst.

POLICE STATIONS

The central police HQ is at Platz der Luftbrücke 6, Tempelhof (46640); other police stations are listed online at www.berlin.de/polizei/dienststellen/polizei-in-den-bezirken/). Police will be dispatched from the appropriate office if you dial 46640. For emergencies, dial 110.

POSTAL SERVICES

For non-local mail, use the *Andere Richtungen* ('other destinations') slot in postboxes. Letters of up to 20g to anywhere in Germany cost €0.70. For postcards it's €0.45. For anywhere outside Germany, a 20g airmail letter or postcard costs €0.90.

Postamt Friedrichstrasse
Georgenstrasse 14-18, Mitte (0228 4333 112). U6, S1, S2, S3, S5, S7, S25, S9 Friedrichstrasse. **Open** *6am-10pm Mon-Fri; 8am-10pm Sat, Sun.* **Map** *p153 N6.* This branch inside Friedrichstrasse station keeps the longest opening hours of the Berlin offices.

Poste restante

Poste restante facilities are available at the main post offices of each district. Address them to the recipient 'Postlagernd', followed by the address of the post office, or collect them from the counter marked *Postlagernde Sendungen*. Take your passport.

PUBLIC HOLIDAYS

On public holidays (*Feiertagen*) it can be difficult to get things done in Berlin. However, most cafés, bars and restaurants stay open – except on Christmas Eve, when almost everything closes.

New Year's Day Neujahr *1 Jan*
Good Friday Karfreitag *Mar/Apr*
Easter Monday Oster Montag *Mar/Apr*
May Day Tag der Arbeit *1 May*
Ascension Day Christi Himmelfahrt *May/June*
Whit Monday Pfingstmontag *May/June*
Day of German Unity Tag der deutschen Einheit *3 Oct*
Christmas Day Erster Weihnachtstag *25 Dec*
Boxing Day Zweiter Weihnachtstag *26 Dec*

SAFETY & SECURITY

In 2018, Berlin's crime rate was on the decline. Most central areas of the city are safe even at night, as long as you use common sense, although pickpockets are not unknown around tourist areas and Alexanderplatz becomes something of a crime hotspot after dark. Visitors who are obviously gay or non-German should avoid the poorer suburbs to the east of the city where right-wing extremism is prevalent. For the police, *see above*.

SMOKING

Many Berliners smoke, though the habit is in decline. Smoking is banned on public transport, in theatres and many public institutions. Many bars and restaurants have closed-off smoking rooms. Smaller, one-room establishments may allow smoking but must post a sign outside denoting their status as a *Raucherkneipe* (smoker pub). There are no restrictions on smoking at outside tables, which are well used, even in winter.

TELEPHONES

Dialling & codes

All phone numbers in this guide are local Berlin numbers (other than those for Potsdam in the West of the Centre chapter, which begin 0331); if you're dialing from *outside* Berlin, you will need to add the code for the city (030). Numbers beginning 0180 have higher tariffs, and numbers beginning 015, 016 or 017 are for mobile phones.

To phone Berlin from abroad, dial the international access code (00 from the UK, 011 from the US, 0011 from Australia), then 49 (for Germany) and 30 (for Berlin), followed by the local number.

To phone another country from Germany, dial 00, then the relevant country code: Australia 61; Canada 1; Ireland 353; New Zealand 64; United Kingdom 44; United States 1. Then, dial the local area code (minus the initial zero) and the local number.

Public phones

Most public phones give you the option of cards or coins, and from Telekom phones (the ones with the magenta 'T') you also can send SMSs. Phonecards

can be bought at post offices and newsagents for various sums from €5 to €50.

Operator services

For online directory enquiries, go to www.teleauskunft.de.
International directory enquiries *118 34*.
Operator assistance/German directory enquiries *118 33 (118 37 in English)*.
Phone repairs *080 0330 2000*.
Time *0180 4100 100 (automated, in German)*.

Mobile phones

Check with your service provider about service provision and roaming charges while you're in Germany, though those with service in the EU should automatically have service in Germany. US mobile phone users should also check their mobile/cell's compatibility with GSM bands. German SIM cards can be purchased easily enough from supermarkets or corner internet shops. (We recommend the latter, as the personnel can help with set-up.) A typical starter pack costs around €15 and comes with an adequate amount of SMS, calls and data, which can be topped up if necessary.

TIME

Germany is on Central European Time, which is 1hr ahead of Greenwich Mean Time. During summer 'daylight saving time', Germany is 2hrs ahead of Greenwich Mean Time, which means, in effect, that Berlin is 1hr ahead of London throughout the year; 6hrs ahead of New York; 9hrs ahead of San Francisco, and 9hrs behind Sydney.

TIPPING

A 10% service charge is included in restaurant bills, but it's common to leave a small tip too. In a taxi, round up the bill to the nearest euro.

TOURIST INFORMATION

EurAide *DB Reisezentrum, Hauptbahnhof, Tiergarten (www. euraide.de). S5, S7, S75 Hauptbahnhof.* **Open** *Mar, Apr 11am-7pm Mon-Fri. May-July 10am-8pm Mon-Fri. Aug-Oct 10am-7pm Mon-Fri. Nov 11am-6.30pm Mon-Fri. Dec 10am-7.30pm Mon-Fri.* **Map** p98 L5. Staff advise on sights, hostels, tours and transport, and sell rail tickets.

VisitBerlin *2500 2323, www.visitberlin. de.* Berlin's official (if private) tourist organisation has information points at Kurfürstendamm 22, Charlottenburg; Brandenburg Gate; Hauptbahnhof (ground floor, Europaplatz exit); Tegel Airport (next to gate 1); and at the base of the TV Tower at Alexanderplatz. All are open daily. The website is comprehensive.

VISAS & IMMIGRATION

A passport valid for 3mths beyond the length of stay is all that is required for UK, EU, US, Canadian and Australian citizens for a stay in Germany of up to 3mths. Citizens of EU countries need only show their ID cards. Citizens of other countries should check with their local German embassy or consulate whether a visa is required well before they plan to travel. For stays of longer than 3mths, you'll need a residence permit (*Aufenthaltserlaubnis*).

Index

Credits

CREDITS

Crimson credits
Text Anna Geary-Meyer, Victoria Gosling, Callie Payne
Layouts Emilie Crabb, Patrick Dawson
Cartography Gail Armstrong

Series Editor Sophie Blacksell Jones
Production Manager Kate Michell
Design Mytton Williams

Chairman David Lester
Managing Director Andy Riddle

Advertising Media Sales House
Marketing Lyndsey Mayhew

Acknowledgements
Anna Geary-Meyer would like to thank Verena Spilker from Transnational Queer Underground; Victoria Gosling would like to thank Leighton Cheal, Luke Lalor, Jenna Krumminga, Ulrike Kloss and Michelle Arrouas; Callie Payne would like to thank Kaila Sarah Hier for her help on the Berlinale box. Thanks and acknowledgements are also due to all contributors to previous editions of *Time Out Berlin*, whose work forms the basis for this guide.

Photography credits
Front cover santirf/istock.com
Back cover LaMiaFotografia/Shutterstock.com
Interior Photography credits see p203.

Publishing information
Time Out Berlin Shortlist 4th edition
© TIME OUT ENGLAND LIMITED 2019
February 2019

ISBN 978 1 780592 65 7
CIP DATA: A catalogue record for this book is available from the British Library

Published by Crimson Publishing
21d Charles Street, Bath, BA1 1HX (01225 584 950, www.crimsonpublishing.co.uk) on behalf of Time Out England.

Distributed by Grantham Book Services
Distributed in the US and Canada by Publishers Group West (1-510-809-3700)

Printed by Replika Press, India.

While every effort has been made by the authors and the publishers to ensure that the information contained in this guide is accurate and up to date as at the date of publication, they accept no responsibility or liability in contract, tort, negligence, breach of statutory duty or otherwise for any inconvenience, loss, damage, costs or expenses of any nature whatsoever incurred or suffered by anyone as a result of any advice or information contained in the guide (except to the extent that such liability may not be excluded or limited as a matter of law).

All rights reserved. No part of this publication may be reproduced, stored in a retrieval system, or transmitted in any form or by any means, electronic, mechanical, photocopying, recording or otherwise, without prior permission from the copyright owners.